THE
IROQUOIS
RESTORATION

THE
IROQUOIS
RESTORATION

IROQUOIS DIPLOMACY ON THE
COLONIAL FRONTIER, 1701–1754

RICHARD AQUILA

WITH A NEW INTRODUCTION BY THE AUTHOR

UNIVERSITY OF NEBRASKA PRESS
LINCOLN AND LONDON

♾ The paper in this book meets the minimum requirements of American
National Standard for Information Sciences—Permanence of Paper for
Printed Library Materials, ANSI Z39.48-1984.

First paperback printing: 1997

Library of Congress Cataloging-in-Publication Data
Aquila, Richard, 1946–
The Iroquois restoration: Iroquois diplomacy on the colonial frontier,
1701–1754 / Richard Aquila.
p.   cm.
Originally published: Detroit: Wayne State University Press, 1983. With
new introd.
Includes bibliographical references and index.
ISBN 0-8032-5932-8 (pbk.: alk. paper)
1. Iroquois Indians—Government relations.   2. Iroquois Indians—
History.   3. Indians of North America—Government relations—To 1789.
I. Title.
E99.I7A68   1997
973'.049755—dc21
97-18524   CIP

Reprinted from the original 1983 edition by Wayne State University Press,
Detroit.

TO MARIE

Contents

List of Illustrations

Preface

I first became interested in the Iroquois in 1968 when I read Francis Parkman's fascinating book, *The Jesuits in North America*. His account of the Iroquois' seventeenth-century wars against the Hurons and Eries presented a vivid picture of the Iroquois at the height of their power. Yet Parkman, in *The Jesuits* and later works, never explained fully what happened to the Iroquois after 1700. Parkman picked up the Iroquois' story in the mid-eighteenth century and attributed their demise to the expulsion of the French from North America in 1763. In the process, he neglected an important question—what were the Iroquois doing between 1700 and 1754?

More recent scholars have used the same approach or else have focused on other periods or topics in Iroquois history. George T. Hunt, in *The Wars of the Iroquois: A Study in Intertribal Trade Relations* (1940), explores economic causes of the Iroquois' seventeenth-century warfare. Allen W. Trelease limits his study of the Iroquois to *Indian Affairs in Colonial New York: The Seventeenth Century* (1960). Anthony F. C. Wallace takes an ethnohistorical look at one Iroquois tribe in his *The Death and Rebirth of the Seneca* (1972). Barbara Graymont provides a detailed study in *The Iroquois in the American Revolution* (1972). And Bruce Trigger includes valuable information about the seventeenth-century Iroquois in his book, *The Children of Aataentsic: A History of the Huron People to 1660* (1976). Yet despite these excellent works and others done by historians and anthropologists, there is still a gap in Iroquois history. No substantial work fully examines the patterns and

1

implications of Iroquois diplomacy during the early 1700s. The question remains—what were the Iroquois doing between 1700 and 1754? This study, which focuses on Iroquois diplomacy during the first half of the eighteenth century, is my attempt to answer that question.

A few comments should be made about my use of quotations and primary sources. In an effort to make the text clearer and more readable, I have modernized archaic abbreviations and standardized the use of Indian tribal names. In no case, however, has a change been made at the expense of accuracy. As a further aid to the reader, I have included a glossary of important names, tribes, and places at the end of the book.

I wish to thank all those who helped me complete this study of the Iroquois. The Center for the History of the American Indian, the Newberry Library, Chicago, provided a fellowship which allowed eleven uninterrupted months to complete much of this project. Ball State University provided funds for maps and illustrations. Charles E. Martin, staff cartographer at Ball State University, provided cartographic assistance. Professor Bradley Chapin, my graduate advisor at Ohio State University, gave me the opportunity to pursue my interests. Professor Mansel G. Blackford contributed scholarly advice, encouragement, and friendship. Professors William T. Hagan, Francis Paul Prucha, and Francis Jennings offered valuable suggestions on organization. Others helped in different ways to make this study possible. I am grateful to my parents, Mary and Phil Aquila, for their immeasurable contributions and for giving me the chance to succeed; to my mother for her confidence and support; to my father for being my first and best history teacher; to my brother Phil for perspective and comic relief; to Professors Daniel B. Ramsdell and Virginia Platt for starting me down the path toward a career in history; to Professor Edmund J. Danziger for sparking my interest in

American Indian history; to Professor Stephen Leonard and the History Department at Metropolitan State College, Denver, for professional advice and encouragement; to Jim Meighan, who introduced me to the dream, and to Donald Bain, who certainly was more than just an excellent typist. Most important of all, I wish to thank Marie Aquila, who, as a colleague, critic, scholar, editor, friend, and wife, made this study of the Iroquois both possible and worthwhile.

Richard Aquila

Introduction to the Paperback Edition

The "Phantom" Iroquois Empire

Since *The Iroquois Restoration* was first published in 1983, there has been a proliferation of books and articles about the Senecas, Cayugas, Onondagas, Oneidas, and Mohawks—the Five Nations that comprised the Iroquois Confederacy. This new introduction identifies some of the main issues now being addressed in Iroquois history and explains how *The Iroquois Restoration* fits into the growing literature on the subject.

Recent scholars have approached Iroquois history and culture from a variety of angles, hoping to gain a better understanding of the role played by the Iroquois on the colonial frontier. Of particular interest have been questions involving the Iroquois' alleged wilderness empire, the Five Nations' degree of unity, their specific relations with Indian and white neighbors, and the overall significance of the Iroquois in American history.

Perhaps the most radical reinterpretation involves the long-accepted notion that the seventeenth- and eighteenth-century Iroquois established a vast wilderness empire that stretched from their New York homelands to the Mississippi. Over the years, most writers have portrayed the Five Nations as political and diplomatic geniuses, as well as brutal conquerors. "The Five Nations think themselves by Nature superior to the rest of Mankind," observed the British colonial official Cadwallader Colden in 1727. "This opinion gives them that courage, which has been so terrible to all the Nations of North America; and they have taken such Care to impress the same Opinion . . . on all their neighbors [who] . . . yield the most submissive Obedience to them."[1]

By the nineteenth century, the idea of an Iroquois empire had become common wisdom. New York politician De Witt Clinton praised the Iroquois as "the Romans of the Western World," while ethnologist Lewis Henry Morgan and historian Francis Parkman offered details about how the Five Nations created an invincible and politically astute confederacy that conquered neighboring tribes and lands.[2]

Twentieth-century writers perpetuated the Iroquois mystique. Randolph Downes called them "overlords." William Brandon noted that the Iroquois' "power and glory during the eighteenth century reached the highest point attained [by] any Indian nation north of Mexico." Most recently, Stephen Saunders Webb described how dependent tribes "provided warriors for the wars of the Iroquois, paid tribute to the prestige of the Five Nations annually at Onondaga, and, often, were a source of the slaves who served the Iroquoian aristocracy in house and field."[3]

The first cracks in the Iroquois empire interpretation opened up in the late 1960s, when scholars trained in ethnohistory began rethinking earlier assumptions. Anthony F. C. Wallace was one of the first to reappraise Iroquois relations with their Indian and white neighbors. Later studies by Francis Jennings and Richard L. Haan, along with *The Iroquois Restoration*, did even more damage to the alleged empire. The revisionists portrayed a Confederacy riddled by factionalism. They described warriors who lost as often as not. They demonstrated that the Iroquois did not control Indian neighbors to the south and west. They revealed that Iroquois success was usually more the result of diplomacy, adaptation, and necessity than of military genius or strength. They even proved that Indian and Euro-American politicians of the seventeenth and eighteenth centuries had concocted the imperial Iroquois myth to further their own goals.[4]

In March 1984, a scholarly conference on "The 'Imperial' Iroquois" was held in Williamsburg, Virginia. Most of the one hundred persons in attendance came away agreeing with a statement made by Francis Jennings in the first session: "The theme of this conference is a myth," he announced. "The Iroquois never had an empire." Subsequent books by scholars such as Daniel K. Richter and James H. Merrell proved Jennings right beyond a reasonable doubt.[5]

But, if the revisionists solved one main issue, they left others unresolved. For example, if the Iroquois did not have an empire, then what exactly did they have? Most scholars now point to a fictional empire, but disagree on the specifics of what caused the fiction. Jennings believes that the "Ambiguous Iroquois Empire" was actually the Covenant Chain, an intercultural alliance between New York and

6

the English colonies and the Iroquois and their Indian allies that dates back to the late 1670s. Richter agrees that the so-called Iroquois empire "was not really an empire at all, but rather a system of alliances in which, at best, the Five Nations were first among equals by virtue of their ability to serve as brokers between English governments and Indian nations."[6]

While accepting the general assumption that the Covenant Chain was the reality behind the Iroquois empire, Richard L. Haan warns that the Chain was even more ambiguous than most scholars realize. Questioning the prevailing notion of a monolithic Covenant Chain, he suggests that multiple chains were made by various Iroquois leaders and factions.[7]

The emphasis that most revisionists place on the Covenant Chain not only obscures what was really behind the alleged Iroquois empire but diverts attention away from the historical significance of the myth. *The Iroquois Restoration* demonstrates that the Iroquois' imperial reputation always rested on more than just the Covenant Chain. It also brings into focus the impact that the Iroquois and their fictional empire had on American history.

Intimations of a vague Iroquois empire danced in the heads of Indians, as well as French and English colonial officials, long before the Covenant Chain even came into existence. The Five Nations' claim to fame was built in part upon their impressive victories against the Hurons, Neutrals, and other tribes of the upper Great Lakes country during the 1640s and 1650s. Neighboring tribes spoke in terror of the "Mohawks"—a New England Algonquian term that meant "eater[s] of human flesh." One Massachusetts Bay colonist reported in 1674 that local Indians were so afraid of the Iroquois "that the appearance of four of five Maquas [Mohawks] in the woods would frighten them from their habitations." Settlers of New France likewise lived in fear. "If we do not go to humiliate these barbarians," warned a French colonist in 1660, "they will destroy the country and drive us all away by their warlike and carnivorous nature."[8]

The Five Nations' political structure and diplomatic goals reinforced the notion of an Iroquois empire. The Confederacy with its League Council at Onondaga reminded European onlookers of an expansionist, European-style nation-state. Iroquois rhetoric added to the imperial image. According to Francis Jennings, the Five Nations' founding principles—*The Great Law of Peace of the Longhouse People*—asserted that "alien peoples must bow to Iroquois terms." Clearly, the

Iroquois entertained dreams of empire. Not necessarily a European-style empire, says Jennings, but an empire nonetheless, wherein the Five Nations would establish hegemony through "voluntary association, military conquest, and combinations of the two in confederation with tributary allies."[9]

Despite these imperial hopes and a reputation for military prowess, the Iroquois never came close to establishing an actual empire. By the 1660s, the French and their Indian allies were contesting Iroquois claims to the Great Lakes country, while the Susquehannocks were handing Iroquois warriors defeats in the South.[10]

The Iroquois' dream of empire took a step toward reality in the late 1670s with the forging of the Covenant Chain, whereby New York's Governor Edmund Andros and officials from other English colonies enlisted the Five Nations' support to avoid a general Indian uprising on the colonial frontier. In return for their help, the Iroquois achieved recognition as England's most-favored Indian nation.[11]

The Chain enabled both the English and the Iroquois to further their imperialistic ambitions. Richter has shown that the new alliance allowed Andros "to pacify the natives, simplify English-Indian relations, and—because the governments of Massachusetts, Maryland, and Virginia all participated in treaty negotiations as subordinate partners to New York—to establish the preeminence of the duke's province in Anglo-America." The Five Nations benefitted just as much. Richter maintains that the Chain established the Iroquois' "long-lived dominance in the intercultural diplomacy of the Northeast." It also secured the Five Nations' borders, and provided the Iroquois with thousands of potential English and Indian allies. In addition, the Chain offered economic benefits, allowing Iroquois hunters, traders, and diplomats to travel safely throughout the Great Lakes country.[12]

The Covenant Chain undoubtedly advanced the myth of the Iroquois empire. But, significantly, the Chain was the result, not cause of the fiction. Andros was willing to hammer out the new alliance because he already recognized the Five Nations' worth. The Iroquois' alleged political organization and reputation as warriors made them a potentially valuable English ally. The Indians' geographic location was equally important. Not only did the Five Nations' homelands serve as a strategic buffer between New France and England's middle colonies, but Iroquoia's central location allowed the Five Nations to develop important political, economic, and social contacts with Indian and white neighbors throughout the eastern woodlands.

8

The Iroquois Restoration demonstrates that the Iroquois' reputation as shrewd diplomats and invincible warriors was based on more than just the Covenant Chain. The fictional empire was the product of several specific Iroquois actions and reactions during the seventeenth and eighteenth centuries. Furthermore, this fictional empire was not as ambiguous as most revisionists claim. There was no cultural misunderstanding about the nature of the Covenant Chain or Iroquois empire. The Five Nations and their Indian and white neighbors understood exactly what was going on. They all knew the Iroquois empire was an illusion, but they accepted that illusion and operated on the assumption it was a reality.

The English not only accepted but often promoted Iroquois claims to empire. Officials realized that the alleged Iroquois empire provided a foundation for English claims to the Ohio country. English colonists also knew that they needed the Five Nations for protection against French and Indian enemies, as well as for diplomatic and economic reasons.

The French accepted, although to a lesser extent, the concept of the imperial Iroquois. Along with recognizing Iroquois sovereignty, the French approved at least some of the Iroquois' claims over lands and tribes of the Ohio country. The French were willing to cooperate, because they—like the English—needed the Five Nations. As friends, the Iroquois could be valuable trading partners and allies who could contribute to French expansion. As enemies, the Five Nations, due to their proximity and numbers, could terrorize New France and facilitate English plans to undermine the French colony.

Even rival tribes in the Great Lakes country frequently went along with the myth of the Iroquois empire. Pennsylvania Indians had little choice, since the fiction of Iroquois supremacy was foisted upon them by a more powerful Iroquois Confederacy in cahoots with a devious Pennsylvania government. They either had to accept Iroquois domination and gain whatever advantage they could from a bad situation, or else flee farther to the West. Ohio tribes had more options. Due to their numbers and distant location, they did not have to cooperate with the Iroquois. But, they realized they had much to gain by paying lip service to the alleged empire. Iroquois allies could be extremely useful against Indian and white enemies. The Iroquois, because of geography and politics, also held the key to Ohio tribes' relations with the English. Without Iroquois consent, Ohio Indians could not join the Covenant Chain or partake in English trade.

9

Naturally, the Iroquois were more than willing to go along with the fiction that they controlled neighboring Indians and lands. By giving the impression of empire, the Five Nations remained England's most-favored Indian nation, and they increased their prestige among their French and Indian neighbors.

The Iroquois Restoration demonstrates that the Five Nations did not have an actual empire. But they did have an empire of sorts—not a European-style empire with military control over other tribes, nor even an Indian-style empire based solely on an ambiguous Covenant Chain. Instead, it was a "Phantom Iroquois Empire"—a deliberate fiction created by the skillful application of diplomacy, warfare, politics, trade, and self-serving propaganda. The idea of an Iroquois empire took hold and achieved a life of its own, extending a shadowy influence over neighboring peoples and lands. This phantom-like empire affected political and economic relationships, altered settlement patterns, and helped determine the outcome of the British-French contest for the Ohio country. Its impact sent reverberations across space and time. Although the Iroquois empire may have been a myth, that myth influenced reality. And *that* is what is important historically.

The nature of the Iroquois empire is not the only issue that divides scholars. They also debate the Five Nations' degree of unity. Much of the controversy swirls around the question: was the Confederacy capable of developing and implementing "policies" that would be followed by individual tribes and members? Richard L. Haan says no, arguing that the decentralized nature of Iroquois politics prevented the Confederacy from developing any concerted policies. "What successes the Iroquois achieved were due in no small measure to their image of unity and to the ignorance of English officials about the factional nature of decision-making among the [Iroquois]," concludes Haan. "In reality, by 1750 Iroquois influence in the Northeast was splintered. Iroquois society always had divisions, but the failure of leaders to develop a clear response to English and French overtures in the eighteenth century made the [Iroquois] quite incapable of controlling their own diplomatic future."[13]

Most revisionists take a more moderate position. While agreeing that the Five Nations did not have a European-style centralized government, they stress that common goals and circumstances often provided a degree of unity to Iroquois actions. "A generation of experience with the Confederacy's mechanisms for coordinating policies had hardly transformed the peoples of the Longhouse into a mono-lith; traditions of localism, factionalism, and individual leadership still thrived," cautions Daniel K. Richter. "Nonetheless, the policies pursued by various headmen, kin groups, factions, and villages showed a striking consensus on basic issues." By the 1720s, even the various Anglophile and Francophile factions among the Five Nations were practicing what Richter terms the "Modern Indian Politics." He ex-plains that the Iroquois' dealings with their Indian and white neigh-bors "all echoed the same refrain: in northeastern North America, peace and balance must be preserved at all costs; autonomy and spiri-tual power must be found in diplomacy rather than war; military im-pulses must be channeled away from the region. For a time, the song played well."[14]

My findings are similar to Richter's. The Iroquois' "Restoration Strategies" were a unified policy only in the loosest sense of the term. Common circumstances, conditions, and goals among the Iroquois people provided a unity to their actions throughout the first half of the eighteenth century. Sometimes the Confederacy implemented the strategies. Other times, individual tribes or persons followed the strategies. When taken together, these actions of the Confederacy, member tribes, and individual Indians followed the same basic pat-terns during the first half of the eighteenth century.

Another area of disagreement among revisionists involves Iroquois relations with their Indian and white neighbors. Most scholars agree on the basics: after 1701, the Five Nations maintained neutrality with the English and French, kept peace with nearby tribes, and made war on southern tribes. Experts disagree, however, on details. Why and how did the Iroquois establish neutrality? What was the exact rela-tionship between the Five Nations and the tribes of the Ohio coun-try? Did the Iroquois have an actual policy of war on southern tribes or was it merely individual war parties heading southward? How did the Iroquois develop control over Pennsylvania Indians?

My book answers these questions by analyzing Iroquois diplomacy on the colonial frontier. It details how and why the Iroquois estab-lished a guarded neutrality between the two European powers; it ex-plains their need for a rapprochement with the tribes of Canada and the Great Lakes country; it examines their plan to create hegemony over Pennsylvania Indians and lands; and it reveals the motives be-hind the Five Nations' constant warfare against southern tribes.

The significance of the Iroquois Confederacy in American history

11

has been another source of controversy in recent years. One group of scholars, putting a new spin on the old "Iroquois as Romans of the Western World" myth, maintains that the Iroquois were the real founding fathers of American democracy. "Throughout the eighteenth century," explains Alvin Josephy, "the republican and democratic principles that lay at the heart of the Five Nations' system of government had been included among the studies of the enlightened philosophers of Europe and America who were seeking more just and humane ways for men to be governed." Other writers, such as Donald Grinde Jr., Bruce Johansen, and Bruce Burton, have recently elaborated on the argument, concluding that the origins of the American Revolution, as well as the United States Constitution, can indeed be found in the laws of the Iroquois Confederacy.[15]

Most scholars and writers, myself included, totally reject these attempts to trace the origins of American democracy back to the Iroquois League. "There is . . . little or no evidence that the framers of the Constitution sitting in Philadelphia drew much inspiration from the League," insists Dean Snow, an expert on Iroquois politics and culture. "It can even be argued that such claims muddle and denigrate the subtle and remarkable features of Iroquois government. The two forms of government are distinctive and individually remarkable in conception. It serves no legitimate long-term purpose to confuse the two, or to attempt to make either a derivative from the other. Yet the temptation to demonstrate that the United States Constitution was derived from a Native American form of government remains, for ephemeral political purposes, too strong for some to resist."[16]

Yet, just because the Iroquois did not directly influence the development of American democracy does not mean that they did not have an impact on American history. Quite the contrary. *The Iroquois Restoration* demonstrates that the Five Nations had a profound effect on the flow of American history throughout the seventeenth and eighteenth centuries.

The Iroquois' historical significance is linked to their alleged wilderness empire. Looking back in time, we cannot find evidence of an actual empire that stretched from New York to Illinois. But we can find evidence that the Five Nations created the impression that they controlled a vast empire that reached all the way to the Mississippi. We can also find proof that the Iroquois' Indian and white neighbors aided and abetted the Iroquois' pretensions. So, while the Iroquois empire may have been more myth than reality, it was significant none-

12

theless. Like many ideas in history, this idea of an Iroquois empire helped shape events. Before it was through, the "Phantom Iroquois Empire" cast a very long shadow on the pages of American history.

Ball State University
February 6, 1997

NOTES

1. Cadwallader Colden, *The History of the Five Indian Nations of Canada Which Are Dependent On the Province of New York, and are a barrier between the English and the French in that part of the World* (1727), reprint (New York, 1904), xvii.

2. De Witt Clinton, *Discourse Delivered before the New-York Historical Society, At Their Anniversary Meeting, 6th December, 1811* (New York, 1812), 8, 9, 23; Lewis Henry Morgan, *League of the Iroquois* (1851), reprint (Secaucus, New Jersey, 1972), 8; Francis Parkman, *The Conspiracy of Pontiac* (1851), reprint (New York, 1962; Lincoln, Nebraska, 1994), 38–39.

3. Randolph Downes, *Council Fires on the Upper Ohio: A Narrative of Indian Affairs in the Upper Ohio Valley until 1795* (Pittsburgh, 1940), 20, 27, 42–74; William Brandon, *The Last Americans: The Indian in American Culture* (New York, 1974), 226; Stephen Saunders Webb, *1676: The End of American Independence* (New York, 1984).

4. Along with the revisionist interpretations of the Iroquois empire by Anthony F. C. Wallace, *The Death and Rebirth of the Seneca* (New York, 1969); Francis Jennings, *The Ambiguous Iroquois Empire: The Covenant Chain Confederation of Indian Tribes with English Colonies from Its Beginnings to the Lancaster Treaty of 1744* (New York, 1984); Richard Haan, "The Problem of Iroquois Neutrality: Suggestions for Revision," *Ethnohistory*, XXVII (1980): 317–30; and Richard Aquila, *The Iroquois Restoration: Iroquois Diplomacy on the Colonial Frontier, 1701–1754* (Detroit, 1983; reprint, Lincoln, Nebraska, 1997), see also Bruce G. Trigger, *The Children of Aataentsic: A History of the Huron People to 1660*, 2 vols. (Montreal, 1976); Leroy V. Eid, "The Ojibwa-Iroquois War: The War the Five Nations Did Not Win," *Ethnohistory*, XXVI (1979): 297–324; and Dorothy V. Jones, *License for Empire: Colonialism by Treaty in Early America* (Chicago, 1982).

5. Copies of the papers presented at "The Imperial Iroquois: The 44th Conference on Early American History," March 30–31, 1984, are on file at the Institute of Early American History and Culture, Williamsburg, Virginia. Participants included Francis Jennings, William Fenton, Wilcomb E. Washburn, W. J. Eccles, Barbara Graymont, William Sturtevant, Daniel K. Richter, James H. Merrell, Mary Druke, Richard L. Haan, Theda Purdue, Douglas Boyce, Charles Hudson, Michael McConnell, Ives Goddard, James

Axtell, and Richard Aquila. Jennings's remarks are cited in Daniel K. Richter and James H. Merrell, editors, *Beyond the Covenant Chain: The Iroquois and Their Neighbors in Indian North America, 1600–1800* (Syracuse, New York, 1987), 6. A product of the conference, the volume is an excellent overview of revisionist approaches to the Iroquois. Richter elaborates on the revisionist position in *The Ordeal of the Longhouse: The Peoples of the Iroquois League in the Era of European Colonization* (Chapel Hill, North Carolina, 1992). Other recent works that question the myth of the Iroquois empire include: Francis Jennings, *Empire of Fortune: Crowns, Colonies, and Tribes in the Seven Years' War in America* (New York, 1988); Michael K. Foster et al., eds., *Extending the Rafters: Interdisciplinary Approaches to Iroquoian Studies* (Albany, New York, 1984); and Richard White, *The Middle Ground* (New York, 1991).

6. Jennings, *The Ambiguous Iroquois Empire*, xvii; Richter, *Ordeal of the Longhouse*, 126, 137.

7. Richard L. Haan, "Covenant and Consensus: Iroquois and English, 1676–1760," in Richter and Merrell, eds., *Beyond the Covenant Chain*, 41–57.

8. See Aquila, *The Iroquois Restoration*, chap. 1; Jennings, *The Ambiguous Iroquois Empire*, chap. 6; and Richter, *The Ordeal of the Longhouse*, chap. 3. The colonists' quotations appear in Richter, 31, 64.

9. Jennings, *The Ambiguous Iroquois Empire*, 93, 94.

10. See Aquila, *The Iroquois Restoration*, chap. 1 and Jennings, *The Ambiguous Iroquois Empire*, chap. 7.

11. Jennings, *The Ambiguous Iroquois Empire*, chap. 8; Richter, *The Ordeal of the Longhouse*, 135, 136. Haan argues that the Covenant Chain did not take shape until nearly a decade later; see "Covenant and Consensus," particularly pp. 43–50.

12. Richter, *The Ordeal of the Longhouse*, 136–37.

13. Haan, "Covenant and Consensus." Quotation can be found on p. 57.

14. Richter, *The Ordeal of the Longhouse*, 6, 7, 65, 169, 170, 215, 236–39.

15. Alvin Josephy, *The Patriot Chiefs: A Chronicle of American Indian Resistance* (New York, 1976), 28–29; Donald Grinde Jr., *The Iroquois and the Founding of the American Nation* (San Francisco, 1977); Donald Grinde Jr., and Bruce Johansen, *Exemplar of Liberty: Native America and the Evolution of Democracy* (Los Angeles, 1991); Bruce Johansen, "Native American Societies and the Evolution of Democracy in America, 1600–1800," *Ethnohistory*, XXXVII (1990): 279–90; Bruce Johansen, *Forgotten Founders: Benjamin Franklin, the Iroquois, and the Rationale for the American Revolution* (Ipswich, Massachusetts, 1982); and Bruce Burton, "Iroquois Confederate Law and the Origins of the U.S. Constitution" *Northeast Indian Quarterly*, III, no. 2 (Autumn, 1986): 4–9.

16. Dean Snow, *The Iroquois* (Cambridge, Massachusetts, 1994), 154, 238 n.14. For a detailed rebuttal to the myth of the Iroquois origins of the U.S. Constitution, see Elisabeth Tooker, "The United States Constitution and the Iroquois League," *Ethnohistory*, XXXV (1988): 305–36, and Elisabeth Tooker, "Rejoinder to Johansen," *Ethnohistory*, XXXVII (1990): 291–97.

Introduction to the First Edition

Today, when most people think of American Indians, they visualize the war bonneted, horse-riding Plains warrior made famous by dime novels, Wild West shows, television programs, and Hollywood movies. In reality, however, Great Plains Indians like the Sioux and Cheyenne may not have been as historically important as the Iroquois of the Eastern Woodlands. For over 100 years, the Iroquois played a major role in the development of the colonial frontier, influencing westward expansion, the fur trade, and colonial warfare.

This book is a history of Iroquois diplomacy during the first half of the eighteenth century. Part I provides background information and surveys the rise and fall of Iroquois power during the 1600s. Since historians such as Francis Parkman, George T. Hunt, Allen W. Trelease, Lawrence Henry Gipson, and others have done superb jobs in detailing the Iroquois' seventeenth-century wars, I see no reason to duplicate their work. Instead I briefly describe which wars were fought, why they occurred, why they ended, and how they affected the Iroquois. Part II provides an in-depth analysis of Iroquois involvement with Indians and whites between 1701 and 1754. It ends in 1754, because the coming of the Seven Years' War and the eventual expulsion of the French from North America mark the beginning of a new phase in Iroquois diplomacy.

My thesis is that Iroquois power was at its nadir after King William's War and that after 1700 the five Iroquois nations of New York, by design or circumstance, established a program aimed at restoring the power and prestige of the

Iroquois Confederacy. It would be misleading to insist that the Iroquois' "Restoration Policy" was premeditated. But it would also be wrong to conclude that Iroquois actions between 1701 and 1754 were merely haphazard. The Iroquois recognized their problems, interests, and needs and moved accordingly to meet them. Whether or not the Restoration Policy was premeditated depends upon which strategy is being discussed, what time period is being dealt with, and what specific event is occurring. The Restoration Policy was at various times the product of necessity, fortuitous circumstance, common need, chance, and rational geopolitical decisions. During the first half of the eighteenth century, the Iroquois were in the right place at the right time. Sometimes their Indian and white neighbors put them there. Other times they placed themselves there. In either case the Iroquois were smart enough to recognize opportunities and able enough to take advantage of them.

Iroquois actions and reactions led to the evolution of a program aimed at restoring Iroquois economic, political, and military strength. This program was a unified policy only in the loosest sense of the term. Common circumstances, conditions, and goals among the Five Nations provided a unity to Iroquois actions throughout the first half of the eighteenth century.

The Iroquois Restoration Policy comprised four major strategies. First, the Five Nations followed a policy of neutrality toward the English and French and tried to use both European powers to further their own interests. Neutrality enabled the Iroquois to receive various forms of economic and military assistance from both sides. Neutrality also allowed the Iroquois to trade with the English and French, and it secured Iroquoia from enemy attack. Second, the Iroquois sought a rapprochement with the powerful tribes of the upper Great Lakes country and Canada. Peace with the western tribes enabled the Iroquois to hunt safely in the West, to open trade with the western Indians, to prevent

16

the western tribes from invading Iroquoia, and to obtain powerful allies against Indian and white enemies. The Iroquois' ties to the western tribes also enhanced their diplomatic value as intermediaries between western Indians and whites. Friendly relations with the domiciliated Indians of Canada secured the Iroquois' northern borders, provided the Iroquois with additional military allies, and facilitated the growth of economic and social relations between the Iroquois and northern Indians. Third, the Iroquois cooperated with the Pennsylvania government to gain hegemony over the tribes and lands of Pennsylvania. The Iroquois then profited from land sales and received military and economic assistance from the colony. Hegemony also allowed the Iroquois to form beneficial alliances with the tribes of Pennsylvania. And fourth, the Iroquois followed a policy of war toward southern tribes. This warfare allowed the Iroquois to promote political, economic, and military relations with the French and western tribes, who were also at war with southern Indians. Southern raids enabled the Iroquois to develop closer ties to Pennsylvania Indians, who became allies against the southern Indians. And the southern wars provided young Iroquois warriors with the opportunity to achieve social and political advancement through success in battle.

Throughout the first half of the eighteenth century, the Iroquois generally adhered to their Restoration Policy. Sometimes the League Council implemented the strategies. On other occasions, individual Iroquois tribes or persons followed the policy. When taken together, actions of the Iroquois League Council, tribes, and individual Indians followed the same basic pattern during the first half of the eighteenth century.

The Restoration Policy allowed the Five Nations to recoup much of their political, military, and economic power. At the same time it mitigated factional strife among the Five Nations and gave Iroquois society the chance to recover

17

from the devastation of King William's War. The Restoration Policy propped up the Iroquois Confederacy during the first half of the eighteenth century and greatly affected the Iroquois' Indian and white neighbors. The Iroquois Restoration Policy worked remarkably well until 1745, but after that date external forces and internal divisions combined to undermine the program's effectiveness.

This study provides a comprehensive diplomatic history of the Iroquois from the mid-1600s until 1754, with the emphasis on the period 1701–1754. It reevaluates Iroquois relations with the English and French and explains how the Iroquois developed symbiotic relationships with both powers. It analyzes Iroquois contacts with Indians of the Eastern Woodlands. It explains how the Iroquois gained control over nearby tribes, why they waged war on southern Indians, and how they became allies of northern and western tribes. It presents a new interpretation of the Iroquois' role as middlemen in the fur trade. It shows how the Iroquois' external relations reflected and affected the evolution of their society in the seventeenth and eighteenth centuries. This case study also reveals cultural conflict and consensus between Indians and whites during the colonial period and demonstrates how the two groups interacted to achieve their goals. Finally, it shows that the Iroquois played a significant role in the European settlement of North America. The story of the Iroquois on the colonial frontier is an important chapter in American history, but it is not the final chapter involving the Iroquois. The Iroquois, unlike many eastern Indians, have retained their tribal identity and some of their original lands. Iroquois people, residing on reservations in New York State, still hold traditional councils and celebrate many of the old ceremonies. Iroquois history has become part of America's heritage.

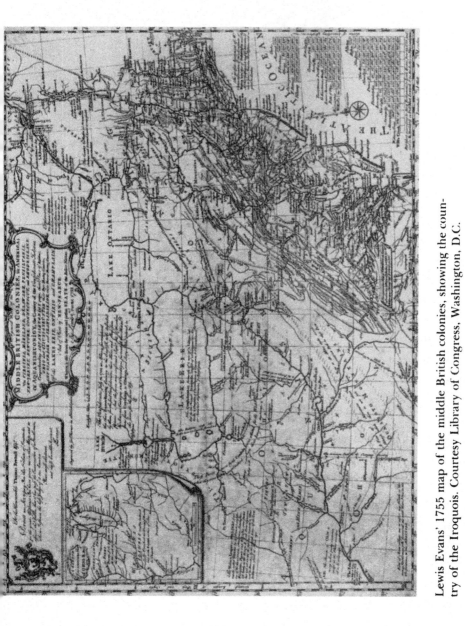

Lewis Evans' 1755 map of the middle British colonies, showing the country of the Iroquois. Courtesy Library of Congress, Washington, D.C.

Iroquois council at the home of William Johnson, near Albany, in the mid-1700s, shown in a painting by E. L. Henry, *Johnson Hall.* Courtesy John B. Knox and the Albany Institute of History and Art.

Iroquois captive being tortured. From David Pietersz de Vries, *Korte Histo-riael* (Hoorn, 1655). Courtesy Rare Books and Manuscripts Division, The New York Public Library, Astor, Lenox and Tilden Foundations.

TEE YEE NEEN HO GA ROW Emperour of the Six Nations

Chief Hendrick, or Tee Yee Neen Ho Ga Row, a Mohawk chief and one of the "Four Indian Kings" who visited London in 1710. Portrait by I. Verelot, engraved in London. He holds a wampum belt in his right hand; the wolf at his side indicates his membership in the wolf clan. Courtesy Library of Congress, Washington, D.C.

SA GA YEATH QUA PIETH TOW, King of the Maquas

Brant, or Sa Ga Yeath Qua Pieth Tow, another of the "Four Indian Kings" who visited London in 1710. Portrait by I. Verelot, engraved in London. Courtesy Library of Congress, Washington, D.C.

The original French castle by the lake at Ft. Niagara, built ca. 1726–27 (surrounding grounds are modern). Courtesy Old Fort Niagara Association.

William Johnson played a major role in maintaining the Covenant Chain between the English and the Iroquois. Portrait by T. Adams, engraved in London in 1756. Courtesy Library of Congress, Washington, D.C.

PART I

Background:
The Iroquois in the
Seventeenth Century

1

Early Iroquois Expansion

The twelve canoes were moving slowly along the northern shore of Lake St. Peter in the St. Lawrence River. Father Isaac Jogues, sitting comfortably in a lead canoe, had every reason to feel satisfied. The morning of August 2, 1642, was still young, and the party of four Frenchmen and about thirty-six Hurons could travel many miles before sunset. The Jesuit had been at Trois Rivieres and Quebec gathering desperately needed supplies for his mission among the Hurons of the upper Great Lakes. Now he was returning to his wilderness church.

As the canoes reached the western end of Lake St. Peter, Jogues began noticing the numerous islands that dotted the river and the bank that seemed to be overflowing with dense forest growth and tall bulrushes. Jogues' canoe, like the others, stayed close to the shore to avoid the fast current. The stillness, broken only by the paddles dipping into the water, was suddenly interrupted by ungodly, bloodcurdling screams. Hideously war-painted Iroquois warriors rushed from an ambuscade, swarming like hornets over Jogues' party. The French priest, trying to save a comrade, was quickly overwhelmed by the attackers. Several Iroquois began beating him with war clubs and then pounced on the fallen Jesuit, ripping out his fingernails and tearing open his hands with their teeth. The fighting was over within minutes—time that must have seemed eternal for Jogues and his men. The priest and twenty-one others were carried off to Iroquois villages where they were again beaten and tortured. The Jesuit's ordeal continued for several months.

Jogues' captivity and eventual martyrdom, as told to Europeans in *The Jesuit Relations,* contributed to the image of the Iroquois as a sadistic, savage people who revelled in torture, cannibalism, and desecration. New France's Indian allies held similar views: the term Iroquois is an Algonquin word meaning "rattlesnake" or "terrifying man." The French and Indians undoubtedly had good reasons for viewing the Iroquois as they did, but their opinions certainly did not present a total picture of the people they called Iroquois. In reality the Iroquois were not animallike savages who killed and tortured for pleasure. They were the most important and sophisticated Indian group on the northern colonial frontier. Their friendship or enmity influenced European settlement of North America and affected the outcome of the English and French struggle for empire.

The Iroquois were actually five confederated tribes: the Mohawk, Oneida, Onondaga, Cayuga, and Seneca. After 1712, the Tuscarora moved north from Carolina and were admitted into the League of the Iroquois as the sixth tribe. The Iroquois also were known to the French and English as the Five Nations, and then later as the Six Nations. The confederated tribes, speaking an Iroquoian language, called themselves the *Ho-de-no-sau-nee,* the "People of the Longhouse." (Hereafter, to avoid confusion, they will be referred to as the Iroquois or the Five Nations.)

Throughout most of the seventeenth and eighteenth centuries, the Five Nations' population never exceeded 15,000. Their homelands—Iroquoia–ran parallel to and south of Lake Ontario. Prior to 1650, Iroquoia stretched from the Mohawk River to the Genesee River. After that date the western boundary was extended to the Niagara River. The Mohawks, the most eastern tribe, lived on the south bank of the Mohawk River. To their west were the Oneidas, located on the shores of Oneida Lake. Next came the Onondagas, settled on the Onondaga River. Farther west were the Cayugas, situated near the eastern shore of Cayuga Lake. And farthest to the west were the Senecas, living near the Genesee River. The Tuscaroras were assigned homelands within Oneida territory.

Except for land cleared for villages and cultivation, Iroquoia was covered with lush forests of hemlock, maple, elm, pine, and oak. Trails and paths, sometimes only six inches wide, notched the woodlands, weaving a network of avenues throughout Iroquoia. The Central Trail (running approximately along the present route of the New York State Thruway) connected principal villages and provided access to Canada and the West. The Central Trail was intersected at various points by smaller cross-paths, which ran like tributaries to more remote areas of Iroquois territory. Other Indian trails heading south alongside the Susquehanna River and its branches converged at Tioga and formed the Great Southern Trail into Pennsylvania and Virginia. Trained runners could cover up to 100 miles per day along these routes. For over 200 years, Iroquois traveled these wilderness highways to hunt, trade, conduct diplomacy, and wage war throughout the Eastern Woodlands.

The Five Nations were primarily an agricultural people. After men cleared the fields surrounding the village, women would cultivate corn, beans, and squash, the mainstays of the Iroquois diet. Wild nuts and berries gathered by the women, along with fish and game brought home by the men, rounded out Iroquois meals. Various yearly celebrations, such as the Planting Festival, the Green Corn Festival, and the Harvest Festival, were linked to the production of crops.

Before contact with the white man, the Iroquois had obtained shelter and clothing from the natural environment.

31

They used poles and large slabs of elm bark to construct the large, rectangular longhouses, which could house fifty or sixty persons. Entering one of these multi-family dwellings, one could look down a dark, fifty- to one-hundred-foot-long corridor and see small fires smoldering every ten to fifteen feet. Compartments housing the immediate family and perhaps some relatives (the inhabitants were usually related along matrilineal lines) were located on the sides of each fire. They were accustomed to the noisy, crowded, smoke-filled, and frequently lice-infested conditions. Each clan posted its totem or crest above a longhouse's entrance. This practice allowed the Indians to locate and visit kinfolk throughout the Five Nations. Iroquois men hunted animals, like deer, bear, and beaver, to obtain skins for moccasins, leggings, skirts, and other garments. But contact with whites soon changed the Iroquois lifestyle. By 1700, Iroquois frequently wore woolens and ornaments manufactured by whites, and, by mid-century, many Iroquois were living in log homes modeled after those of their white neighbors.

A large Iroquois village, sometimes called a "castle," might have up to 3,000 residents. Matrilineal clans selected chiefs to represent them on the village council. These chiefs—the influential men of the community—handled the day-to-day problems of farming, water supplies, nearby hunting and fishing rights, and the raising of war parties. The village council met publicly and generally carried out the wishes of the majority.

Each of the Five Nations also had a tribal government, although tribal councils met infrequently. A tribal council comprised all village chiefs and dealt with matters such as war and peace, land sales, and tribal policy. The council's decisions were not binding on the individual villages. For all practical purposes the tribe was not a political organization. It was merely a collection of towns and related individuals speaking the same language.

The tribes, villages, and clans were joined together in the

Iroquois Confederacy, or the League of the Iroquois. This kinship organization provided the Five Nations with a loose governmental structure at the inter-tribal level. The Iroquois likened it to a longhouse stretching from the Hudson to the Genesee. The Senecas, living farthest west, were "Keepers of the Western Door," while the Mohawks to the east were "Keepers of the Eastern Door." The Onondagas, living in the heart of Iroquoia, became "Keepers of the Central Fire." The League dates back to the late 1500s or early 1600s, when, according to legend, Deganawidah the Prophet convinced the five tribes to stop their bickering and incessant warfare and live beneath the shade of the "Great Tree of Peace." Deganawidah implored all men to be brothers, and, preaching the "Great Law of Righteousness, Civil Authority, and Peace," formed a union among the numerous Iroquois settlements scattered in the forests of central New York.

Annually in late summer or early fall, the League Council met at Onondaga, the Confederacy's capital in central New York, near the present-day site of Syracuse. Fifty sachems, or civil chiefs, appointed by clan matrons from each of the Five Nations, comprised the Grand Council. Although the number of sachems in each tribe varied, the sachems voted as a tribal block, so each nation had only one vote. Unanimity was necessary to reach a decision.

The League Council provided the Five Nations with a weak central government, more like that of the United States under the Articles of Confederation than the Constitution. The sachems dealt with matters involving the entire Confederacy, such as war and peace, relations with whites and foreign Indians, land sales, and important economic and domestic issues. The Grand Council could not interfere in a tribe's internal affairs, nor did it have the power to enforce its decisions. If individual tribes or members of those tribes did not wish to comply with League decisions, they did not. The League Council governed with the Iro-

33

quois people's advice and consent. The Council led the Five Nations by persuasion and consensus, not fiat.

The Iroquois Confederacy was important for its symbolic rather than actual power. The Confederacy symbolized the Five Nations' unity and worked to end serious conflicts among its members. The League Council provided the means for making group decisions that influenced the beliefs and actions of the Confederacy's tribes and individual members. Equally significant, the League Council served as a mechanism for negotiations with European neighbors. Colonists saw the Grand Council as a European-style, democratic, centralized government. Many Americans still insist that the Iroquois Confederacy was a prototype for American democracy and federalism. Actually the League was neither democratic nor centralized in the European sense. It was a kinship state designed to promote unity and harmony among its related members. Yet sometimes perceptions are more important than realities. Whites perceived the League Council as a central government and negotiated with it, thereby increasing its significance.

The Iroquois used belts of colored beads, known as wampum, in political dealings with Indians and whites. Originally Indians made wampum beads out of shells, but by the mid-1600s, wampum usually consisted of glass beads manufactured by whites. Wampum belts were used primarily as mnemonic devices. Beads were arranged to form various designs and symbols that had specific meanings. Wampum was employed to record treaties, specify important points, and guarantee a speaker's words. Belts were kept in the care of a "Keeper of the Wampum," who could decode the symbols and repeat verbatim what had transpired when the belts first passed over the council fire.

The Five Nations were as adept at war as they were at politics. The decision to wage war could be made by sachems, tribal chiefs, or even individuals. During the 1640s, the Iroquois launched a series of wars against the tribes of the upper Great Lakes. The Five Nations, aiming at the dispersion, destruction, or control of the Indians living west of Iroquoia, consecutively defeated the Hurons, Neutrals, and Eries and sent other tribes like the Miamis, Illinois, and Potawatomies fleeing westward.

The attacks were, in part, economically motivated. During the first three decades of the seventeenth century, the people of the Five Nations obtained firearms, powder, blankets, pots, knives, and other trade goods from the Dutch and English in exchange for furs, mostly beaver. Before long the manufactured products that were once luxuries for the Indians became necessities. By 1640, the Iroquois, having trapped out their homelands, had to find a new source of furs for the valuable beaver trade. Their search led them to lands claimed by the Hurons and other Great Lakes tribes and sparked the series of wars sometimes called the Beaver Wars. For the rest of the century the Iroquois employed threats and violence to force their way into the fur-rich territories of their Indian neighbors. The Iroquois were ready, if necessary, to destroy the western tribes in order to control the furs of the upper Great Lakes country.[1]

The Iroquois' culture provided further motivation to make war on the western tribes. Honor, glory, and social success could best be achieved on the warpath. The individuals who were held in great esteem by the tribe or who were chosen "Pine Tree Chiefs" or civil leaders often achieved their status by establishing reputations as successful warriors. In fact, by the mid-eighteenth century, Iroquois war chiefs sometimes held more power and public support than the hereditary civil sachems. Other cultural factors also made war important for the Iroquois. At times the people of the Five Nations waged war to get revenge. On other occasions war parties captured prisoners for adoption or torture, for the Iroquois traditionally replaced all mourned dead. The dead could be replaced in two ways. A prisoner of war could be adopted into a dead man's

35

family, taking the place of the deceased in the Iroquoian longhouse and society. The dead warrior could also be replaced in a spiritual sense. That is, a captive could be tortured to death by the dead warrior's family and friends. Frequently the victim was eaten, thereby becoming literally a part of the family. Prisoners were sometimes taken for another reason. When warfare or disease caused a serious loss of population, the Iroquois sought to replenish their numbers through mass adoptions. Occasionally, entire villages were adopted.[2]

Psychological reasons may have contributed to Iroquois warfare. Some anthropologists suggest that the League effectively blocked all fratricidal strife among the Five Nations, so that the Indians' pent-up frustrations and hostilities had to be focused upon those outside the Confederacy. The "League of Peace," paradoxically, caused the Iroquois to lash out against neighboring Indians and whites.[3]

The Iroquois were successful in their seventeenth-century Indian wars for several reasons. Their homelands gave them a strategic and geographic position from which they were able to control the portal of the Great Lakes and the sources of waterways flowing both to the Mississippi and the Atlantic. This position allowed them to control traffic between Montreal and the interior, as well as passage to the lower Great Lakes, the Ohio Country, and the frontiers of New York, Pennsylvania, Maryland, Virginia, and the Carolinas.[4]

Another reason for their success is that they usually possessed military superiority over their enemies. One reason for this superiority was the League of the *Ho-de-no-sau-nee*, which united the five Iroquois tribes into one confederacy. Historians have sometimes overstated the ability of the League to get the Five Nations to contribute warriors for a united war effort. But on occasion, the Five Nations, through the League, did unite for a combined attack against a common enemy. The League also served other

36

important functions. It brought a period of internal peace to its five members, which allowed each to pursue other interests, such as trade wars or raids against hostile tribes, while not having to worry about intra-League fighting. At the same time the League provided the Five Nations with a more effective socio-political organization than most of the other tribes of the Eastern Woodlands. This organization allowed the Five Nations, unlike some of their enemies, to withstand, and adapt to, the pressures of war and social change.[5]

The Five Nations were usually better armed than their Indian enemies. Because of their location, they had easy access to firearms and powder. During the early 1600s, if the Dutch declined to trade guns for furs, the Five Nations would take their trade to the English, the Swedes, or the French. The western tribes did not have this leverage, for the only Europeans with whom they came into contact were the French. By the mid- and late 1600s, Iroquois warriors, regularly receiving arms and ammunition from the English, were at least as well armed, and frequently better armed, than their foes.[6]

The Iroquois' success in seventeenth-century warfare can also be attributed in part to their intense motivation, which stemmed from economic necessity, as well as from their cultural heritage. The Iroquois had to conquer their neighbors in order to acquire the furs needed for their vital trade with the Dutch and English. Such a do-or-die situation provided the determination needed for success. No doubt, their culture, with its stress on glory and honor through war, provided additional motivation for Iroquois males to succeed in battle.

Furthermore, the Five Nations had a psychological advantage working for them. Every new Iroquois victory struck added terror into the hearts of their enemies. By the mid-1630s, the Hurons were so frightened of the Iroquois that, at times, a mere rumor of an approaching Iroquois war party was enough to send an entire village fleeing into the woods in search of hiding places. On other occasions, the sight of suspicious-looking footprints was all that was needed to set the Hurons scurrying in fright. Other tribes reacted in similar ways. Even the French lived in dread of Iroquois attacks. In 1684, a Jesuit confided to the governor of New France, La Barre, "The French man who came here told me that whilst you were at La Famine a false alarm reached Montreal that the Iroquois were coming; that there was nothing but horror, flight, and weeping at Montreal."[7]

The first wave of Iroquois warfare against the western tribes subsided by the mid-1660s. When the war clouds cleared, several important results were evident. The Iroquois were the dominant force in the Western Country, a territory that extended from Iroquoia in the east, to the lands north and south of Lake Michigan in the west. The Western Country was bounded by the Ohio River valley in the south and the Ottawa River valley in the north. The wars had nearly emptied this region of its native population. The Five Nations had conquered or dispersed the Huron, Tobacco, Neutral, and Erie nations, while other tribes had fled to safer lands in the north or farther west. The constant threat of Iroquois attacks had driven the Miamis west and northward into the Wisconsin area, while it caused the Illinois to withdraw to the western side of the Mississippi River. Other nations, like the Fox, Sac, Mascouten, and Kickapoo, fled from lower Michigan in terror of the advancing Iroquois.[8] This exodus left the Western Country to the Iroquois. After years of fighting, the Five Nations had finally secured control of vast lands which could provide the beaver furs needed for the vital Albany trade.

The victory over the western tribes did not come cheaply: the cost was paid in blood. In 1657, a French Jesuit wrote, "Their [the Iroquois'] victories have so depopulated their towns that there are more foreigners in them than natives." The Iroquois balanced off their war casualties through mass adoptions of foreign Indians. Head counts made by travelers in Iroquoia between 1660 and 1684 show that Iroquois warriors consistently numbered around 2,300. The composition of the Five Nations' war parties may have changed as adopted warriors replaced the dead Iroquois men, but the Iroquois' total strength in manpower had survived. When the opening round of the Iroquois' wars in the Western Country came to a close in the mid-1660s, Iroquois power was still intact.[9]

Equally significant was the fact that after years of constant warfare, the Iroquois finally controlled the Western Country and its wealth of furs. The Iroquois' victories in the West, however, had not solved all their problems. Smallpox plagued the Iroquois people in 1662 and left the survivors in a depressed and weakened condition. The Susquehannocks, a powerful tribe living on the lower Susquehanna River, were threatening Iroquois villages and trade. Algonquin tribes of the Northeast were raiding Iroquoia. And, to make matters worse, the French, taking a harder line against the intractable Iroquois, had imported the famous Carignan-Salieres Regiment to invade Iroquoia. In 1666, the French carried out their plans with two successful expeditions against Mohawk villages.[10]

The Five Nations were being threatened from all directions, and they knew all too well that they could not win on all fronts. Realizing that they already had defeated the western tribes, that they controlled the Western Country, and that the French were an almost unbeatable foe, the Iroquois decided to concentrate their energies on the Susquehannocks, an enemy that could be defeated. Before taking on the Susquehannocks, the Five Nations wanted to remove the threat of a two-front, or even a four-front, war. So they opened negotiations with the Algonquin raiders. The Iroquois sent ambassadors to the Algonquins and even got the English to intervene on their behalf. A peace treaty, securing the Iroquois' northeastern borders, was ratified in 1672.

39

Next, Iroquois deputies trekked northward to Canada to ask for peace. In 1667, the Five Nations and the French and their Indian allies agreed to bury their hatchets and pledge themselves to a lasting peace. This treaty ended the possibility of war on the Iroquois' northern and western borders.[11]

Meanwhile, some of the Five Nations had already begun to focus their attention on the Susquehannocks, since the destruction of that tribe would secure the Iroquois' southern border. Between 1667 and 1679, Iroquois warriors continuously raided the Susquehannocks and other Indian enemies to the south. The Iroquois' hostilities with the Susquehannocks were rooted in sixteenth-century blood feuds. By the 1600s, the feuding had escalated into full scale warfare due to economic rivalry in the fur trade. The proximity of the two tribes, along with their warlike cultures, contributed to the perpetuation and escalation of the hostilities.[12]

The Five Nations soon learned that the Susquehannocks' extermination would not be easy. The Virginia and Maryland colonies took an active interest in the affairs of the Susquehannocks, for that tribe supplied them with furs and peltry. As a result the Susquehannocks were able to obtain an abundance of firearms and even cannons for their castles. These weapons cancelled out any superiority the Five Nations might have had in firepower. The war dragged on until the late 1670s. Then it came to a sudden close, with the mysterious defeat of the Susquehannocks. Historians still debate whether the Iroquois or other forces were responsible for the Susquehannock defeat. Most likely, Virginia and Maryland frontiersmen contributed to the demise of the Susquehannocks, who, ironically, were English allies. Settlers probably attacked the Susquehannocks to avenge murders committed by marauding Indians. The Susquehannocks repeatedly insisted that Senecas had committed the atrocities. But angry frontiersmen, to whom all Indians were the same, may have turned with a vengeance on the nearby, friendly Susquehannocks. Historical evidence supports this scenario.

Governor Nicholls of New York reported that the Iroquois attacked the Susquehannocks as the latter were retreating along the Virginia frontier. In 1679, an Oneida sachem told a Virginia official, "The Susquehannas are all destroyed for which we return you many thanks." Regardless of how the destruction of the Susquehannocks occurred, the result was the same. The Susquehannock Nation was no more. Any survivors were dispersed or incorporated into the Five Nations.[13] In this manner the southern border of Iroquoia was secured.

From 1667 until 1679 the Five Nations were not, however, warring exclusively on the Susquehannocks. On occasion Iroquois warriors attacked other tribes to the south and west. In 1677, the governor of Virginia sent Henry Coursey to Iroquoia to ask the Five Nations to stop raiding the various tribes of Virginia and Maryland. The Iroquois agreed to halt their southern raids, and concluded a treaty in 1677. During this period some of the Five Nations also made raids into the Western Country. One such raid occurred in 1670, when some Senecas attacked an Ottawa village. The French quickly stepped in as mediators and restored the peace.[14]

The Iroquois-French Treaty of 1667 and the Iroquois' preoccupation with the Susquehannock War brought a relative calm to the Western Country. Between 1667 and 1680, French Indians (i.e., Indian allies of New France) and *coureurs de bois* took advantage of this respite to reoccupy their lands east of the Mississippi River. The Iroquois were angry about the western Indians' return. The Five Nations needed the Western Country as a source of furs. That was one of the reasons why their warriors had first driven out potential rivals from that area. But now those enemy tribes had moved back and were again hindering Iroquois hunters. After the Susquehannock problem was settled in 1680, the Iroquois were more determined than ever to rid the West of all rivals. So Iroquois warriors picked up their weapons and began their second wave of western warfare. The truce with the western tribes was over. Although the Iroquois did not know it at the time, their military supremacy in the Western Country was almost over too. They, and not the western tribes, would be the losers in this new struggle for the beaver hunting grounds.[15]

The Iroquois opened the fighting with several impressive victories against western tribes. In April, 1680, a war party numbering about 550 men attacked an Illinois village. The ferocious warriors smashed through the Illinois' defenses, sending the Indians into a panic-stricken retreat. The relentless Iroquois pursued their victims and clubbed them into submission. When the fighting was over, the Iroquois had killed or captured 1,200 Illinois men, woman, and children, while losing only 30 of their own warriors. Another Iroquois war party met with a similar, though not nearly so spectacular, success when it captured a hunting party from the *Bay des Puants* tribe. Afterwards Du Chesnu, the intendant of New France, solemnly remarked, "The victory achieved by the Iroquois rendered them so insolent that they have continued ever since that time to send out divers [*sic*] war parties."[16]

The Iroquois continued to do well in their encounters against the western tribes, and by 1687, Iroquois victories over the Illinois, Miamis, Ottawas, and Hurons had the western Indians reeling.[17] But just at the moment when a total Iroquois victory in the West seemed imminent, the French decided to intervene. At that point the long struggle, which later became entwined with King William's War, had begun.

2

The Twenty Years' War

The Iroquois war against the western tribes and their French allies lasted from the late 1670s until 1701. Although it began as an Indian war between the Five Nations and the western tribes, the conflict eventually escalated into a full-scale colonial war, with the French and their Indian allies fighting the English and the Iroquois. Three main stages are evident in the fighting that occurred between 1680 and 1701. (For the sake of simplicity, this twenty-year period will be referred to as the Twenty Years' War.)

The first stage, 1680–89, found the Iroquois on the offensive. Iroquois raids during the first part of this decade had the French and Indians on the retreat. The French received a further setback in 1684 when the governor of New France, La Barre, made an unsuccessful attempt to invade Iroquoia. Nonville assumed the governorship in 1685 and immediately made plans to avenge his predecessor's humiliating defeat. His troops invaded the Senecas' homelands on June 30, 1687. During the next ten days, the French and Indian army destroyed four villages and the surrounding fields of corn and squash. But the Senecas had wisely chosen to retreat, so their power remained intact. Before the year was out, the Senecas and their Iroquois confederates had Montreal under a partial siege, and the

French regime in Canada was on the verge of paralysis due to famine, sickness, and the numerous Iroquois depredations. On July 26, 1689, over 1,500 Iroquois warriors attacked the village of Lachine, just six miles upstream from Montreal. Since Nonville's garrison at Montreal could offer no effective resistance to the invaders, the results were disastrous. When a French rescue party finally arrived from Montreal, it found only smoldering houses and French bodies lying dead on the battleground or tortured on posts. Pierre Charlevoix, an early eighteenth-century Jesuit, described the Iroquois raid on Lachine as follows: "[The Iroquois] found all the people asleep, and began by massacring the men; then they set fire to the houses. By this means, all who had remained in them fell into the hands of these Indians. . . . [The Iroquois] opened the bodies of pregnant women, to tear out the fruit they bore; they put children alive on the spit, and forced the mothers to turn and roast them. They invented a number of other unheard-of tortures; and thus, in less than an hour, 200 persons of every age and both sexes, perished in the most frightful tortures." Charlevoix added that afterwards the Iroquois came within a league of Montreal, "everywhere committing the same ravages and perpetuating the same cruelties and, when weary of these horrors, they took 200 prisoners, whom they carried off to their villages and burned."[1]

In all fairness to the Iroquois, the raid at Lachine was basically no different in conception or style than Nonville's raids into Seneca territory, which had taken place earlier in the month. The only real difference was that the Iroquois' attack was successful.

Immediately following the Lachine raid, Iroquois power seemed to be at its peak, but the winds of change were already beginning to blow. Before 1689 was over, Canada would have a new governor, and the Iroquois would have new problems.

The war's second act opened in 1689, when two noteworthy events occurred: the English openly entered the war, which then became intertwined with the colonial conflict, King William's War, and Count Frontenac returned to Canada to assume control of the French war effort. Frontenac's return proved to be the more important of the two events. He opened with a successful attack on Schenectady. His forces then repelled a poorly organized English-Iroquois retaliatory effort. Within a year of his arrival, Frontenac had begun to turn the war around.

The years 1693–97 were characterized by French and Indian victories, Iroquois defeats, and English reluctance to fight, all of which forced the Iroquois on the defensive. On January 25, 1694, Frontenac sent 600 French and Indians to invade Mohawk country. They took the Mohawks by surprise; when the fighting was over, 300 Mohawks had been captured, three of their castles burned, and their winter food supply destroyed. Soon thereafter, many Iroquois, realizing that the English would not help them, began asking for peace. In 1695, Frontenac regained control of Fort Cataraqui, located at the eastern end of Lake Ontario. From the fort, he was able in 1696 to launch another massive attack into Iroquoia. This action convinced the Iroquois that the old count could invade their homelands at will. English-French hostilities ended the next year with the Treaty of Ryswick. Frontenac, however, refused to recognize the Five Nations as English subjects and demanded that they make a separate peace before the war could be stopped with the French and Indians.[2]

The final stage of the Twenty Years' War lasted from 1697 until 1701. During this period the Iroquois were under constant attack from the French Indians and feared a total loss. By the end of 1699, the Iroquois realized that they had few alternatives left. They knew the English could not be counted on for assistance and realized they could not defeat the French and Indians alone. To make matters worse, the Iroquois began hearing rumors of a French-

English conspiracy to destroy the Five Nations. In dismay some Iroquois turned to what they felt was their only remaining option. They decided to negotiate a separate peace treaty with the French and Indians.

On March 21, 1700, two Iroquois Indians arrived in Montreal to meet with Governor Callieres, who had replaced Frontenac in September, 1699. They indicated that they were not commissioned to negotiate for the Five Nations, but promised that fully empowered deputies would be arriving in July. The suspicious Callieres was not satisfied with the unconvincing reasons given by the two messengers to explain the long delay before the Iroquois deputies' arrival.

Most likely not all the Iroquois were responsible for sending the two messengers to Montreal. Some Iroquois, even as late as July, constituted a pro-English faction that was opposed to any peace negotiations with New France. Clues indicate that the two messengers represented only the Iroquois peace faction, that is, the group or party among the Iroquois that sought peace through direct negotiations. The messengers had no authority to act for the entire Five Nations. Also, the messengers' vague replies about the Five Nations' reasons for not coming to Montreal until July show that they could not speak for all Iroquois. Lastly, since only six deputies from two of the Five Nations arrived in July to discuss peace, it seems probable that the two original messengers were not speaking on behalf of all the Five Nations when they arranged the conference. Otherwise, more deputies from all Five Nations would have arrived as promised.

Although there is some question as to who sent the two messengers, there is no doubt that their mission was a success. They not only got Callieres to agree to a summer date for the negotiations, but they also got him to declare a cease-fire until the peace talks could be held.[3]

While the Iroquois peace faction was arranging the negotiations with New France, the English were becoming increasingly concerned over the status of the Five Nations. On April 20, 1700, Governor Bellomont of New York wrote to the Board of Trade, making it clear that should the Iroquois defect to the French side, the English would be forced off the continent within two months. Robert Livingston, an Albany Commissioner of Indian Affairs, visited Iroquois villages in April and reported that the Five Nations were dejected and were contemplating a separate peace treaty with the French. He added that although all the Indians feared the French, the Mohawks, in particular, had felt the wrath of the French enemy: nearly two-thirds of the Mohawks had already defected to the French and more might follow. He pointed out that French Jesuits controlled some of the Five Nations and that many Iroquois people might desert to the French side. Livingston recommended to Bellomont that steps be taken to maintain the Indians' loyalty. He felt that New York could stop the western tribes' raids on the Iroquois by opening up a trade with those far Indians. Livingston also recommended that New York build forts to protect the Iroquois and station Protestant missionaries throughout Iroquoia to convert the Five Nations and neutralize the Jesuits' presence. Other observers agreed with Livingston that the Five Nations were in a desperate condition, and by May it was evident that the Iroquois had resolved to end their war with New France.[4]

The only question that remained was whether the Five Nations would make peace independent of the English, as the French demanded, or would allow the English to negotiate their peace for them, as the English (who claimed the Five Nations as subjects) wanted.

Members of the Five Nations favoring the English approach met with New York officials on several occasions in June, 1700. These Iroquois promised to remain loyal to the English and condemned those confederates who wanted to make a separate treaty with New France. Pro-English sachems maintained that the Five Nations would not treat

47

separately with the French and Indians if New York inter-
vened and stopped the western tribes' attacks on the Iroquois. These Iroquois made it clear that they wanted to
remain loyal to the English and would do so as long as New
York helped them against the western or far Indians.[5]

Western Indian raids against the Iroquois in May and
June probably undermined the position of those Iroquois
wanting to negotiate with New France. In March, the
French governor had agreed to a cease-fire until peace talks
could be held in July. Yet, the western tribes' hostilities had
not stopped. The pro-English faction among the Five Nations most likely used the cease-fire violations to show those
Iroquois who had not yet committed themselves to either
faction that the French and Indians could not be trusted.
By July, very few Iroquois were willing to attend the scheduled peace conference at Montreal. The two Iroquois messengers who had arranged the July talks back in March had
promised that deputies from the Oneidas, Onondagas, Cayugas, and Senecas would meet with the French governor.
But when the time came, the pledge was not met. Many
Iroquois had been convinced by Governor Bellomont not to
negotiate with the French. Yet not all the Five Nations were
willing to follow the governor's advice. Some Iroquois were
determined to carry out the separate peace talks with New
France's Governor Callieres.[6]

On July 18, two Onondaga deputies and four Seneca deputies arrived at Montreal to attend the scheduled conference. Though they claimed to represent all the Iroquois
nations except the Mohawks, it seems more likely that they
were sent by the peace faction only. Even their excuse as to
why the Oneidas and Cayugas did not send their own deputies seemed flimsy. They claimed that they represented the
four upper Iroquois nations who had resolved to treat without the pro-English Mohawks and that the reason no Cayugas or Oneidas were present was because "Bellomont
having sent Peter Schuyler to dissuade them from going

down to Montreal, the deputies of those two cantons had gone to learn the reason of his opposition to their voyage."[7]

The truth of the matter is that had the Cayugas and Oneidas really wanted to negotiate with New France, they would have, regardless of the governor's protests. What probably happened was that after the Iroquois' peace faction realized that the Cayugas, Oneidas, and Mohawks would not negotiate with the French, they decided to send deputies to the scheduled conference anyway. These deputies could maintain that they were commissioned by all the Five Nations except the Mohawks (who were most loyal to the English because of their proximity) to reach a settlement which the entire Confederacy would later find acceptable.

The six Iroquois deputies presented five wampum belts to Governor Callieres. Each belt represented a major point that the Iroquois wanted to make. Handing the first belt to the French governor, the deputies' spokesman said that the Five Nations had heard that the Treaty of Ryswick had established peace between England and France, and between all the Indian allies of both nations. Yet French Indians were still killing Iroquois people. He added, "The hatchet is still hanging over our heads; we come to learn from our [French] Father whether he will withdraw it or have it taken away from his allies." Callieres replied that the Iroquois had been misinformed by Bellomont: they were not included in the Treaty of Ryswick. They had to conclude a separate agreement with the French and Indians if they wanted the fighting to stop.

The Iroquois deputies then presented a second belt to the French governor, asking why the western tribes had repeatedly violated the cease-fire agreed to in March. The Iroquois spokesman said, "I request you, Father, to take the hatchet out of their hands so that they may strike no more; if I do not defend myself, it is not for want of courage, but because I wish to obey you." Callieres probably could not believe his ears. Here were his long-time foes suddenly say-

49

ing they did not wish to disobey him. The governor, maintaining a calm facade, replied that in March he had taken steps to prevent any further attacks by the western Indians, but that the Five Nations' constant stalling, plus an Iroquois attack on the Miamis, had provoked the western tribes. Callieres added that he regretted the attacks on the Iroquois, and, if the Five Nations were sincere in their requests for peace, they should send ambassadors from all Five Nations within thirty days to conclude a treaty.

The Iroquois responded with a third wampum belt, promising they would come within thirty days to make peace. The deputies then gave Callieres another belt and requested that the Jesuit Bruyas and two soldiers, Maricourt and Joncaire, accompany them on their return to Iroquoia. The deputies argued that such a French delegation would "convince the cantons that their [French] Father sincerely desired peace." The deputies added that the three French ambassadors would also be able to bring back to Canada all the Frenchmen being held as prisoners in Iroquois villages.[8]

This request was a masterful stroke by the Iroquois deputies. They realized that many Iroquois would interpret the French ambassadors' arrival at Onondaga as a sign that the French had come begging for peace, and more Iroquois might, therefore, be willing to negotiate a French treaty independent of the English. The selection of the Jesuit and the two soldiers had been carefully planned. The deputies knew that the French were eager to proselytize among the Iroquois and that many Iroquois were equally intent on receiving the Catholic missionaries. The deputies also were aware that Maricourt and Joncaire would be well received by the Iroquois. Both of them, but especially Joncaire, were held in esteem by the Five Nations. Joncaire had first come into contact with the Iroquois when he was captured in a battle by the Senecas, probably in 1687. La Potherie, who was Joncaire's contemporary, explained that Joncaire "was taken in a battle; the fierceness with which he fought a war

50

chief who wished to bind him in order to burn his fingers until the sentence of death could be carried out, induced the others to grant him his life, his comrades having all been burned at a slow fire. They [the Senecas] adopted him, and the confidence which they had in him thenceforth led them to make him their mediator in all negotiations." The Senecas later bestowed their greatest honor on Joncaire by making him a tribal sachem; and the Frenchman held their respect until the day he died.[9] One of the ironies of history is Joncaire's present anonymity. Americans have made heroes out of Davy Crockett and Daniel Boone, but overlook Joncaire, one of the first frontiersmen of them all and perhaps the greatest. The fact that Joncaire was a Frenchman, and therefore an enemy of the English, might explain why Americans have long neglected him, but it certainly does not justify it.

The French governor agreed to the Iroquois' request that Bruyas, Maricourt, and Joncaire be sent to Iroquoia on the condition that some deputies remain in Montreal as hostages until the three Frenchmen returned safely. Four of the deputies volunteered to stay behind.

The Iroquois deputies then presented the final wampum belt to the French governor as a pledge of peace. They promised that their people would not listen to any Englishmen who tried to convince them not to make a separate peace treaty with New France. The conference was then adjourned. Soon afterwards, two of the Iroquois deputies, along with Father Bruyas and the soldiers Maricourt and Joncaire and a small French escort, set out for Iroquoia.[10]

If the Iroquois deputies were hoping that the arrival of the three Frenchmen would impress the Five Nations, they were not disappointed. The three French ambassadors were welcomed enthusiastically by the war-weary people of the Five Nations. An Iroquois welcome party met the French delegates at Lake Gannentaha and triumphantly led the French to their Confederacy capital, Onondaga,

51

where the party entered the town amid volleys of mus-
ketry. The loud reception was topped off by a lavish feast.
On August 10, the three ambassadors made their first appearance before the League Council. Sachems from all the
Five Nations except the Mohawks were present and listened attentively as the Frenchmen delivered their messages. The ambassadors condoled the Iroquois for warriors
slain in past wars. They then told their Iroquois hosts,
"Children. It is now peace between the great Kings over
the great water. Let it likewise be peace between you and
us and the Rondachses, the Waganhaes, Twightwees, Tion-
dadees, and all our other Nations of Indians." The
Frenchmen declared that they wished to exchange prisoners and place a Jesuit mission in Iroquoia. The sachems
agreed to send deputies to Canada to arrange the peace
and exchange of prisoners, but hedged on accepting a
mission.[11]

The turnabout in the Five Nations' position on separate
negotiations with New France was probably caused by two
factors. First, the French deputies' arrival at Onondaga convinced the Iroquois, as the peace faction hoped it would,
that the French sincerely desired peace. The reaction of
English officials to the French ambassadors' arrival was
equally, if not more, important in convincing most of the
Iroquois to negotiate with New France.

As soon as Governor Bellomont had learned about the
Frenchmen's visit, he dispatched John B. van Eps to Onondaga to warn the Five Nations not to be deceived by the
French. When van Eps reached the Iroquois capital, he
learned the talks between the French and the Iroquois had
already begun. Van Eps cautioned the sachems that the
governor of New York had ordered them not even to speak
to the French. The imperious tone of Bellomont's message
shocked the League Council and made the sachems even
more determined to negotiate with New France. The Five
Nations had long believed that they were not subjects of the

English king, but were instead equal allies. Bellomont's message, as delivered by van Eps, was a challenge to Iroquois sovereignty. The French convinced the Iroquois Council that Bellomont's message proved that the English looked upon them as subjects. Joncaire even suggested that the reason the English did not want the Iroquois to make peace was that they wanted to see the Five Nations weakened through continued warfare. The sachems became even more indignant and determined to negotiate with the French when they received news that a governor from New England was furious about their talks with the French and had threatened to destroy them should they make a separate peace. Undoubtedly, many of the Five Nations decided to support the peace faction's position of negotiating a treaty with New France in response to these English attitudes. Unwittingly the English had pushed many Iroquois into the waiting arms of the French.[12]

On August 11, 1700, Joncaire left Onondaga for Seneca country, where he had spent many years as an adopted prisoner. The Senecas welcomed him back warmly, as a son and ambassador, and agreed to hand over all French captives to him. But to his chagrin, many prisoners refused to return to Canada. They had been adopted into Seneca families and had grown accustomed to Seneca ways, and they had no intention now of abandoning their new lives.

Meanwhile, back at Onondaga, the League Council decided to carry out the negotiations with New France. The governor's envoy, van Eps, was allowed to sit in on the deliberations. He received a good indication of the direction in which the sachems were heading when Teganissorens, a member of the peace faction, rose to act as the Council spokesman. Teganissorens announced that the Iroquois were going to comply with the French request that each nation immediately send deputies to Canada. Shortly thereafter, Bruyas and Maricourt, accompanied by Onondaga and Cayuga deputies, left for Montreal. A few days later,

Joncaire arrived with six Seneca deputies and some released prisoners. In all, only thirteen French prisoners had agreed to return to Canada.[13]

The French ambassadors had failed to bring back many prisoners of war, but they had succeeded in convincing most of the Five Nations to agree to separate negotiations with the French. However, not all of the Five Nations had agreed to talk peace. The Mohawks had not taken part in any of the conferences, and the Oneidas' sincerity in wanting peace was suspect. The Oneidas had not even sent deputies as promised, but had merely sent wampum belts, insisting that their chief deputy was ill. Overall, though, prospects for peace between the Iroquois and the French and Indians never looked better. The efforts of the Iroquois peace faction along with the French actions and the English responses had pushed most Iroquois to the point where they were willing to negotiate directly with the French, as evidenced by the League Council's adoption of the resolution calling for resumption of peace talks with New France. At the same time though, most Iroquois were not yet ready to abandon their longtime English allies. Some Iroquois remained convinced that the English could help the Five Nations. Even as the Iroquois peace delegation made its way northward toward its rendezvous with the French governor, other Iroquois were seeking assistance from the New York governor. On August 27, several Iroquois sachems met with Governor Bellomont and asked for protection from the western tribes allied to New France. They also requested that Protestant missions be established in Iroquois villages, that better trade policies be established at Albany, and that forts be built throughout Iroquoia to protect the Five Nations. The sachems promised that if the governor granted their requests, the Five Nations would not deal separately with New France.

Bellomont replied that he thought the Five Nations should stop fighting the western tribes and should, instead, bring those nations into the Covenant Chain through trade. (The Covenant Chain was a military, political, and economic alliance between the English and the Iroquois and other pro-English Indians.) The governor then promised to establish a fort at Onondaga if the Five Nations would help build it. Lastly, he recommended that the Iroquois seize all Jesuits who were among them and bring them to Albany as prisoners.

The sachems answered that they wanted the fort at Onondaga, but they would not seize any Jesuits, since such a move might interfere with peace talks with the western and northern tribes.[14] These sachems, from all appearances, sincerely wanted New York's help. They hoped Governor Bellomont would protect them by building the fort and intervening with the western tribes. The pro-English Iroquois promised that their nations would turn their backs on French overtures if the governor met their demands. At the same time though, the sachems were careful not to do anything that might ruin negotiations with New France. That probably explains why they were so reluctant to capture any Jesuits, as Bellomont had requested. In short, most of the Five Nations were now willing to talk to both the English and the French, and would deal with whomever had the most to offer.

When the Iroquois peace delegation arrived at Montreal in early September, 1700, it received a welcome fit for heroes and dignitaries. Some of the Indians living near Montreal must have felt twinges of jealousy as the nineteen Onondaga, Cayuga, and Seneca deputies, who also spoke for the Oneidas, were saluted with blasts from the French *patararoes,* short cannons set up vertically and plugged to make a very loud noise.

On September 3, the conference between the Iroquois deputies and Governor Callieres of New France began. The Iroquois spokesman opened by stating that the Confederacy was willing to comply with French desires for

55

peace. The Iroquois deputy then carefully explained several points. First, as proof that the Iroquois wanted peace, they had already stopped a group of 200 of their warriors from attacking French Indians in retaliation for earlier raids. Second, the Iroquois wanted all their prisoners of war returned by the French. Third, the Iroquois desired to trade with the French at Fort Cataraqui. Fourth, they hoped the French would place a smith at the fort to repair Iroquois guns and goods. And fifth, the Iroquois wanted a guarantee of French protection should the English attempt to chastize them for seeking a separate peace. The Iroquois demands clearly show the Five Nations' strategy. They wanted peace and the return of all their prisoners from the French, but they also wanted assurances that after the peace they would still have access to trade goods, smiths, and protection.

Governor Callieres responded favorably to all the Iroquois requests. He commended the Indians for recalling their warriors and promised that they had nothing more to fear from the western tribes. He suggested that should a violation of the peace occur, the aggrieved party should come to him, and he would act as a mediator who would right the wrong. The governor agreed to provide low-priced trade goods and smiths for the Five Nations, and he promised to ask the king for permission to protect the Iroquois from any English retaliatory actions. Callieres then thanked the Iroquois for returning thirteen French prisoners of war and recommended that the entire Five Nations meet with the French and their Indian allies the following August to formally ratify the peace and exchange all prisoners.

Next, the French Indian allies who were present, such as the Hurons, Ottawas, Abenakis, and Praying Iroquois (i.e., Indians from the Five Nations living in Canadian missions), promised to stop warring on the Iroquois. Not all were eager to do so, but Callieres, nevertheless, got them to agree. A preliminary treaty between the Five Nations and

56

the French and Canada's Indian allies was signed on September 8. The deputies from the Onondagas, Cayugas, and Senecas were either authorized or took it upon themselves to sign for the Oneidas and Mohawks.

The conference was then adjourned, with all parties promising to return in August, 1701, to conclude the general peace. The French immediately sent messengers westward to spread the news of the peace, to order the northern and western tribes to return all prisoners of war, and to send deputies to the scheduled August conference. Meanwhile, the Iroquois deputies set out on their journey home. They had one important task left. Although they had signed a preliminary treaty of peace and had arranged for a grand ratification conference the following August, they still had to convince all of the Five Nations to accept their transactions.

On October 16, 1700, Governor Callieres proudly informed Home Minister Ponchartrain that he had concluded peace with the Iroquois, and that the final ratification and exchange of prisoners would occur next August. Callieres was particularly pleased at the outcome because the Iroquois were making peace despite English disapproval. He added that he was even willing to accept the Iroquois as a neutral party, favoring neither the French nor English, for he was confident that the Jesuits could eventually win over the Iroquois to the French side.[15]

The French had another reason to be pleased with the peace treaty. For a long time New France had considered establishing a fort at Detroit. However, the constant threat posed by the Iroquois had made most French officials leary of attempting that project. But the peace opened the way for the construction of Fort Detroit. Some French officials believed that a fort at Detroit would check Iroquois power. According to La Mothe de Cadillac, who later became the commandant at Fort Detroit, "the strength of the [Iroquois] savages lies in the remoteness of the French, and that ours increases against them with our proximity. For it is certain

57

that, with a little Indian corn, these [Iroquois] people have no difficulty in traversing two hundred leagues to come and take someone's life by stealth. . . . But, on the contrary, when we are the neighbors of that tribe and are within easy reach of them, they will be kept in awe and will find themselves forced to maintain peace."[16]

While the French were pleased that the Iroquois were at last concluding a peace, the English were not yet fully aware of the turn of events. Governor Bellomont, when informed by the Onondagas that they no longer wanted a fort built in their town, attributed their change of mind to the schemes of some Albany residents. Actually, the Onondagas did not want the fort because they felt they no longer needed protection from the French and Indians. If anything, they probably believed they had more to fear in the coming months from the English than from former French and Indian enemies.[17]

Throughout early 1701, there were signs that the Five Nations had approved of their deputies' actions and were determined to ratify the peace treaty with the French and Indians at the upcoming August conference. In March, Iroquois deputies arrived at Montreal and complained that the Ottawas, a western tribe, had violated the cease-fire and captured a Seneca chief. Governor Callieres promised that he would try to settle the Iroquois-Ottawa dispute, and, if possible, would order the Seneca's release.[18] This incident shows that the Iroquois did not wish to fight the Ottawas. Instead, they relied upon mediation of the French governor in the hope that peace arrangements would not be ruined.

The Iroquois' decision to ratify the French peace agreement in August may also help explain why the Onondagas concluded a "lasting peace" with the Pennsylvania government in April, 1701.[19] The Onondagas, concerned about how the English colonies would react to the Five Nations' peace treaty with New France, quite possibly made a treaty of friendship with Pennsylvania to help offset any bad feelings that might develop after August.

By late spring English colonial officials knew that the Five Nations were planning to sign a separate treaty with New France. In June the governor of New York sent envoys to Onondaga in an attempt to change the Iroquois' minds. At about the same time Governor Callieres sent Father Bruyas, Joncaire, and another ambassador to Onondaga to remind the Iroquois about the ratification meeting scheduled for August. The ambassadors arrived only to find the English envoys already in the village. Yet despite the presence of the Englishmen, the French ambassadors were greeted enthusiastically by the Iroquois people. Father Bruyas warned the League Council that if the Iroquois deputies did not attend the Montreal conference as promised, Iroquois requests for peace would no longer be honored. The implied threat was obvious. Father Bruyas then reminded the Indians of their pledge to exchange all prisoners of war at the August meeting. Finally, he told them that a new French and English war might soon erupt, in which case they were to remain neutral.

The League Council met privately to consider the messages brought by the English envoys and the French ambassadors. Three days later they were ready to give their answer. The English and French representatives were summoned before the Council, and Teganissorens of the peace faction was selected by the sachems to serve as the Five Nations' spokesman. Teganissorens came right to the point: the Five Nations would honor their promise to meet with Governor Callieres in Montreal in August and would then exchange prisoners of war. But then he added, "Five delegates are about to set out for Montreal, two others will go to Albany; I myself will remain on my mat, to show all the world that I take no side, and wish to preserve a strict neutrality."[20]

59

The message was clear: the Five Nations would negotiate with both the English and the French, but would remain neutral. The League Council had several reasons for deciding to carry on simultaneous talks with the English and French. The Council was probably divided along factional lines. The peace faction must have argued strenuously that the English could not prevent the Five Nations' total destruction should they renege on their pledge to ratify the peace agreement with the French and Indians. No doubt the pro-English sachems were just as insistent that the Five Nations, for economic and military reasons, could not risk a total break with the English. The decision to negotiate with both the English and the French was probably the only alternative acceptable to all parties. Furthermore, the very nature of both the decision-making process and the structure of the League of the Iroquois required compromise if they were to function at all.[21] Therefore, it is little wonder that the League decided to send deputies to Montreal and Albany.

The League Council may also have had other motives for the decision. Perhaps some sachems believed that the Five Nations could play the French and English against each other, and in the process could extract concessions from each side. Moreover, some sachems may have hoped that a treaty with each could provide insurance against duplicity on the part of either.

Whatever their motivations, the decision was final. The Iroquois would carry out the promises made the previous September and send deputies to meet the French at Montreal in August. At the same time, the Iroquois would dispatch other deputies to talk with the English at Albany.

Early in July the three French ambassadors left Onondaga for Montreal, accompanied by deputies from the four upper Iroquois nations, plus around 200 Iroquois men, women, and children. The Mohawks promised that their deputies would follow shortly thereafter. At long last, the

Five Nations were on their way to Montreal to ratify a general peace treaty with the French and Indians. The Iroquois reached Montreal on July 21, and were welcomed by the roar of cannons and the greetings of French officials.

The scene was repeated the following day when nearly 800 of New France's western and northern Indian allies arrived at Montreal. Again the French cannons and officers saluted their welcome. The Indians climbed out of their canoes and soon went to work building temporary wigwams and shelters for their delegates and people. Before long, a heterogeneous community of Indians stood before the palisades of Montreal, where empty green fields had been only a few days earlier.

Yet despite their presence, most of the deputies were not yet ready to ratify the "Grand Peace Treaty." First they wanted to settle some issues with the governor. For the next few days, Callieres met with his Indian allies and discussed their grievances. He learned that many of the western and northern tribes did not want to make peace with the Iroquois, nor did they want to return their Iroquois prisoners. He also learned that many Indians were disgruntled, because the Iroquois had not brought or restored their prisoners. This showed a lack of good faith.[22]

In response to these charges, an Iroquois spokesman replied that his nation had earnestly tried to return all prisoners, but the young men of their villages had control of them. To further complicate the matter, most of the prisoners were captured in childhood, did not know their own parents, and were now attached to their adopted families. The French tribes were not satisfied with the explanation, for they felt they had the same problems, but had returned their prisoners anyway. The Iroquois replied that they resented those who doubted their sincerity. It was clear to Governor Callieres that the prisoner issue was a definite obstacle to a permanent peace.

The health of the Indians presented another problem for

the French governor. Throughout the conference, fever plagued the Indians, who were crowded together in their makeshift villages. Many Hurons grew sick and died; before long some Indians began to suspect witchcraft as the cause of the illness all around them. The governor realized he had to act fast. He held a series of private conferences with various tribal leaders and made plans for a public signing of the articles of peace. Callieres hoped to impress upon the Indians the significance of this proclamation by making the ceremony a great occasion and celebration. He wanted the event to be the grandest council ever witnessed by Indians. The governor scheduled much pomp and left little to circumstance as he began making preparations. A broad, level field outside the city was selected as the site for the conference. An arena, bordered by a double fence 128 feet long and 72 feet wide, was then laid out. A distance of 6 feet separated the two fences. Next a covered hall, 29 feet long and almost square shaped, was erected on one end of the arena. On August 4, the day of the ceremony, the hall was filled with French officials and their ladies, while 1,300 Indians were arranged in perfect order within the fenced enclosure. The symmetry was completed by having uniformed French guards encircle the arena.

Spectators must have been fascinated by the sight. There were French officers in their bright dress uniforms, replete with military decorations and highly polished buckles and implements. There were French ladies and officials in their finest formal wear. And there were Indians from all over the Eastern Woodlands. There were Iroquois from New York and Canada; Hurons and Ottawas from Michilimackinac; Weas from Chicago; Mascoutens, Sacs, Puants, Menominees, Foxes, Potawatomis, and Kickapoos from Green Bay; Crees from the north; Miamis and Mohegans from the St. Joseph River; Ojibwas from Lake Superior; and Illinois from the Illinois Country. There were also Abenakis from the East, as well as representatives from other scattered Indian bands from the Western Country and Canada. All these Indians had come to ratify the Grand Peace Treaty. And like their white counterparts, they were dressed in their finest attire.

The governor began the conference by explaining that the Grand Peace Council was convened to ratify the peace agreed upon the preceding September. Callieres buried the war hatchets so deeply that they could never be taken out. He told the Indians that from then on they must all live like brothers and "if by chance one should strike another, the injured brother must not revenge the blow, but come for redress to him, Onontio, their common father."[23]

After his speech was translated into several Indian languages, the Indians shouted their approval. Wampum belts were distributed to the Indian deputies, who rose in order, and delivered brief replies to the governor. The Indian allies of New France returned their Iroquois prisoners of war, but said they were making peace merely to please Onontio.

The French were greatly amused by the Indians' attire and behavior. Charlevoix reported that one Algonquin chief was dressed like a Canadian voyageur. Another Indian "had his face painted red and wore an old rusty wig, profusely powdered and ill combed, which gave him an air at once frightful and ridiculous." Charlevoix added, "As he had neither hat nor cap, and wished to salute the Governor-General in French style, he took off his wig. A great outburst of laughter followed, which did not disconcert him, for he doubtless took it as applause."[24] No doubt, the Indians were just as entertained by the pretentiousness of the French gallery, costumes, and demeanor.

When the French Indians had finished their speeches, Iroquois deputies rose to deliver their orations. One sachem maintained that they "would convince the most incredulous of their fidelity, sincerity, and respect for their common father." The Iroquois added, "Onontio, we are pleased with all you have done, and we have listened to all you have said. We assure you by these belts of wampum that we will stand fast in our obedience. As for the prisoners whom we have not brought you, we place them at your disposal, and you will send and fetch them."[25]

The calumet of peace was smoked by all the deputies, and then the Grand Peace Treaty was brought forward and signed by all. Afterwards, huge kettles of boiled oxen were carried in, and a great feast began. The night ended with fireworks and salutes by cannon fire. It was truly an occasion for celebration: the Twenty Years' War between the Iroquois and the French and Indians was over at last.

Governor Callieres met with the Iroquois deputies once more before their departure. On August 7, he stressed that he would not stand for their reneging on the pledge to return all French and Indian prisoners of war. He ordered that they be returned to Joncaire. Afterwards, if the prisoners wished to remain in Iroquoia, they would be free to do so. Finally, Callieres reminded the Iroquois that they were to remain neutral should war again break out between the English and the French. After complaining, to no avail, about the fort the French were building at Detroit, the Iroquois agreed to comply with all the governor's requests. They then set out for their homelands.

Shortly thereafter, the Mohawk deputies arrived at Montreal and ratified the peace treaty and other points that the deputies from the four upper Iroquois nations had agreed to earlier. According to Charlevoix, "Some time after, Joncaire arrived with very few prisoners, the others absolutely refusing to follow him. It was believed, or the authorities chose to pretend to believe, that this was no fault of the Iroquois, and there the matter rested."[26]

The most obvious result of the Grand Treaty was that it brought an end to the Twenty Years' War. The Iroquois had been fighting against the French and Indians since 1680, and the warfare, particularly during the last ten

64

years, had been quite costly to the Five Nations. The conclusion of peace provided the Iroquois with a much needed respite, and allowed them the time to recover from the ravages of war and to reassess their policies toward both their Indian and white neighbors. In the years following the 1701 agreement, the Iroquois developed better economic and political ties with the French and western Indians. The Five Nations accepted French Jesuits into their villages. They began trading with the French. They received French smiths to mend guns and other implements. And they negotiated military and economic alliances with many western tribes.

The Iroquois-French treaty also resulted in the movement of Indians into the Western Country. A major cause of the Twenty Years' War had been the Iroquois' insistence on exclusive hunting rights in the Western Country. But after twenty years of fighting, the Iroquois were no longer in any condition to contest the hunting claims of other tribes. By signing the Grand Peace Treaty, the Iroquois acknowledged the right of western and northern tribes to live and hunt on the western lands. Hurons, Miamis, and other western Indians immediately took advantage of this concession.

In addition, the Iroquois-French treaty provided for the exchange of prisoners. Actually, the Iroquois received more prisoners than they gave up. Historians have used this fact as proof that the Iroquois did not sincerely want peace, or to show that the treaty was a victory for the Iroquois. Neither point is necessarily true. Admittedly, the Five Nations never released the number of prisoners agreed to by their deputies. But that does not mean that the Iroquois were intentionally deceiving the French and Indians. The Five Nations did make an effort to comply with their deputies' promises. Most captives, though, refused to return to their original homes, and the League Council did not have the authority to order their removal from Iroquois families. Those prisoners who did wish to go home were handed over to Joncaire, and

65

he escorted them back to Canada. The Iroquois Confederacy was unable, not unwilling, to comply with the promises made by their deputies to release all captives.

The decision to ratify the French treaty probably helped calm the stormy waves of factionalism within the Confederacy. By 1701, certain groups, such as the one led by Teganissorens, were determined to have peace with New France. Had the League Council opposed such measures, the result might have been increased factional strife, which might have even erupted into a civil war.

At the very moment when the Iroquois deputies were en route to the Grand Council at Montreal, other deputies were already in Albany negotiating with English officials. On July 14, 1701, Iroquois deputies told the lieutenant governor of New York, John Nanfan, that the Five Nations had recently made peace with several western tribes. The Iroquois spokesman then informed the lieutenant governor that the Praying Iroquois living at Sault St. Louis near Montreal refused to come home to Iroquoia.

The deputies met again with Nanfan on July 19. They complained that the French were encroaching upon their lands and were building a fort at Detroit without Iroquois consent. Then, in a surprise move, they deeded to the English all of their western hunting grounds which lay north and south of Lake Erie between Iroquoia and Lake Huron, a territory 800 miles long and 400 miles wide. All that the Iroquois asked in return was that the English guarantee their right to hunt safely on these lands. The Iroquois were looking ahead to the day when the French and western Indians might try to prevent the Iroquois from hunting in the Western Country.

The deputies assured the lieutenant governor that the Five Nations had no love for Jesuits, and they again asked Nanfan to stop the French from building a fort at Detroit and from taking possession of their western hunting grounds. The lieutenant governor, accepting the Western

Country on behalf of his king, promised to provide protection for Iroquois hunters in the West. The conference was then adjourned.[27]

The English-Iroquois treaty was as important as the Grand Council Treaty to the Five Nations. The Iroquois hoped that the Albany talks would assure the continuance of peace with New York and the other colonies. Some Iroquois were probably concerned about the English response to the separate treaty with New France. The renewal of the Covenant Chain at Albany would demonstrate that the Five Nations had no intention of abandoning their English allies. To strengthen their relationship with the English, the Iroquois deeded their western hunting lands to the English king, and reiterated their contempt for the French. Each action was aimed at convincing the English that the Five Nations still considered themselves friends of the English and enemies of the French.

The Five Nations had another practical reason for negotiating a treaty with the English in 1701: they hoped that the renewed English alliance would protect them against French duplicity or further threats by the western Indians. While the Iroquois deputies treated with the English at Albany, they knew other Iroquois were heading to Montreal to ratify a treaty that would open up the Western Country to the French and Indians. Therefore, the deputies at Albany desperately sought assurances that the English would protect Iroquois hunters in the Western Country. They achieved their goal by deeding those hunting grounds to the English in exchange for English promises to protect Iroquois hunters in the West. The Five Nations used the English in another way. Aware that they could not prevent the French from building a fort at Detroit, they asked the English to do it for them.

The treaty may also have been a means to conciliate pro-English factions within the League. The pro-English sachems probably would not have consented to ratification of

67

the French treaty had not the League Council agreed to a treaty with the English. The existence of such determined pro-English groups might account for the Mohawks' tardiness in arriving at Montreal to ratify the French treaty. Since most of the Mohawks who lived in New York were staunchly pro-English, it seems likely that the Mohawk deputies were members of the Iroquois' pro-English faction. Before leaving for Montreal, they could have stopped at Albany to make sure that the Iroquois Confederacy had renewed the Covenant Chain with the English. The Mohawks may not have been willing to ratify the French treaty until the English alliance was reconfirmed. The Mohawk deputies' presence at Albany on July 19 would explain why they were unable to reach Montreal before August 8.

The Iroquois-English treaty made at Albany on July 19, and the Iroquois-French Grand Council Treaty concluded in Montreal on August 4–7, make up the Iroquois Peace Settlements of 1701. They are proof that the Confederacy had decided that the Five Nations would no longer be exclusive allies of the English. Instead the Iroquois were going to negotiate with both the English and French and accept whatever benefits each side had to offer. In subsequent years the Five Nations would perfect this technique to the point where they would play the French and English against each other in order to obtain what they needed from each side.

The origins of the Iroquois' policy of neutrality can be found in the Peace Settlements of 1701. The treaties marked the first time that the Confederacy had agreed to remain neutral in the event of an English-French war. In the eighteenth-century colonial wars, Iroquois warriors frequently fought with the English against the French, or joined the French against the English. So the Settlements of 1701 certainly did not establish a permanent Iroquois neutrality. They did serve, however, as a precedent for neutrality. While the Iroquois of later years did not always adhere

68

to neutrality, they did always consider it, for the Settlements of 1701 had established neutrality as a viable option.

The Settlements of 1701 show that a new balance had been achieved by various factions within the Confederacy. Pro-English factions no longer dominated the League Council. To be sure, they still existed, as evidenced by the Mohawks and Oneidas who were reluctant to ratify the French peace treaty, but they were weakened by the ravages of war. The Twenty Years' War had killed off many pro-English sachems. Also the heavy losses and lack of English support had convinced many Iroquois that peace with New France was the best alternative to ensure the Confederacy's future.[28] By 1701, the pro-French faction and peace faction could no longer be ignored in Iroquois councils. An indication of their strength is the fact that they were able to convince the League Council to negotiate a treaty with New France, despite English arguments to the contrary. That in itself is proof that pro-English sachems no longer controlled the League Council.

The Settlements of 1701 demonstrated the Iroquois Confederacy's autonomy and significance. By concluding separate treaties at Montreal and Albany, the Iroquois showed that they were a sovereign Indian nation. The treaties also helped set the stage for future colonial wars. The Iroquois' deed to the western hunting lands gave the English a claim to the Ohio Country. When the French later contested the English claim, war resulted.

The Settlements of 1701 were important to the Five Nations' future and signaled the beginning of a new era in Iroquois history. After 1701, Iroquois relations with their English, French, and Indian neighbors would never be the same.

3

The Effects of the Twenty Years' War on the Iroquois

The Peace Settlements of 1701 brought the Twenty Years' War to an end. Yet, victory celebrations were conspicuously absent in Iroquois longhouses and villages. The Five Nations had come out on the losing end of the Twenty Years' War, so there would be no status quo ante bellum in Iroquoia. The Twenty Years' War was a turning point in Iroquois history. Before the war, the Iroquois had been a proud, strong, and prosperous people. After the war they found themselves struggling for their very existence. The effects of the war on the Five Nations would be made apparent in the years immediately following the Settlements of 1701.

The Iroquois' military strength had been broken by 1701. The constant warfare of the past twenty years had taken its toll, both physically and mentally, on the Iroquois. Comparative studies of their population before and after the war list 2800 warriors in 1689 and only 1,230 in 1698. One Iroquois sachem told the governor of New York in 1696, "We are become a small people and much lessened by the war." A New York official counted 1,800 warriors among the Five Nations in 1712. This large increase was probably the result of adoption from other tribes, as well as natural increase. Yet even this increase was not enough to offset the large numbers of Indians who were repopulating the Western Country during these years. As late as 1722, Governor Burnet of New York realized that the "importance of the Iroquois had lessened due to the diminution of their numbers."[1]

Obviously, war casualties contributed greatly to the decrease in the Iroquois' population, but there were also other factors. Numerous Iroquois defected to the French side during the war. In 1700 Robert Livingston reported that perhaps as many as two-thirds of the Mohawks had moved to Canada, where they received clothing, protection, and religious instruction from the French. Disease was another factor contributing to the decreasing population. Two major smallpox epidemics swept through Iroquois villages in 1696 and 1717. Lack of food also caused death for many Iroquois. The French made several successful forays into Iroquoia during the Twenty Years' War, burning villages and destroying food supplies. New York colonists were able to replace only a portion of the food destroyed. Food shortages during the winters of 1687, 1689, 1694, and 1696 led to many deaths either from starvation or from lowering the people's resistance to disease.[2]

The Twenty Years' War left psychological scars on the Iroquois people. The Five Nations were tired of fighting and realized that they were no match for the French and Indians. English officials described the Iroquois as being in a "staggering condition," and "weary of war," or "discouraged by the lack of British help," and "terrified of the French." In 1703, Robert Livingston informed the Board of Trade that for the previous two years the Iroquois had been asking him to go to England and "give your Lordships an account of their condition." Livingston portrayed them as a dejected people: "The late war and the great loss which they sustained in their youth hath almost dispirited them, and during the peace the French . . . [have tried] to gain them to their side, or to terrify them . . . of French power." The Five Nations felt helpless. During the war many of their homes had been smashed and burned, and the English had done little to help them. The Iroquois realized that they were on their own. They also knew that they could do little to protect themselves if war broke out again. These realizations added to the despair that was so visible throughout their villages during the early 1700s.[3]

Following the Twenty Years' War, the Iroquois people had to cope with severe drinking problems. The war certainly was not the sole cause of drunkenness. Prior to the war many Iroquois had problems with alcohol, but the war and its disastrous results might have provided additional reasons to drink. The high consumption of liquor after the war sometimes made the people ungovernable and uncontrollable. On several occasions sachems warned English officials that liquor was causing many problems in the Five Nations' villages and unless it was prohibited, it might lead to civil war and a breakup of the Confederacy.[4]

The Twenty Years' War affected the Iroquois people in another way: the Five Nations seemed almost paranoid in the years immediately following the war. Wild rumors of English plots to destroy the Five Nations spread quickly from one Indian town to another. Incredible stories of supposed French and English designs on the Iroquois' homelands were constantly being passed among the tribesmen. Even fellow League members became subjects of suspicion. Tales of witchcraft and treachery circulated from village to village. In their weakened condition, the Five Nations felt vulnerable to all possible dangers and fell prey to even the most far-fetched rumors of apocalyptic destruction. The English repeatedly assured them that the rumors were untrue, but the Iroquois could take no chances. In their war-weakened condition, any story was believable and could possibly mean the end of the once mighty Iroquois.[5]

72

In contrast to their illusory fears about the French and English conspiracies, the Iroquois did have to face two serious threats to their existence. The western Indians and the French provided real reasons for fear. The Twenty Years' War had established the western tribes as a menacing foe. Before the war, the Five Nations had dominated the western Indians, but after the war things were different. Governor Bellomont spoke incredulously about the turn of events. He noted that at one time 100 Iroquois would have sent 1,000 western Indians running, but now the western Indians feared the Iroquois so little that "they will venture to fight them [Iroquois] upon the square." The change was due to several factors: the Iroquois were so weakened by the last war that they were unable to fight back; the French provided the western tribes with training and supplies, whereas the English were of little help to the Iroquois; and the western Indians had more warriors. The Iroquois, whose own armies had decreased in size, spoke in awe of the western tribes, describing them as being "as numerous as the sand on the sea shore." The distraught Iroquois realized they no longer could defeat the western tribes by themselves.[6]

The French posed another threat to the Iroquois' existence. The Five Nations, before the war, had usually held their own against New France. They respected French power, but hardly feared it. But the Twenty Years' War changed all that. Battered by the French and Indians, the Iroquois were no longer a match for either. To incur French wrath after 1700 was the same as asking for destruction. Iroquois respect for French power was joined by an immense fear of it. English officials were aware of the Iroquois' fears. The Five Nations even asked the English to build forts and station troops within Iroquoia to ensure their security and protection. This was a drastic change in Iroquois policy. Prior to the war, the strong and proud Iroquois had guarded their territorial integrity by refusing to allow English forts on their land. Their weakness after 1700 convinced the Five Nations that their position concerning forts within Iroquoia had to be altered.[7]

During and following the Twenty Years' War, the Iroquois were also being threatened by French Catholicism. Jesuits had first visited Iroquoia during the 1640s in hopes of converting the Five Nations. The government of New France used the missionaries, whom the Indians called the "Black Gowns," for political, as well as religious, purposes. French officials understood that through religion the Jesuits could gain the Iroquois' friendship, and then through friendship New France could win the Indians' political loyalty.[8]

The priests met with success in both the religious and political arenas. Between 1680 and 1714, they baptized many Iroquois and convinced some to move to missions in Canada where the converted Iroquois came to be known as the Christian or Praying Iroquois. No doubt, some of the converts moved to the Canadian missions for materialistic or political reasons. Yet many were true believers in the gospel preached by the Black Gowns. One such convert was described in 1696 by Father Jacques de Lamberville. With macabre pride, Lamberville informed a colleague, "You will . . . be pleased to hear what happened to a Christian Iroquois of our mission at the Saut, named Marguerite, who was captured and burned . . . in Iroquois country." Lamberville explained that the Iroquois first cut off several of her fingers and slashed her body all over, but Marguerite "uttered not a groan." She simply prayed to God and the Virgin Mary and "exhorted her Iroquois countrymen to embrace the [Catholic] faith." Lamberville added, "After her whole body had been burned [and] her scalp removed, and she was untied, instead of running hither and thither, [as] captives who are burned generally do, she knelt once more at the foot of the stake, where, while she continued her prayers, her torturers struck her on the head several times with bars to make an end of her; but in vain." The Iroquois finally "brought her martyrdom to an end by fire."[9]

The Jesuits established missions in Canada and Iroquoia. One of the most successful Canadian missions was Sault St. Louis, also called Caugnawaga, located near Montreal. In 1711, the Jesuit Joseph Germain described the Caugnawaga mission as "consisting of 5 or 600 Iroquois. These are families who have left their own country, because they were not free to form a church and to lead a Christian life there, on account of the insults offered by their infidel countrymen and the English." By the mid-1680s, the Jesuits also had missions within Iroquoia. Father de Lamberville's Onondaga mission was particularly important. From his headquarters in the Iroquois capital, Lamberville could baptize many Iroquois, as well as monitor and influence the League Council. Father Millet served similar functions at his Oneida mission. The missionaries fled to Canada during the Twenty Years' War, but when the fighting was over, they returned to Iroquoia and resumed their religious and political activities.[10]

The success of the missions in both Canada and in Iroquoia greatly affected the Five Nations. Not only did the introduction of the new religion undermine native beliefs and customs, but the defection of converts to missions in Canada helped splinter Iroquois society. Clans and families broke up as Praying Iroquois moved northward. The exodus of the Christian Iroquois was partly responsible for the dwindling population of the Five Nations. This adherence to French Catholicism by some Iroquois sharpened factional lines and divided Iroquois society.

Iroquois solidarity was further splintered by rising factionalism. After the Twenty Years' War, some of the Five Nations remained loyal to their English allies, while others, fearing French and Indian strength, developed closer ties to the French. The latter group, which represented a pro-French faction among the Five Nations, was condemned as

75

"traitors" by the English. Although Jesuits were responsible for bringing many Iroquois over to the French side, Joncaire was perhaps the most highly regarded Frenchman among the Five Nations. According to Charlevoix, "The missionaries doubtless contributed [to maintaining the Iroquois-French peace] . . . but they were greatly aided by the conduct of Sieur Joncaire, and the harmony maintained with them by that officer. Joncaire, adopted by the Senecas and highly esteemed by the Onondagas, kept moving constantly from one canton to the other; he informed the missionaries of everything . . . and thus succeeded in baffling all the plans . . . of the English. He charmed the Iroquois by his frankness; he spoke their language as well as they, a thing that gratified the Iroquois wonderfully."[11]

Factionalism, of course, was nothing new to the Iroquois. It had roots in the long-standing family or group rivalries so commonly found among Indian tribes.[12] What was significant, however, was the impact this heightened factionalism had on the Five Nations, as various families or individuals joined either the English or French side. To a degree factionalism created conditions which enabled the Iroquois to strengthen themselves. The existence of strong factions meant that neither the pro-English nor pro-French groups could dominate the League Council. The Confederacy was forced, therefore, to adopt a middle, or compromise, policy. This led the Five Nations to a policy of neutrality, which provided the Iroquois with years of peace and the opportunity to restore their power and prosperity. The existence of factions also kept the English and French guessing about the direction the League would take. In effect, the League of the Five Nations, because of the political stands of the opposing factions, was brought into a balance between its two European neighbors. At times, when the pro-French faction was dominant, the Confederacy tilted in favor of the French; at other times, when the pro-English faction grew in strength, the League leaned back toward the English.

The English and French were forced to contribute gifts and supplies to ensure Iroquois friendship and neutrality.

Factionalism, however, also weakened the Iroquois. By the early 1700s, French and English factions could be found among all Five Nations. The Senecas and Onondagas were especially noted for their influential pro-French factions. These factions divided the Iroquois people and made it difficult for them to agree on a policy during war or peace. The tensions caused by the opposing factions sometimes threatened to uproot the League's symbolic "Great Tree of Peace," whose "shade" had brought friendship and brotherhood to the Five Nations since the inception of the Confederacy. Most of the problems centered on what positions the League members would assume toward the French, the Jesuits, the English, and neighboring tribes. Some Iroquois remained loyal to their longtime English allies, but the many defeats suffered at the hands of the French and Indians, along with political considerations, persuaded most Iroquois to adopt either a pro-French or a neutral position after 1700.

The war shattered the Iroquois economy, which was based largely on the fur trade. During the war the Iroquois were unable to go on regular hunts, since they had to remain in Iroquoia to protect their families and villages from the enemy. The fierceness of the French Indians also made hunting in the Western Country a dangerous proposition. The Iroquois economy continued its downward trend throughout the early years of the eighteenth century. The Iroquois' decline in power resulted in their loss of the Western Country to the French and Indians. After 1700, the French began erecting forts at strategic locations throughout the West. These posts served three main functions: they were visible symbols of New France's claim, based on discovery and occupation, to the Western Country; they were agencies which kept the western tribes loyal and prevented the Iroquois from reestablishing control

77

over the West; and they were points of departure for expeditions seeking mineral wealth or the Northwest Passage. In 1700, the French constructed a strong warehouse and fort at Michilimackinac. The next year they built a fort at Detroit, an important pass leading into Lake Huron and the rich fur regions of Michigan. The French established Fort St. Louis, or Kaskaskias, on the Illinois River in 1700, as a claim to the Illinois territory. The French forts and the western tribes that settled near them for trade and security intimidated the Iroquois and inhibited them from hunting freely in the Western Country.[13]

The weakened Iroquois rapidly lost control of the western fur trade. After 1700, when *coureurs de bois* and western Indians swarmed throughout the West trapping valuable fur-bearing animals, the fort system became the mainstay of the French trade in the region. As early as 1700, the Michilimackinac outpost was known as the trade capital of the West. By 1703, this important role had switched to Fort Detroit. The western tribes congregated there, as they had done earlier at Michilimackinac, to barter their furs for much-needed European goods. Other posts like Fort St. Louis, Fort Niagara, and Fort Cataraqui also served as successful trade centers. Cadwallader Colden of New York recognized the problem these forts posed to the Iroquois. He explained that the French had Fort Cataraqui at the northeast end of Lake Ontario to keep a check on the Iroquois, and Fort Niagara to command the western trade and overawe the Senecas, as well as several other forts among the upper nations of Indians on the "chief passages as the Indians come from their hunting to intercept the fur trade and to keep an awe and command over them." The Five Nations knew that the increased efforts of the French were harmful to their own aspirations in the West. One sachem expressed the concern of many Iroquois in 1701 when he asked New York's lieutenant governor, "Where shall we hunt if the French take possession of our beaver country?"[14]

78

Ironically, it may have been the English traders at Albany, and not the French, who applied the *coup de grace* to whatever hopes the Iroquois had about retaining control over the western fur trade. To compensate for fewer furs being brought in by the Iroquois, Albany merchants began trading with merchants in Montreal. The Caugnawagas (Praying Iroquois) often served as the carriers in this valuable trade. To Albany they brought the furs, which had been obtained by Montreal merchants from western Indians, and exchanged them for English goods. These goods they then carried back to the Montreal traders, who used them in the western fur trade. By 1720, the Montreal-Albany trade was flourishing. It enabled the French to obtain British goods, which were better quality and lower priced than French products, for trade with the western Indians. The flow of trade—from Albany to Montreal to the Western Country—totally bypassed the Iroquois. The Montreal-Albany trade was temporarily stopped during the administration of Governor Burnet in New York in the early 1720s, but, after 1729, it resumed and thrived once again.[15]

The western tribes profited the most from English and French trade policies. By 1700, the Iroquois had lost their position as the chief gatherers of furs in the Western Country to western Indians, who supplied pelts to both the French and English. When Iroquois men attempted to hunt in the West, they had to contend with both the increased competition from friendly tribes and constant attacks by hostile ones. Those Iroquois lucky enough to return from a successful hunt were confronted with two more problems: a lower demand for beaver furs because of changes in European fashions; and exorbitantly priced, scarce trade goods at Albany. The end result was poor economic times for the Five Nations.[16]

In the end, the Twenty Years' War staggered the Iroquois. It drained their strength, smashed their economy,

79

and splintered their solidarity. The war left the Five Nations in a vulnerable and precarious position. The Iroquois'
situation forced them to reevaluate their policies toward
Indian and white neighbors. Prior to the war the Iroquois
had been strong enough to employ their war clubs to
achieve their goals in the Western Country. But the war
weakened the Iroquois so much that they could no longer
club their French and Indian enemies into submission.
They realized that a rapprochement with the French and
Indians was now imperative for their survival, and that the
only real weapon left to achieve such a settlement was diplomacy. If the Iroquois were to survive and if they were to be
free to hunt in the West, then they had to improve their
diplomatic relations with the French and the western tribes.
The Iroquois could not afford continued warfare.

After 1701, the Five Nations moved in several directions
toward restoring their power and prosperity. It would be
misleading to portray the Five Nations as convening one
day in 1701 to deliberately map out the course that would
lead to their restoration, but it would also be wrong to insist
that the actions of the Five Nations during this period had
no direction or purpose. More likely, Iroquois positions
were the result of conscious Iroquois actions, as well as
timely Iroquois reactions. Sometimes the Iroquois initiated
events. Other times they merely reacted, albeit shrewdly, to
events as they occurred. Looking back, we can now see that
distinct patterns developed in Iroquois relations with Indians and whites. A policy aimed at restoring Iroquois economic, political, and military power was evolving during the
early years of the eighteenth century. This policy was a
unified program only in the loosest sense of the term. It
resulted from similar political, military, economic, social,
and geographic conditions found among the Five Nations
after 1701. These common circumstances provide a unity to
Iroquois actions throughout the first half of the eighteenth

century. The Iroquois Restoration Policy was at times followed by the Confederacy as a whole. On other occasions, it was used by individual tribes or persons within the League. The program comprised four major strategies: 1) a policy of neutrality toward the English and the French; 2) friendly relations with tribes of the Western Country and Canada; 3) hegemony over the Indians and lands of Pennsylvania; and 4) a policy of war toward the southern tribes living in or near Virginia and the Carolinas.

The Five Nations hoped that these four strategies would enable them to rebuild their war-torn economy and recover prestige among their European and Indian neighbors. How successful they were is the history of the Iroquois Restoration.

PART II

The Iroquois
Restoration, 1701–1754

The Policy of Neutrality

The cornerstone of the Iroquois Restoration Policy was the Five Nations' relationship to the French and English colonies. Throughout most of the first half of the eighteenth century, the Iroquois Confederacy maintained a policy of neutrality toward the English and the French. The Five Nations first assumed this neutral posture with the Peace Settlements of 1701.

Between 1702 and 1708, the Iroquois strictly adhered to their pledges of neutrality. As a result, the Five Nations were able to develop good relations with both their European neighbors. This allowed the Iroquois to trade and negotiate with the English and the French on an annual basis. It also enabled the Five Nations to receive presents, supplies, and assistance from both sides.[1]

The policy of neutrality temporarily broke down in 1709 and 1711 when many Iroquois became convinced that the English were going to conquer New France. In early 1709, New York was brought into Queen Anne's War through an English plan for a joint colonial invasion of Canada. Shortly thereafter, the New York government began to encourage the Five Nations to end their neutrality and join the English colonies in the fight against New France. On July 14, 1709, Governor Richard Ingoldsby of New York met with all of the

Five Nations except the Senecas at Albany to renew the Covenant Chain. The governor told the Iroquois that he wanted the Indians to take part in an upcoming military expedition against Canada. Ingoldsby reminded the Iroquois of their past hostilities with the French, pointing out that the French "have not only seduced your people and enticed them away from your country, but encouraged even your own Brethren to make war upon you, on purpose to weaken you." He continued, "They have set the far Indians upon you and furnished them with arms and ammunition to destroy you. . . . They encroached upon your rights and liberties by building forts upon your land against your wills, possessing the principal passes and hunting places, whereby all your hunting (your only support) was rendered not only precarious, but dangerous." The governor's arguments were convincing: the following day the four Iroquois nations agreed to join the invasion of New France. The Iroquois announced that 150 Mohawks, 105 Oneidas, 100 Cayugas, and 88 Onondagas would take part in the expedition.[2]

At this time there were at most 1,500 Iroquois warriors, so less than one out of three Iroquois Indians agreed to declare war on New France. The Senecas, in particular, were intent on remaining neutral. Since they lived nearest to Canada and had the closest economic and political ties with New France, the Senecas were not eager to see a renewal of Iroquois-French hostilities. On several occasions the Senecas tried without success to convince the other Iroquois tribes not to war on New France. The Senecas' position prevented the entire Confederacy from declaring war on New France, but could not stop the four other Iroquois nations from joining the English expedition.[3]

The joint expedition called for a two-pronged attack on Canada. Colonel Francis Nicholson would lead 1,500 colonial troops, from New York, New Jersey, and Connecticut, along with Iroquois volunteers, overland against Montreal. At the same time, 1,000 New Englanders would join an

86

English fleet for an attack on Port Royal and Quebec. When news of the English plans reached New France, the Canadians began to fear a total defeat. But the war never materialized! The invasion fizzled out, almost before it began. For four long months the English colonists awaited the fleet's arrival. Finally, in October, Governor Dudley of Massachusetts received official word that the war ships had been sent to Portugal instead.

French leaders were overjoyed; English colonial officials were furious; the Iroquois felt betrayed and grew disillusioned with the English when the fleet did not arrive as promised.[4]

The Iroquois had no choice but to ask for French forgiveness. In early 1710, the Onondagas sent deputies to Governor Vaudreuil of New France. They indicated that individual warriors, and not the Confederacy, had taken up the hatchet against the French. No sooner had the Onondagas departed than deputies from the Mohawks arrived, giving the same excuse. The Mohawks even promised that they would never again lift the hatchet against New France. Some Frenchmen believed that the Iroquois had never really abandoned their neutral posture. Father de Mareuil, the Jesuit missionary at Onondaga, maintained in 1709 that the English would not benefit from the Iroquois' declaration of war against New France. According to Mareuil, the Onondagas had reminded the League Council that the Five Nations "lying between two powerful nations each able to exterminate them and both interested in doing so when they no longer needed their help" should devote their attention "to keeping both [English and French] always in the necessity of conciliating them, and consequently preventing either from prevailing over the other." The League Council agreed with this policy and adopted a resolution "to act in the present circumstances according to this rule of policy." Some Iroquois accompanying Nicholson's invasion force apparently acted in accordance with their sachems' wishes. Ac-

87

cording to Father Mareuil, the warriors, fearing that the English would capture Montreal, sabotaged the plan by polluting the troops' water supply with dead animal skins. The unsuspecting English drank the water and up to 1,000 men were poisoned.[5]

The French governor was more skeptical of the Iroquois. Although Vaudreuil agreed to pardon the Iroquois for their role in the attempted English invasion, he knew that some Iroquois, like the Mohawks who lived near Albany, might again side with the English in the future. Vaudreuil, therefore, warned the Iroquois that if they broke their neutrality, they would be attacked by New France's Indian allies. The governor confided to Minister Ponchartrain, "I know that the true means of obligating them [Iroquois] to observe neutrality is to make them apprehend war with the upper nations. I keep them always under that impression, insinuating, and causing it to be insinuated to them, that our Indians await only my orders to declare themselves."[6]

While Vaudreuil was deciding on the best means to keep the Five Nations neutral, English officials were plotting the best ways to use the Iroquois in a second attempt to conquer Canada. In 1710, the disgruntled English colonists sent a petition to England asking for support for an invasion of New France. In conjunction with the petition New York sent Peter Schuyler and four Mohawks to England, hoping that the "colorful" Indians would draw attention to the request. The New Yorkers also felt that the sights of England would impress the Mohawks, who could then convince the rest of the Confederacy to join the attack against New France. The Mohawk ambassadors were enthusiastically received: the queen outfitted them with expensive clothing and held banquets in their honor; they were escorted about London as guests of the nation; they were given tours of the dockyards, arsenals, and landmarks; and they were saluted with cannons by Her Majesty's warships. The Mohawks served the New Yorkers' purposes quite well. They caught

London's attention. More importantly, once attention was riveted on the Mohawks and America, the British agreed to aid the colonists in an attack on Port Royal. Shortly after the successful assault on that French fort, the British consented to plans for a second joint colonial invasion of Canada.[7]

In 1711, the colonies again geared up for a joint expedition against New France. The plans were similar to those of the aborted 1709 venture. This time an English fleet of over sixty ships, commanded by Admiral Walker, was to attack Quebec, while Francis Nicholson was again to lead colonial troops and Iroquois warriors from Albany to Montreal.

At the end of June, the governor of New York sent Captain Abraham Schuyler and David Schuyler to Onondaga to convince the Five Nations to join the expedition. After the Schuylers explained that the British fleet had already arrived, many warriors eagerly agreed to join Nicholson. The Iroquois still must have had doubts about their allies' military competence, however, for Indian leaders reminded the New Yorkers not to delay, since autumn was fast approaching. On August 24, 656 Iroquois warriors arrived at Albany to join Nicholson's expedition. Present were 182 Senecas, 127 Cayugas, 99 Onondagas, 93 Oneidas, and 155 Mohawks.[8]

The large turnout of warriors from all of the Five Nations, including the Senecas, must have pleased the governor of New York. These Iroquois had several reasons for abandoning their neutrality. Many were angry at the French, who they believed were instigating recent western Indian attacks on Iroquois people. Most of the Iroquois also felt that the French were about to be defeated by the English. Hendrick and his fellow Mohawk ambassadors, just returned from London, were telling stories of England's vast resources and power. Furthermore, the recent English victory at Port Royal and the fleet's arrival seemed to indicate that the conquest of Canada was inevitable. Finally, English gifts and promises of aid, as well as Iroquois thoughts of ending the French threat once and for all, were additional encouragements for the Iroquois to take part in the joint colonial expedition. The Five Nations felt that they had everything to gain by joining the English, who seemed unstoppable.[9]

Not all Iroquois, however, were prepared to join the English: a large percentage of the Iroquois were determined to remain neutral. The 656 Iroquois accompanying Nicholson's force represented a little more than one-third of all Iroquois warriors. Equally significant, only 182 Senecas (or one-fifth of all Seneca warriors) had agreed to attack New France. The Iroquois maintained that more warriors would have taken part in the expedition, but they had to stay home to protect their villages.[10] This might have been true to some extent, but certainly the defense of Iroquoia did not require two-thirds of all Iroquois manpower. More likely, most Iroquois refused to join the expedition either because they sympathized with the French, or because they did not want to abandon the policy of neutrality.

When the expedition set out for Montreal, Francis Nicholson must have been certain that nothing could go wrong, since the fleet had already embarked for Quebec and warriors from all of the Five Nations had joined the land attack. However, the army was in the field for only a few weeks before Nicholson learned that *everything* had gone wrong. The fleet, carrying almost 12,000 men, met with disaster before reaching Quebec. Fog, stormy seas, and poor leadership were responsible for the sinking of ten ships near the mouth of the St. Lawrence River. In panic, Admiral Walker ordered a hasty retreat to Boston. When news of Walker's debacle reach Nicholson, he threw his hat on the ground and stomped upon it in frustration. Once again, the American and Indian expedition turned back in defeat.[11]

The Five Nations were bitter and depressed about the colonists' second failure. They complained that most of the

warriors who had accompanied the army had not been supplied with firearms and that the French had been warned
about the approach of the force. The warriors felt ashamed
that the invasion had been called off for a second time. The
Iroquois expressed their fears to Governor Hunter. They
told him that forts had to be strengthened, adding solemnly, "God is against us and that we shall receive the first
punishment from him for we can't go forward to reduce
Canada having returned twice."[12]

Fortunately for the Iroquois, the French were again
willing to forgive them for their dalliance with the Nicholson expedition. Governor Vaudreuil believed that many
Iroquois wanted neutrality, and he did not wish to have war
with the Five Nations. He explained to his home government, "It is a matter of importance to us . . . not to be at war
with that tribe if we can possibly help it, and the five Iroquois villages [because of their proximity] are more to be
feared than the whole of New England. If they come [to ask
for forgiveness] I shall take care to speak to them in such a
manner as to show them that I am not obdurate." Vaudreuil guessed correctly how the Iroquois would react after
the defeat. By the end of the year, deputies from all Five
Nations had arrived at Montreal, asking for pardon and
pledging their fidelity in the future.[13]

The war between England and France came to a close in
1713, with the signing of the Treaty of Utrecht. Twice during Queen Anne's War New York had convinced some of
the Iroquois to abandon their neutrality and join the fight
against New France. And twice, English blunders had prevented the invasions from succeeding. The Five Nations
filed away memories of those feeble military ventures; and,
thereafter, they returned to a policy of neutrality between
the English and French. The failures of the English expeditions of 1709 and 1711 convinced many Iroquois that the
English, regardless of their promises or boasts, were not

91

likely to conquer New France. This realization made the Iroquois more determined than ever to maintain a neutral stance.

Fortunately for the Iroquois, the French and English generally remained at peace between 1713 and 1744, so the Iroquois were not pressured or called upon to ally themselves exclusively with either side. Instead, the Confederacy was able to remain neutral for over thirty years. This fact does not mean that all the Iroquois people were always neutral. Individuals and factions continued to harbor pro-English or pro-French sentiments and sometimes acted accordingly. Neutrality was the official policy of the League Council, however, and though individual Iroquois might not always practice what their leaders preached, neutrality served as a guiding principle for the entire Iroquois nation and greatly affected relations between the Five Nations and their Indian and white neighbors.

Iroquois neutrality came under fire again during the mid-1740s, when the European struggle between England and France spilled over onto the North American continent, where it became known as King George's War. The Iroquois were not happy to learn about the war. They recognized their precarious position between the French in Canada and the English in New York, and were determined not to break their long-standing policy of neutrality. English colonial officials, however, had other ideas. In October, 1745, representatives from Massachusetts, Connecticut, Rhode Island, Pennsylvania, and New York arrived in Albany to meet with deputies from the Iroquois Confederacy. All of the Five Nations were represented, except for the Senecas, who were suffering from "an epidemical sickness" that had killed "great numbers" and had prevented the rest from traveling. The English officials wasted no time getting to the point. They wanted to know the Iroquois position concerning the war between England and France. The New England commissioners went a step further: they asked the

Five Nations to honor their alliance by fighting against the French Indians who were attacking Massachusetts frontiers.

The Iroquois deputies were in a bind. They knew that representatives of the Confederacy had recently been to Canada, where they promised the French governor that the Five Nations would remain neutral and not aid the English. They also knew that if they broke their word, their French "father," Onontio, would punish them severely. So the Iroquois tried to avoid committing themselves. Stalling for time, the deputies shrewdly replied, "We are in alliance with a great number of Far Indians and if we should so suddenly lift up the hatchet without acquainting our allies with it, they would perhaps take offense." The deputies explained that before the Confederacy declared war against the French or northern Indians, it first wanted to send a delegation to Canada "to demand satisfaction for the wrongs they have done our [English] brethren and if they refuse to make satisfaction, then we shall be ready to use the hatchet."

English officials tried to pin down the Five Nations. How much time would they give the French Indians to comply? Two months, answered the Iroquois deputies. The colonial representatives disagreed about the Iroquois' position. The Massachusetts representatives accused the New Yorkers of favoring, and perhaps even urging, the Iroquois' delay. Governor George Clinton was furious at the accusation, and upset that the Massachusetts commissioners were carrying on so in front of the Iroquois, thereby demonstrating the colonists' disunity to the Indians. Yet the Massachusetts representatives had made a valid point: Clinton was in no hurry to see his Indian allies hustle off to aid another colony, when he felt they should stay at home in case New York needed help.

Before the conference adjourned, other matters were dealt with. The English and Iroquois renewed their friendship for each other. The Iroquois, at English requests, promised to maintain alliances with western tribes, to keep their people closer together in more compact villages, and to keep their warriors ready for emergencies. The English then promised to protect the Iroquois and provide them with lower-priced goods and ammunition. In private talks the Iroquois assured Pennsylvania representatives that they would help Pennsylvania control the Shawnees who were leaning toward the French. The Iroquois also promised that they would come to Philadelphia in the spring to discuss a possible peace treaty with the Catawba Indians of Carolina. Canassatego, acting as the Confederacy's spokesman, told the Pennsylvania officials that the Five Nations planned to remain neutral in the fighting between England and France. He added that the Iroquois "wish the English of all colonies would agree that we should remain so." The Iroquois would remain neutral "unless the French should come through our settlements to hurt our Brethren the English, which we would not permit."[14]

Events soon proved that the Iroquois had no intention of breaking their neutrality, regardless of what the French and Indians did to the English. In November, just one month after the Iroquois talks with the English, a large French and Indian war party swooped down onto the New York frontier and sacked the town of Saratoga. Governor Clinton immediately began making plans for the defense of his colony. High on his priorities was obtaining the aid of the Iroquois. On November 30, he wrote to the duke of Newcastle, "I have . . . given orders to the Six Nations . . . to take up the hatchet against the enemy." But the Iroquois were not listening. Clinton soon learned from Arent Stevens, New York's official Indian interpreter, that the Five Nations had flatly refused to declare war against the French and Indians. According to Stevens, the Iroquois said that "they and the Cacknawaga Indians in Canada . . . would not . . . make war upon each other, that when Indians went to war with each other they could not make peace with the facility white people did." The Iroquois hoped their refusal did not

94

offend the English. Stevens explained that the Iroquois "desired we should not think the Covenant Chain broken by this refusal as they should not if we refused to assist them in their wars." Governor Clinton, although not pleased with the decision, understood it well. He felt that the Indians' refusal was based on the belief that they would not receive proper military support from the English. Most Iroquois had no intention of being dragged into the war and continued their relations with New France. In April, 1746, New York officials noted that a French priest had settled in Seneca country. The following month, the Albany commissioners complained to the governor that despite the fact that French Indians were terrorizing the Albany countryside, the Iroquois refused to break neutrality.[15]

About the only Iroquois willing to aid the New Yorkers publicly were some Mohawks under the influence of William Johnson, a trader who lived near one of the Mohawk villages. Johnson had arrived in New York in 1738 and quickly established himself as a friend and merchant whom the Indians could trust. He learned the Mohawks' language and customs and was adopted into the tribe as an honorary sachem and advisor. Known to the Mohawks as Warraghiyagey ("the doer of great things"), Johnson succeeded in 1746 in obtaining some support from the Mohawks. In April, individual Mohawk warriors agreed to help garrison the newly rebuilt post at Saratoga. Two months later Johnson told the Mohawks that a large English army would soon be arriving in New York for an invasion of Canada. Johnson later reported that the Mohawks were ecstatic about the news and promised "that they would . . . join heart and hand to fight with us against the French our common enemy whenever called upon."[16]

The rest of the Confederacy did not share the Mohawks' enthusiasm. But the English were determined to get the Confederacy's support, and throughout the summer of 1746 colonial officials did everything they could to obtain

95

that end. In July, Governor Clinton, along with representatives from Massachusetts, almost succeeded in winning over the Iroquois. After meeting with the Five Nations at Albany, Clinton reported that a treaty was made "by which they engaged to join in the war." The governor hardly had time to congratulate himself, though, for within a month the Albany commissioners sadly reported to the governor, "The Six Nations are unwilling to join us in the war against the French and other Indians." The Indians had changed their minds about joining the English when they learned that the northern Indians would not remain neutral in the event of Iroquois hostilities. French threats to destroy the Five Nations if they sided with the English undoubtedly contributed to the Iroquois' decision to remain neutral.

Governor Clinton and other colonial officials were not about to give up on recruiting the Iroquois, so they invited the Five Nations to confer with them at Albany towards the end of summer. If the English were hopeful, the French were concerned. Chabert Joncaire, who had taken over as the French emissary among the Senecas after the death of his father, Joncaire, in 1739, reported to New France's governor that "no dependence is to be placed on the conduct of the Iroquois . . . until they had returned from [Albany]."

The English were pulling out all the stops to win over the reluctant Iroquois. The conference opened on August 19, 1746. In attendance were commissioners from New York and Massachusetts, and deputies from the Five Nations. Representatives from the Missisaugas, a far Nation, were also present. Lieutenant Governor Cadwallader Colden, speaking for the ailing governor, began by renewing the Covenant Chain. Colden told the Indians that the British had captured Fort Louisbourg. He reminded the Iroquois that back in October they had given the northern Indians two months to stop all hostilities against the English. Since then almost a year had passed, and, despite the fact that the northern Indians had continued their raids, the Iroquois

96

were doing nothing. Chiding the Iroquois, Colden said, "As you have not hitherto fulfilled your promise [to war on the northern Indians if they did not stop their raids within the allotted two months], I suspect that they did not come from your hearts." Colden then presented a wampum belt to the Iroquois deputies: "I therefore by this belt demand'an immediate performance of your promises to show that they come from the bottom of your hearts." The lieutenant governor explained that the British colonies were planning to attack Canada by land and sea. He said, "The King your Father expects and orders you . . . to join with your whole force in this enterprise." Colden noted that the English were inviting not just the Iroquois, but all Indians allied to the Five Nations to take part in "this glorious enterprise." He added, "I will furnish your fighting men with arms, ammunition, clothing, provisions, and everything necessary for the war and in their absense shall take care of their wives and children." The conference then adjourned while the Iroquois considered a reply.

On August 23, the Indians delivered their answer. The influence of Cadwallader Colden and William Johnson, along with the promised invasion of Canada, persuaded the Iroquois deputies to accept the English hatchet. An Iroquois spokesman said, "Brethren Corlaer, last year you gave us the hatchet to be made use of against your enemies the French which we accepted and promised to make use of if they should commit any further hostilities upon the English, which they have now done by destroying Saratoga and shedding a great deal of blood. . . . As you now call upon us we are ready and do declare from the bottom of our hearts that we will from this day make use of [the hatchet] against the French and their [Indian] children."[17]

The English were pleased. The Iroquois Confederacy had agreed to abandon its long-standing policy of neutrality and to declare war on the French. Or more correctly, the English *thought* the Iroquois had declared war on the French. Within

97

a short time there was great confusion over whether or not the Iroquois had actually picked up the hatchet. To this day, it is still difficult for us to determine whether the Confederacy went to war against the French. We do know that some members of the Five Nations took part in raids against Canada. What we do not know is whether these raids were sanctioned by the League Council.

Immediately following the conference, New York officials began making arrangements to bring Iroquois warriors into the fighting. Governor Clinton appointed William Johnson colonel of the Five Nations and gave him authority to raise and equip war parties against the French and Indians. Johnson did his job well. Over the next several months he constantly had warriors from all the Five Nations out against the French. Johnson's encouragements and promises of money for French scalps and prisoners induced many Iroquois to join the war parties.[18]

Yet, despite Johnson's recruiting success, many people had reason to believe that the Confederacy was not honoring its declaration of war against New France. The New York Assembly complained that, although Iroquois were raiding the French, they were refusing to attack northern Indians allied to New France. The Assembly eventually became so upset that it stopped paying Iroquois warriors for French scalps. Some colonists even questioned whether the Iroquois had ever declared war against the French and Indians. Conrad Weiser, Pennsylvania's official Indian interpreter and consultant for Indian affairs, maintained in the summer of 1747 that the Confederacy had not declared war. Weiser felt that William Johnson never got the entire League to take up the hatchet against the French, although be was able to get the support of the Mohawks and some stragglers from each nation. Other evidence also indicates that the Iroquois Confederacy did not follow through on its promise to fight the French. In March, 1747, the French and Indians declared war on the Mohawks and warned the

98

other Iroquois nations not to get involved. This shows that the French believed only the Mohawks were responsible for prior attacks in Canada. The following month Chabert Joncaire reported from his post among the Senecas that all of the Five Nations, with the exception of the Mohawks, had "accepted the hatchet from the English," but had no intentions of using it. Joncaire explained, "they took [the hatchet] only to get rid of [the English, who were constantly after them to declare war]." The fact that Joncaire was still living among the Senecas is further proof that not all Iroquois were hostile toward the French.[19]

The question remains then: did the Iroquois Confederacy abandon neutrality and declare war on the French? The answer seems to be yes: the Confederacy did agree to take up the hatchet. The catch is that the promise was never carried out. For all practical purposes, the Iroquois Confederacy, despite its declaration of war, never broke its neutrality in regard to England and France. Most likely, the Iroquois deputies were sincere when they agreed to join the English in a war against the French, having been lured into the declaration by English promises of support and a large-scale invasion of Canada. But the Indians quickly began having second thoughts when they realized that the proposed invasion was not going to occur. The Iroquois would have known for sure that the English army was not coming by the summer of 1747. And astute Iroquois leaders probably suspected as early as the fall of 1746 that something was amiss, since the promised support from an English army had not yet materialized. The more some sachems became convinced that the English invasion of Canada was not going to occur, the less they supported war against Canada. Because of these attitudes on the part of some sachems, the League Council, which required unanimity for all decisions, would have been unable to sustain the earlier position of war against the French. Only a position of neutrality would have been able to win support from all factions within the Confederacy. By late summer of 1747, the Iroquois Confederacy had resumed a neutral position in the war against the English and French. For the duration of King George's War, the four upper nations of Iroquois remained neutral, thereby forcing the League Council to be neutral officially, while the Mohawks and some warriors from each tribe enlisted with the English to fight against the French.[20]

King George's War stretched the Iroquois' policy of neutrality nearly to the breaking point. English colonial officials such as George Clinton, Cadwallader Colden, and William Johnson pressured many members of the Five Nations into a pro-English position, while Albany traders, not wanting to see their lucrative trade with Montreal disrupted by warfare, joined French officials in convincing other Iroquois to remain neutral. The resulting actions of the pro-English and pro-French factions among the Five Nations worked to the advantage of the Confederacy. Iroquois warriors, by participating in the fighting against the French, gave the English the impression that all Five Nations had taken up the English hatchet. At the same time, sachems from the four upper cantons assured the French that the Confederacy as a whole was still neutral. Iroquois neutrality may have been teetering on the brink of ruin, but it had not yet fallen.

By the end of the summer of 1748, news reached the colonies that King George's War was over and that a ceasefire had gone into effect. If the Iroquois were hoping for a return to normalcy, they were soon disappointed. The war had created new conditions that would ultimately contribute to the demise of the Iroquois policy of neutrality.

The Iroquois worked hard to repair damage done to the neutrality policy by King George's War. After 1748, the Iroquois did all they could to reestablish good ties with the French. One of the main obstacles in the path to friendship was the issue involving the exchange of prisoners. The English, who claimed the Iroquois as subjects according to Article 15 of the Treaty of Utrecht, maintained that they—and not the Iroquois—should discuss the matter with the government of New France. The French, refusing to acknowledge England's right to act as an intermediary, insisted that the Confederacy negotiate for itself. Otherwise, Iroquois captives would not be freed. The Five Nations, anxious to secure their warriors' release, were in no mood to be caught in the sticky web of European politics. The sachems decided to comply with the French request, but only after they covered themselves with the English. The Mohawks turned their French prisoners over to the New York government, which could then supervise their transfer back to Canada. The entire Confederacy then took part in direct negotiations with New France to obtain freedom for all Iroquois warriors captured in the war. Iroquois-French relations improved considerably between 1748 and 1754. During those years, French envoys regularly traveled throughout Iroquoia and distributed gifts, while members of the Five Nations made frequent visits to Canada, where they received presents from the French government. The Iroquois once again were on good terms with the French. This enabled the Iroquois Confederacy to pursue its policy of neutrality without interruption from 1748 until 1755.[21]

Despite the friendly relations with New France, the Iroquois Confederacy was still a long way from trusting the French. After 1748, the Five Nations were particularly concerned about French designs on the Western Country.

King George's War had altered the status quo in the Western Country. Prior to the war the French had supplied most of the Indians living along the upper Great Lakes or lower Ohio River and its tributaries. When the war cut off New France's supply of trade goods, many tribes were forced to turn to the English for manufactured products. Some Indians established a direct trade with the English at Oswego, a post situated at the southeast end of Lake Ontario. Others, like the Hurons and Miamis, moved inland

101

and southward to get closer to Pennsylvania traders who had followed Shawnees and Delawares westward into present-day Ohio. Many Iroquois, aware of the opportunities for hunting and trading, joined the rapidly-growing conglomeration of tribes settling on the Ohio River and its tributaries. These Iroquois, by serving as intermediaries, contributed greatly to increased communications and trade between the English and Indians in the Ohio Country. By war's end English traders had supplanted the French in the fur trade with many western tribes.

The French viewed these changes with great concern. They were not about to sit back idly and watch the English profit by trading with tribes in Ohio. After all, most of those Indians were longtime allies of New France. What's more, the French claimed the Ohio Country on the basis of La-Salle's explorations. By 1748, French colonial officials knew what they must do. The English trading post at Oswego had to be neutralized. The western tribes had to be brought back into the French political and economic alliance. And the English interlopers had to be expelled from Ohio. The French could not afford to fail. The stakes were too high. If the English gained possession of the Ohio Country, they would win over the western tribes through trade. To make matters worse, the English would also be in the position to interrupt communication between Canada and Louisiana.[22]

The French moved rapidly to reestablish their authority in Ohio and the West. In early 1749, they threatened the Ottawas, Missisaugas, and other Indians trading regularly with the English. Several months later the governor of New France dispatched Captain Céloron de Blainville, a former commandant at Forts Detroit and Niagara, on a mission to the Ohio Country. Céloron's orders were specific. He would lead a detachment of 200 French troops and 30 Indians from Montreal. The party would follow a water and land route past Fort Niagara and then on to the headwaters of the Allegheny River. Céloron was to descend that river and

102

then follow the Ohio River westward. En route Céloron was to plant lead plates to renew France's claim to the Ohio River and all the lands watered by it. He was also to warn Indians not to abandon their French alliance. And lastly, Céloron was to expel all English traders he found in the area.

Céloron's expedition left Montreal on June 15, 1749. By autumn, it returned. The only things Céloron accomplished were following the proper route and planting the lead plates. The expedition failed to win back the Ohio Indians or expel the English traders. Actually, Céloron was not to blame: his party just was not large enough to threaten either the Indians or the English.

French officials were not pleased to learn from Celeron that the Indians of the Ohio Country were ill disposed toward the French and were still trading with the English. In 1750, the French sent Chabert Joncaire westward to present gifts to the Indians in hopes of bringing them back into the French alliance. But Joncaire received a cold reception, and the tribes of Ohio and the West continued to trade with the English, who offered more abundant, and less expensive, products than the French. By the end of the year, the French, having failed at persuasion, were ready to try force.[23]

Over the next few years the French did their best to exert greater control over the Indians and lands of the West. They strengthened Fort Niagara to better intercept Indians going to Oswego. They encouraged western Indians to harass English traders in the Western Country. They threatened Ohio Indians with destruction if they continued to deal with the English. They even solicited aid from the Five Nations, asking them to recall their people from Ohio. When these measures failed, the French adopted more stringent ones. In 1752, the new governor of New France, the marquis Duquesne, sent a force of Canadians and Indians under the command of Charles Michel de Langlade

103

against a Miami village at Pickawillany (Piqua, Ohio). The force destroyed the town, captured five English traders, and sent the Miamis fleeing. The marquis Duquesne followed up by sending a large army into western Pennsylvania to build forts at strategic locations guarding the Ohio River and its tributaries. The French governor also made it clear to the Iroquois that they were not to stand in his way.

The militant actions terrified the Iroquois and their western Indian allies. Many Ohio Indians began asking the Five Nations to aid them in a war against the French. But the Iroquois—living right next door to Canada—realized the foolishness of that approach. The Iroquois knew that their policy of neutrality provided them with the best means to check French expansion. The Confederacy could remain at peace with Canada and still enlist English support to counter the French.[24]

The only problem with the Iroquois' plan was that ever since the end of King George's War, the English had been more concerned with trade and expansion into Ohio than they were with the Iroquois. The Five Nations did not like being ignored by the English, especially now that the French were making threatening noises. Some Iroquois decided to rectify the situation. In June, 1753, Chief Hendrick and sixteen other Mohawks traveled to New York City and demanded an audience with Governor Clinton. The governor, somewhat shaken by this unscheduled visit, agreed to meet with the Indians. Hendrick reminded Clinton of his tribe's longtime allegiance to the English. He then warned that if the New York government did not stop ignoring the Five Nations, the Covenant Chain would break. Hendrick then said his people needed protection from the French. He also complained that much of the Mohawks' land was being taken fraudulently by New York colonists. Clinton's evasive reply angered the Mohawks. Hendrick shouted back the Mohawks' defiant response: "The Covenant Chain is broken between you and us." And the Mohawks stormed out of the meeting.

104

When news of the Mohawks' actions reached William Johnson, he quickly arranged a meeting with Hendrick and other tribal leaders. Johnson, an adopted Mohawk, felt no need to be polite. He severely reprimanded the Indians for their behavior toward Governor Clinton, adding that the officials were surprised "to find that you, whom they looked upon as most sincere friends, should use such loud and foul words that almost shook and soiled that firm and bright [Covenant] Chain." The Mohawks, having calmed down, apologized for their treatment of Governor Clinton and offered to renew the Covenant Chain with William Johnson and the other Iroquois nations.[25]

As is so often the case, the squeaky wheel gets the oil. Specifically in this case, the complaining Iroquois soon got the attention. In September, 1753, William Johnson met with the Iroquois Council at Onondaga and renewed the Covenant Chain between the English and Iroquois. He then asked the Five Nations to beware of their friendly relations with the French, warning that the French were trying to divide the Confederacy. An Onondaga Indian (known to whites as the Red Head) gave the Iroquois' reply. He expressed gladness that the Covenant Chain was renewed, because it was "almost eat through with rust." The Iroquois also made sure that Johnson understood their concern with French advances into the West. The Red Head explained, "it is not with our consent that the French have committed any hostilities at Ohio, we don't know what you . . . French and English together intend[. We] are so hemmed in by both, that we hardly have a hunting place left."[26]

The Indians had no way of knowing, but as they spoke to William Johnson, their problems were being discussed by the Board of Trade back in England. The Board members, astounded by Chief Hendrick's and the Mohawks' confrontation with Governor Clinton, had taken notice of the Iroquois' complaint that the English were ignoring them. They decided to recommend a conference between the Five Na-

105

tions and the colonial governments of New York, Virginia, Pennsylvania, Maryland, New Hampshire, Massachusetts, and New Jersey. The Board members warned colonial officials to satisfy the Iroquois' demands as much as possible and to pay the Iroquois for all fraudulent land patents. The Board of Trade suggested that the Covenant Chain be renewed and that presents, some of which would be provided by the crown, be handed out to the Five Nations. The Board members were not acting for altruistic reasons. They believed that Iroquois friendship was essential to British interests in North America. Not only were the Five Nations a strong and influential ally, but they also provided Great Britain with a claim to the Ohio Country. The Five Nations' claim to Ohio, based on the right of conquest, allowed the English to counter French claims to that territory. The English argued that the Iroquois, according to the Treaty of Utrecht, were English subjects. Therefore all Iroquois lands belonged to the English Crown.

The Albany conference, planned by the Board of Trade, convened in June, 1754. Deputies of the Confederacy met with representatives from New York, Massachusetts, New Hampshire, Connecticut, Rhode Island, Pennsylvania, and Maryland. The English sought to reaffirm their friendship with the Five Nations and to make plans for strengthening colonial defenses. The Iroquois hoped to secure English aid and support against French encroachments in the West.

Before the conference officially opened, Iroquois sachems met with New York's new governor, James De-Lancey, and members of his council. On June 27, Mohawks from the Lower Castle said they hoped this governor would not ignore the Five Nations like Clinton had. They then complained about New York colonists who were stealing Mohawk land through fraudulent deeds. DeLancey promised he would look into the matter. The next day Indians from Canajoharie (the Upper Mohawk Castle) and several sachems from each of the other Five Nations met with the

106

governor. They also asked him not to neglect them, and pointed out that the French had taken advantage of the period during which Clinton had ignored the Five Nations by drawing many Iroquois to settle at the Swegatchy mission (on the present site of Ogdensburg, New York).

The Albany Congress officially opened the next morning, Saturday, June 29. Governor DeLancey delivered a general speech to the Five Nations on behalf of the king and the colonies. The governor renewed the Covenant Chain and presented gifts to the Iroquois. He asked the Confederacy to keep the alliance strong and to extend it to include more tribes. DeLancey then recommended that the people of the Five Nations live closer to one another. He explained, "We are informed that you now live dispersed from each other contrary to the ancient and prudent custom of your Forefathers; and as you are by this means, exposed to the attempts of your enemies, we therefore in the most earnest manner recommend to, and expect it from you, for your own safety, to collect yourselves together, and dwell in your National Castles." The governor said he was especially concerned about the many Onondagas who had gone off to live at Swegatchy.

The next point made by DeLancey dealt with the Ohio Country. He explained that the French were making "continual encroachments upon us both . . . to the northward and westward." The governor carefully reminded the Iroquois, "Your Fathers by their valor above 100 years ago, gained a considerable country [to the west], which they afterwards of their own accord put under the protection of the King of Great Britain. The French are endeavoring to possess themselves of this whole country." DeLancey warned the Iroquois that if the French were to continue their advance they would not only disrupt English trade with the Ohio Indians, but would cut the Iroquois off from all contact with the western tribes and lands. The governor added, "We want to know whether these things appear to you in the same light as they

107

do to us, or whether the French [actions] . . . be done with your consent."

With Chief Hendrick acting as their spokesman, the Indians gave their reply on July 2. The Mohawk chief said the Confederacy was pleased to renew the "ancient chain of friendship" and would do its best to bring additional tribes into the alliance. Hendrick admitted that the Iroquois were living dispersed, as DeLancey had said, and he promised that the Five Nations would attempt to recall their people. The wily Hendrick added, "You have asked us the reason of our living in this dispersed manner. The reason is, your neglecting us for these three years past." Showing his flair for the dramatic, Hendrick picked up a stick and tossed it behind his back, saying "You have thus thrown us behind your back, and disregarded us, whereas the French are a subtle and vigilant people, ever using their utmost endeavors to seduce and bring our people over to them." The message was clear to the English. If they continued to ignore the Iroquois, they would lose the Five Nations to the French.

Hendrick then dealt with the situation in the Ohio Country. He explained that the Iroquois never gave the French permission to encroach on those lands. Hendrick said, "The governor of Virginia and the governor of Canada are both quarrelling about lands which belong to us, and such a quarrel as this may end in our destruction." He carefully pointed out that neither the French nor the English had the right to settle on the Ohio lands without the Five Nations' consent.

Hendrick's response to the English questions was over. But the Iroquois now had some additional comments to make. Hendrick complained that the English allowed Albany merchants to trade supplies and ammunition to the French in Canada, "which further enables the French to carry on their designs in Canada." He then warned the English that they had to strengthen themselves if they hoped to hold back the French. He said, "look at the

108

French, they are men, they are fortifying everywhere, but we are ashamed to say it, you are all like women, bare and open without any fortifications."

Hendrick sat down, knowing that his points had been well taken. But there was still one more matter to be discussed. The Iroquois wanted William Johnson to manage Indian affairs within the colony of New York. Johnson had been the liaison between the Five Nations and New York during King George's War. But after the war Johnson resigned when he realized the stingy assembly would not provide the funds necessary to do the job.

A Mohawk, known to the English as Abraham, rose to address the congress. He reminded the English that the Iroquois had previously asked the government to reinstate Johnson, adding, "We long waited in expectation of this being done, but hearing no more of it, we embrace this opportunity [to] . . . desire that Colonel Johnson be reinstated and have the management of Indian Affairs . . . for we love him, and he us." The conference was then adjourned so the English delegates could draft a reply.

On July 3, the English responded. Governor DeLancey, once again speaking for all the commissioners, promised that the English would stop neglecting the Iroquois. He made it clear that the English would respect Iroquois ownership of the western lands and would do all they could to prevent French encroachments in Ohio. He added, "you did put this [Ohio] land under the King our Father, he is now taking care to preserve it for you. . . . yet the property or power of selling it to any of His Majesty's subjects . . . we always consider as vested in you."

DeLancey assured the Iroquois that the English would follow their advice and begin building forts to defend their frontiers. What he neglected to mention was that the English hoped to build the forts at Onondaga and Irondequoit. The English believed that forts located at those strategic locations would guarantee the Five Nations' loyalty.

109

The governor gave an evasive reply to the request that Johnson be reinstated in Indian affairs. Unknown to the Iroquois, political differences with Johnson made the governor unwilling to have him serve as a commissioner. Instead, the governor asked the Iroquois to be patient and give the new Albany Commissioners of Indian Affairs a one-year trial period. Then, if things were not working out, changes could be made.

The Iroquois agreed to everything the governor said. In particular, they thanked the colonial delegates "for the promise of protection given us, of our lands, and the acknowledgement that the right of selling it is in us." The Iroquois then asked that the rum trade be restricted to Oswego and not be allowed in their villages, and the Mohawks requested a church be built at Canajoharie. DeLancey pledged that he would do his best to fulfill the Iroquois' requests.

The conference was nearing its end. About the only business left on the agenda involved land sales. Pennsylvania representatives announced that they were negotiating with the Iroquois for the purchase of a tract of land below the latitude of 42° in Pennsylvania. However, that deal would not be completed until after the conference was over. The other item involved the Mohawks' complaints regarding fraudulent deeds. The delegates agreed to give Governor DeLancey one year to solve those problems.

On July 9, the English and Iroquois representatives met for the last time. Pleasantries and promises were exchanged. Presents were distributed. And the conference was adjourned. The Albany conference was officially over.[27]

The English were satisfied with the proceedings. After the Indians departed, William Johnson explained to the delegates why the Five Nations had to be appeased. According to Johnson, the Iroquois' geographic location was important to both the English and French. He noted that the French had to travel through Iroquoia "in order to perfect

110

that fatal line of communication [between Canada and Louisiana] by means of which to lessen our borders . . . and crowding us into the sea." Iroquois actions also affected English relations with western tribes. Johnson told the colonial delegates, "The eyes of all the western tribes . . . are upon the behavior of the Six Nations, whose fame of power may in some measure exceed the reality, while they only act a timid and neutral part." Finally, the Iroquois provided the English with the means to expand westward. Johnson stated that the Iroquois "don't like that either the French or English should establish themselves there [at Ohio], it being their best hunting ground; they rather expected we should assist in keeping and driving the French off." He added, "I believe, were the French hindered from settling, we could have treated with them for those lands, as they never refused us the pre-emption which is more pleasing to them being without hostility, than for the French to take them as it were by force, and treat them as though they were conquered."[28]

The Five Nations were likewise pleased with the results of the Albany conference. The Iroquois had accomplished what they set out to do. They secured promises that the English would no longer ignore them and would help them check French encroachments in Ohio. Yet despite their gains, the Iroquois did not have to abandon their policy of neutrality. The conference did not win all the Five Nations over to the English side. In fact, if anyone looked close enough, he could see that divisions among the Iroquois were quite apparent. For example, many Iroquois, not wanting to appear pro-English, boycotted the meeting. The colonial delegates noted, "it is a melancholy consideration that not more than 150 men of all the several [Iroquois] Nations have attended this Treaty although they had notice, that all the governments would be here . . . and that a large present would be given." The commissioners also witnessed disagreements between the pro-English Mohawks of Cana-

111

joharie and the rest of the Confederacy and commented on how the French "are continually drawing off the Indians from the British interest, and have lately persuaded one half of the Onondaga tribe with many from the other Nations along with them, to remove to a place called Osweegachee . . . where they have built them a church and fort and many of the Senecas, the most numerous nation, appear to be wavering and rather inclined to the French."[29]

In the months following the Albany Congress, the Iroquois made it perfectly clear to the French and Indians that the conference with the English had not altered the Confederacy's policy of neutrality. The Iroquois, at the end of 1754, were still at peace with the English and French.[30] With the brief exceptions of the aberrations during Queen Anne's War and King George's War, the Iroquois Confederacy maintained a policy of neutrality from 1701 until 1754. By mid-century the rivalry between England and France was again heating up. Before long it would erupt into another colonial war. At that point the Five Nations would be forced to choose sides in the Seven Years' War.

The Iroquois' policy of neutrality resulted directly from the position the Five Nations found themselves in after the Twenty Years' War. With their economy in shambles, military strength drained, and political solidarity shattered, the Iroquois could not afford to alienate either the French or English. Instead the Five Nations turned to both of their white neighbors for aid.

The English, in particular, had much to offer. The Five Nations were aware that English colonists could provide better-quality goods at cheaper prices than the French. Furthermore, English merchants, located at Albany and later Oswego, were closer to the Iroquois than were the French traders at Montreal. Therefore, throughout the first half of the eighteenth century, the Iroquois did most of their trading with the English. Every year Iroquois hunters ranged

112

over hundreds of miles in search of furs and peltry. Upon their return home they sold or exchanged their catches to the English for guns, powder, shot, kettles, tomahawks, knives, cloth, and other manufactured goods. Sometimes an item could be obtained only from the English. For example, strowds were extremely popular woolens (usually bright red) that were made only in England. Strowds were used by the Iroquois for clothing and other coverings and were valued as much for the prestige that the brand name brought its wearer as for the quality.[31] A good comparison might be the attraction that many contemporary Americans have for Pendleton wools.

The Five Nations also received free smithing from the British. As a way to strengthen friendship the New York government frequently provided smiths to mend Iroquois guns, knives, traps, and other implements.[32]

The Iroquois obtained additional economic benefits because of their relationship with the English. They often received presents when they met with officials to negotiate or renew friendship. At times, economic inducements were offered to the Iroquois in order to get their military help. The New Yorkers also hired Iroquois men to carry messages to other tribes or to spy in Canada. In times of crisis such as famine, the Five Nations received emergency economic assistance from the English. And on occasion, the Iroquois, acting either as a group or as individuals, sold land to the English.[33]

The Iroquois depended on the English to defend their hunting rights in the Western Country. The Five Nations deeded their western hunting grounds to the English king in 1701, and in return asked only that the English protect Iroquois hunters on that land. In 1726, the Senecas, Cayugas, and Onondagas signed a similar document, transferring their lands to the crown in exchange for protection of Iroquois hunting rights.[34]

The Five Nations understood the military value of New

113

York and other English colonies. Throughout the first half of the eighteenth century, the Iroquois repeatedly sought New York's support against potential enemies. The Five Nations not only relied on New York as a source of arms and ammunition, but also looked to New York as an ally that could build forts and supply troops to protect Iroquois villages from French or Indian attacks. Whenever the Five Nations had reason to suspect a French attack or received threats from enemy tribes, they went to the New York government for help. One sachem reminded the governor, "We cannot without your assistance put a stop to the French designs."[35]

After 1701, French-inspired rumors of supposed English plots to destroy the Iroquois or to take away their lands occasionally passed through Iroquoia. Each time the Iroquois reminded the English of their Covenant Chain friendship and asked for assurances that the alleged conspiracies were false. The Five Nations realized that they could not withstand an attack from the English any more than they could withstand an attack from the French or the western Indians. Therefore, the Iroquois maintained their alliance with the British as a guard against French, Indian, or even New Yorkers' attacks.[36]

The Iroquois needed the English colonial governments to control the actions of the colonists. The people of the Five Nations were particularly disturbed by the practices of unscrupulous traders. They constantly asked the English governments for cheaper prices for manufactured goods and for fairer trading practices. On numerous occasions after 1701, the Iroquois complained about the scarcity of arms and ammunition and the high cost of powder and shot. As was too often the case, government officials sympathized with the difficulties, but did little to solve them.[37]

The Iroquois people hated being cheated. On occasion violence occurred when traders attempted to cheat their Indian clientele. More often, though, bitter feelings re-

114

sulted from unfair trade practices. Governor Burnet of New York realized the Iroquois had just cause for discontent. In 1726, he ordered Major Abraham Schuyler to live among the Five Nations "to watch the motions of the French, to support our trade with the Far Indians, and to prevent the traders from abusing and imposing on them." But Burnet's good intentions could not stop the bad actions of white traders who were determined to cheat the Indians. In fact, some of the traders who were to blame lived in Pennsylvania, entirely out of the jurisdiction of the New York government.[38]

A later New York governor also sympathized with the Iroquois' problem. On December 21, 1730, Governor Montgomerie informed the Board of Trade that he wanted better regulation of the Indian trade at Oswego in order to stop the unscrupulous traders from cheating the Indians. Yet once again, unfair trade practices continued. Three years later, Governor Cosby of New York told the Iroquois, "Brethren, I am informed that some of our traders at Oswego have cheated the remote Indians by selling them water instead of rum. I will take care that no such thing be done in the future." The Iroquois soon learned that Cosby's promise was worth about as much as the water that traders had peddled as rum. The governor either would not or could not stop the unscrupulous traders. In either case, the Indians wound up being cheated by the traders.[39]

The Five Nations frequently sought help from English colonial governments in order to control the abuses in the liquor trade. Sachems complained that alcohol deprived the Iroquois people of their senses, was ruining their lives and tribes, and was used by traders to cheat them out of their furs and lands. The Iroquois were not exaggerating. The French priest Lafitau reported in 1718 that when the Iroquois and other Indians became intoxicated they went completely berserk, screaming like madmen and smashing everything in their homes. Even relatives and friends were not safe. According to Lafitau, over 100 Iroquois had moved to the Sault St. Louis mission in Canada to avoid the drunken orgies that were commonplace in Iroquoia. Lafitau added, "Although the savages like to drink, they are nevertheless sorry for having done so, because in their drunken fits they lose all they have, and they keenly regret this when they come to their senses."[40]

Certainly not all Iroquois used alcohol, and even those who did probably realized that drinking was causing problems not only for themselves but for their families too. Throughout the first half of the eighteenth century, Iroquois leaders, looking to the English for help, asked officials either to prohibit or regulate the rum traffic. But due to the frontier, with its lawlessness and near-wilderness conditions, regulation proved difficult to enforce, while prohibition was impossible.

The Five Nations also relied on the English colonial governments to protect them from land-hungry colonists. From time to time, colonists would use chicanery, alcohol, or fraud to cheat unsuspecting Iroquois out of their lands. The Iroquois would then turn to government officials to right the wrongs. In 1733, the Mohawks complained to Governor Cosby that the people of Albany were trying to cheat them out of their best farm lands near Fort Hunter (Tiononderoga). After the Mohawks threatened to move to Canada unless the Albany government gave up the fraudulent deed, Cosby sided with the Indians. Shortly thereafter, the deed was delivered to the sachems, who quickly destroyed it. The Mohawks' victory, however, was merely one battle. The Iroquois' struggle against land-jobbers, if it were to be successful, required never-ending vigilance and the cooperation of English colonial governments.[41]

In addition to using the English as a source for economic and military aid and as a means of controlling abuses by English colonists, the Iroquois needed the English for one other reason. The Five Nations frequently used their En-

116

glish ties to improve their relations with other Indian tribes. Sometimes the Iroquois employed their political and military alliances with the English to convince Indian tribes to ally themselves to the Five Nations. On other occasions the Iroquois relied upon their proximity to the English to persuade tribes to accept the Five Nations as friends. For instance, the Five Nations realized that they could use English trade goods to advance their economic and political relations with the western Indians. The western tribes desired English goods, but the Iroquois' homelands stood in between the Western Country and Albany or Oswego. The Iroquois were willing to allow the western Indians passage to the English trade—for a price. The Iroquois demanded peace and an alliance with the western tribes.[42]

During the first half of the eighteenth century, the Iroquois needed the French nearly as much as they needed the English. Like the English, the French were important economically. Many Iroquois traded with the French either in Canada or at French posts like Fort Detroit or Fort Cataraqui. By 1717, the French had established a small trading post near Irondequoit, in Seneca country, and were considering a post at an even more important location—the Niagara portage.

Joncaire had long dreamed of such an outpost. In 1707, he recommended to a representative of the king that a post be built at the portage around Niagara Falls to take advantage of the fur trade with the Iroquois. Joncaire argued that the "Iroquois would trade off there all the moose, deer, and bear skins they might bring, as these peltries could not be transported to the English except by land, and consequently with considerable trouble." Joncaire's recommendation was not followed, because the French feared a Niagara outpost would bring the western tribes too close to English traders at Albany. So for the time being the matter was dropped.

Joncaire's plans for a fort at the Niagara portage became a reality in 1720. In May, Joncaire returned from a winter

117

at Fort Frontenac carrying many furs obtained in trade with Indians. He also had a message that caused many French traders to reiterate the demand for a post at Niagara. Joncaire announced that the Senecas wanted the French to erect a trading post at Niagara and had promised to help maintain and defend the post against any future attacks. Soon thereafter, a crude post was set up at Niagara, and Joncaire was named commanding officer. This post was used for trading with the Iroquois and other tribes. At the same time, it hindered Indians from going to Albany to trade.[43]

For awhile the Iroquois-French trade flourished, but increased English competition and falling prices for furs on the French market caused the trade to taper off in the mid-1720s. The French acted quickly to rejuvenate their Indian trade. In 1725, Longueuil, a French officer who had been adopted by the Onondagas, obtained the Onondagas' consent to erect a new stone fort at Niagara. Actually the Onondagas had no authority to grant the French permission to build at Niagara, which was in Seneca territory. The Senecas even sent a wampum belt to the Onondagas asking them to reject the French request, but the Onondagas did not listen. They agreed to the French request in return for promises of trade and protection.[44]

The Albany Commissioners of Indian Affairs realized the threat that the French plans posed for English traders. On July 8, 1726, they wrote to Governor Burnet to complain about the stone fort being built at Niagara. They also complained about two French ships that had begun sailing on Lake Ontario. The commissioners maintained that the French actions would hurt New York's fur trade, since Fort Niagara was "conveniently situated to intercept all the fur trade of the Upper Nations and even of our Senecas who must pass that place as they come from their hunting who can't avoid passing by that place or so near it that the

French there will trade with them. They are to have a large store of goods there for supplying the Indians."[45]

Some Iroquois shared the New Yorkers' concern over the building of Fort Niagara. The Senecas were reluctant to have the fort at Niagara and complained that it was the Onondagas—and not the Senecas—who had consented to its construction. But Joncaire replied, "since when do you make no longer one body with the Onondagas? You have told us every year that what one Iroquois nation does or says, all the others agree to. Since when is all that changed?"[46]

The French refused to give up their newly constructed stone trading and military post at Niagara, and by the end of the decade, trade once again flourished there. For the next ten years, Iroquois continued to trade with the French at Forts Niagara and Frontenac. By 1738, French trade with the Iroquois was again declining because of New France's suppression of the brandy trade with the Indians, the poor quality of French woolens, and the low price of beaver. Yet the French trade with the Iroquois never stopped entirely. Whenever it was to the Iroquois' advantage, they continued to deal with the French.[47]

The Five Nations profited in other ways from their French connection. The Iroquois frequently received gifts of powder, lead, tobacco, brandy, knives, and other goods from the French, who were trying to preserve the Iroquois' friendship to prevent them from siding with the English. The fine gifts often succeeded in buying the loyalty of the Iroquois. The Five Nations also received provisions and supplies from the French during times of economic distress. In addition, the French provided the Iroquois with smiths to fix their guns, hatchets, kettles, and other manufactured goods. Some Senecas profited by working for the French. Senecas earned wages by carrying French goods over the Niagara portage. The Iroquois benefited economically from

French help in yet another way. The Five Nations knew that the French could order the western tribes not to interfere with Iroquois hunters in the Western Country. This realization was partially responsible for the Iroquois' desire to make peace with New France in 1701. After that date, the Iroquois were pleased to have French guarantees that Iroquois hunters would not be attacked by western Indians.[48]

Aside from their economic motives, the Iroquois had military and political reasons for wanting peace with New France. The Iroquois respected the power of the French and their Indian allies and did not want war with either of them. The Iroquois realized that they needed the French to control the numerous and powerful western tribes. Throughout the first half of the eighteenth century, the Five Nations relied on the French to enforce the Grand Peace Settlement between the Iroquois Confederacy and the Indian allies of New France. When violations of the peace did occur, the Iroquois quickly appealed to the French governor for help.[49]

Some Iroquois believed that they also needed French military protection as a guard against possible English attacks. The French frequently warned the Iroquois about purported English plots to exterminate the Five Nations. Then, the French would offer to defend the Iroquois, thereby winning their gratitude and friendship. In 1708, the French took advantage of the scarcity of gun powder at Albany to persuade some Iroquois that the English were trying to deprive the Five Nations of the means to defend themselves. The French also insisted that the queen of England had asked the French king to join her in destroying the Five Nations and dividing their lands—but the French king was resolved to protect the Iroquois. Over the next forty-five years, the French became quite adept at spreading anti-English rumors. These constant warnings about English treacheries helped convince many Iroquois that they needed the French as a guard against possible attacks

120

by the English. The Iroquois never rejected any French proposals of protection, and, sometimes, they even asked the French to defend them.[50]

Some of the Five Nations needed peace with New France for religious and social reasons. Many Iroquois wanted French missionaries. By 1708, the French had five Jesuits living in Iroquoia. The Black Gowns were forced to leave Iroquoia in 1709, when many Iroquois joined New York in the war against New France. But though they abandoned their missions, they did not forsake their work. After 1709, the Jesuits did most of their proselytizing in Canada and were successful in settling many Iroquois converts in missions near Montreal. One of the more important results of their efforts was the establishment of a mission at Oswegatchie or Swegatchy (on the present site of Ogdensburg, New York). At the conclusion of King George's War, pro-French Iroquois convinced the governor of New France that they wanted a priest to live near them. Needless to say, it did not take much persuasion, and the governor immediately began planning the new mission. Abbe Piquet, described by one French official as "a zealous missionary in whom these [Iroquois] nations have evinced much confidence," was placed in charge of the new outpost. By November, 1749, Iroquois, mostly Cayugas and Onondagas, were settling near the mission. There they received religious instruction and numerous gifts (it is hard to decide which was more inspirational for drawing Indians to the mission), as well as lessons on how to raise cows, hogs, and poultry. The Swegatchy mission was quite successful and won many Iroquois over to the French side.[51]

Some Iroquois wanted Jesuits for more than religious reasons. Many Iroquois had political or economic motives for welcoming the Jesuits. One pragmatic Iroquois man remarked, "If the English sell goods cheaper than the French, we will have ministers; if the French sell them cheaper than the English, we will have priests."[52]

121

There were some Iroquois, however, who sincerely desired the religious teachings of the Black Gowns. In 1711, Father Joseph Germain observed that over 500 Iroquois were living at a mission near Montreal, because their countrymen would not let them practice Catholicism in Iroquoia. Father Nau also noted the religious devotion of the Praying Iroquois. In 1735, he described the Iroquois at Sault St. Louis as excellent churchgoers and singers. Four years later, Nau wrote to his mother, "The [rosary] beads and devotional articles that you have thus far sent have brought joy to the hearts of my poor Iroquois."[53]

After the Christian Iroquois moved to Canadian missions, the Five Nations had another reason for keeping peace with New France. They realized that war would interfere with their social ties to the Iroquois emigrants. In the event of an all out war between the Five Nations and New France, the New York Iroquois and the Canadian Iroquois, who were French allies, might even find themselves shooting at each other. Therefore, it was imperative that the Five Nations remain at peace with New France.

Without a doubt, the Iroquois' need for French and English aid greatly influenced the Five Nations' decision to adopt a policy of neutrality toward the two great powers. But it was not the only consideration. The Iroquois understood that they could further their own needs by playing the English and French off against each other. The Iroquois felt that they could obtain concessions from one side by threatening to take their friendship and business to the other. This ploy was used with considerable success after 1701. The Iroquois were frequently able to obtain better prices from merchants, free smiths, and tighter regulation of the rum traffic and the land sales.[54]

On occasion, the Iroquois used one European power to check the expansion of the other. In 1702, the Iroquois told Governor Cornbury of New York that they were concerned about the French forts at Cataraqui and Detroit. They recommended that the English build forts to offset those of the French. The Iroquois took the same position in 1726. When the French erected a stone post at Niagara, the Iroquois allowed the English to build a fort at Oswego. The French were aware of the Iroquois' strategy. In October, 1728, the Paris government ordered Governor Beauharnois not to build any more forts in Iroquoia. The French leaders reasoned that the cost of a new fort would be more than its worth, for not only would the Iroquois resist a new fort, but they would allow the English to build one right next to it. One French official explained that the Iroquois' policy was that "neither of the two [European] nations should be superior in their country." The Iroquois used a similar approach to check European expansion into the Ohio Country during the 1740s and 1750s. At the Albany conference in 1754, Iroquois leaders indicated to the English that Ohio belonged to the Five Nations and that neither the French nor the English had the right to settle there without Iroquois consent. When the French began building forts in western Pennsylvania and Ohio, the Iroquois asked the English to help them stop the French encroachments.[55]

The Five Nations also used their neutrality to prevent the French and English from fighting each other in the vicinity of Iroquois villages. In 1741, Iroquois deputies reminded the Albany commissioners that the Five Nations "had given the French leave to build the house at Niagara as they had to [New York] to build one at Oswego and desired no molestation . . . be on either side." The Iroquois likewise made their position clear to the French. In 1744, Governor Beauharnois informed a French minister that he could not attack Oswego because of the Iroquois. Beauharnois explained that the Iroquois recently had announced that if both Oswego and Niagara remained undisturbed, the Five Nations would continue their neutrality.[56]

The Iroquois realized the benefits of neutrality. Cadwallader Colden described Consora, a Seneca leader of the

123

early 1700s, as a "very cunning and subtle fellow" who supported the policy of neutrality. According to Colden, Consora believed that the Five Nations should "keep the balance betwixt the two [i.e., the French and English] for if the English should prevail over the French, the Five Nations would be of means to enslave, for then the English would make no more account of them . . . but if the Five Nations would now observe an exact neutrality, they would be courted and feared by both sides." Years later, Secretary for Indian Affairs Peter Wraxall, from New York, made a similar observation about the Five Nations and their policy of neutrality. He wrote, "to preserve the balance between us and the French is the great ruling principle of the modern [Iroquois] Indian politics."[57]

The Iroquois had a very practical reason for following a policy of neutrality between the English and French: there was no feasible alternative. Since the Iroquois needed both powers for economic, political and social reasons, they could not afford to alienate either side. Furthermore, the Iroquois were not powerful enough to wage successful warfare against the English or French. Iroquois military strength had been decimated by the Twenty Years' War. To make matters worse, major disasters such as smallpox epidemics in 1717, 1732, and 1733, and famines in 1741 and 1742 further weakened the Iroquois' military strength.[58] In addition, factionalism splintered Iroquois society and dictated that the Confederacy follow a neutral policy.

During the first half of the eighteenth century, there was no unanimity among the Five Nations about relations with the English and the French. There was an English party and a French party in every village. The bases for these factions were a complicated blend of political, military, economic, social, and religious considerations. The Senecas, who lived closest to New France and thus had the most to gain or lose, were especially pro-French in their politics. Other members of the Five Nations also voiced a pro-

124

French position whenever it was to their advantage. At the same time, many Mohawks (who lived closest to the English) and other Iroquois adopted a pro-English posture.[59] As a result, the Confederacy, which depended upon compromise for survival, was forced to steer a middle course. The various factions usually prevented the League Council from adopting either a pro-French or pro-English position. Instead, the League had to favor neutrality in order to avert intra-League political strife and perhaps even a civil war.

The English had numerous reasons for accepting the Iroquois' decision to remain neutral. Some New York businessmen and officials realized that neutrality could benefit New York's economy. By 1702, many Albany traders and New York merchants were involved in the notorious Montreal-Albany trade, and they saw Queen Anne's War as a threat to their profitable Canadian commerce. If New York and the Five Nations were dragged into the war against New France, the resulting turmoil on the New York frontier would undoubtedly interrupt all trade. Therefore, these New Yorkers were eager to see the Iroquois remain neutral. As long as the Iroquois continued to be neutral, New France would not attack the New York countryside and the Montreal-Albany trade would continue.[60]

English colonists realized that they could not afford to lose the Five Nations' friendship. Many New Yorkers made huge profits by trading with the Iroquois. Others needed the Iroquois to open up trade with the western tribes. They knew that the western Indians could not reach Albany without going through or near Iroquois territory. So the New Yorkers relied on the Iroquois to give the western Indians a free and safe passage through Iroquoia. On occasion, New York officials and businessmen also used Iroquois Indians to invite western Indians to trade at Albany. Some officials and colonists realized that English colonial economic expansion could be facilitated through the purchase of lands from the Five Nations.

125

The English also had military reasons for wanting to retain the Five Nations' friendship. They needed the Iroquois as allies and intelligence gatherers in wars against the French and Indians. The English colonists were also aware of the strategic importance of the Iroquois' location. Situated between New France and the middle English colonies, Iroquoia was the perfect defensive barrier against French and Indian attacks.

Equally important, the English needed the Iroquois for political reasons. Colonial governments frequently used the Iroquois either to control other Indians or to expand the English Covenant Chain to include more tribes. Iroquois intermediaries were used to conduct negotiations between the English and western tribes. And the Iroquois were sometimes sent out to make peace with western tribes, thereby bringing them into friendship with the English. The English also used the Iroquois to check French expansion. Whenever the French tried to expand their power and control over the Great Lakes region, the English would turn to the Iroquois to counter the French actions. The English received Iroquois permission to build forts within Iroquoia to counterbalance those of the French. They also had guarantees that the Confederacy would try to prevent French expansion. After 1748, the English used their Iroquois alliance to oppose French claims to the Ohio Country. The English recognized Iroquois ownership of the Ohio Country, based on the right of conquest. They insisted that those lands, therefore, belonged to the crown, since the Iroquois were English subjects.[61]

The French, like the English, were willing to accept Iroquois neutrality in order to retain the Five Nations' friendship. The French realized that the Iroquois could help them in many ways. The French were aware of their military importance. Despite the Iroquois' setback in the Twenty Years' War, most French officials did not want to risk another war with the Iroquois, whose proximity and numbers still made them a threat to New France's survival. Although the French were not eager to fight the Iroquois, they were eager to have those Indians fighting on their side. Governor Vaudreuil believed that the men of the Five Nations could be used to force other Indians to remain at peace with New France. This strategy proved quite successful; and Iroquois warriors were frequently employed in raids against tribes hostile to New France. The Iroquois helped New France's military position in another way. Praying Iroquois were resettled in communities in Canada. These Caugnawagas assisted the French in wars against the English or other enemies. At the same time, the Praying Iroquois and their villages served as buffers, insulating Canadian settlements from attack.[62]

The French also understood that as long as the Iroquois-French peace remained in effect, the Five Nations would not aid the English in a war against New France. Furthermore, if the French could fully win over the Iroquois, the English would be in a desperate situation. The French believed that by improving their own relationship with the Iroquois, they could weaken the English position. Governor Montgomerie of New York was wise to French designs. In 1730, he wrote to the Board of Trade, "The Six Nations is a barrier between Canada and New York, New Jersey, Pennsylvania, Maryland, and Virginia, that the former security of these provinces in the late war with France, has been owing to that barrier; if the French therefore should try by any arts alienate the affections of those nations, all these provinces, in case of another war between the two crowns, must be exposed to all the miserable effects of a barbarous enemy."[63]

The French, like the English, benefited economically from their friendship with the Iroquois. Throughout the first half of the eighteenth century, the French traded with the Iroquois, and men of the Five Nations served as middlemen in the Montreal-Albany trade. The French also used

127

the Iroquois to prevent western Indians from trading at Albany. Sometimes Iroquois were employed to harass western Indians as they passed through Iroquoia en route to Albany. On other occasions the French obtained the Iroquois' permission to build forts which would block the western and northern Indians' routes to the Albany trade.[64]

The French received additional benefits from their friendship with the Five Nations. They obtained valuable information concerning English movements, and they used the Iroquois to check English expansion. The French cautioned the Five Nations not to give the English lands for forts or settlements, because, as one governor warned, the Englishman "has no other object in view than to make himself stronger, perhaps in order some day to crush you [Iroquois]." By mid-century, the French also needed Iroquois cooperation to prevent the English from winning over the tribes of the Ohio Country. Since travel and communication routes between Canada and Ohio passed through territory controlled by the Iroquois, the French, not wanting to lose Ohio, could not afford hostilities with the Iroquois.[65]

Both the French and English needed the Iroquois.[66] And neither wanted to risk alienating the Five Nations by refusing to accept their position of neutrality. As a result, the path was cleared for the Iroquois to pursue their goals by employing the neutrality policy.

5

Rapprochement with the
Western and Northern Tribes

Iroquois relations with the various tribes of the Western Country and Canada underwent a dramatic change in the eighteenth century. Throughout the 1600s, the Five Nations had waged almost continuous warfare against western tribes such as the Miami, Illinois, Ottawa, Huron, Potawatomi, Sac, and Fox and northern tribes such as the Caugnawagas, Abenakis, and Nipissings. But by the turn of the century, the Iroquois found themselves in a weakened position and realized they could no longer afford continued hostilities with either the western or northern Indians. This realization led to the introduction of a new peace policy toward the tribes of the West and Canada. A rapprochement with the western tribes would promote peace between the Five Nations and the far Indians, facilitate travel, hunting, and trade for all Indians in the Western Country, and enable the Iroquois to attract western tribes to the English Covenant Chain, thereby reducing the potential strength of the French and western Indian axis that had long been an enemy to the Five Nations. The rapprochement with the northern tribes would secure the Iroquois' northern border and promote the growth of economic, military, and social relations between the Iroquois and northern Indians.

The Iroquois needed the Western Country as a source for furs. Iroquoia had been depleted of beaver by 1640, so after that date the Western Country was the Iroquois' primary hunting ground. The Five Nations had won the right to hunt in the Western Country by defeating the Hurons, Neutrals, and Eries in a series of wars during the mid-seventeenth century. The survivors of the Iroquois attacks retreated westward, where they were joined by other tribes of the Great Lakes region such as the Illinois, Miami, Fox, Sac, Kickapoo, and Mascouten, who decided to flee rather than defend their homelands against the fierce Iroquois invaders.

The dispersion of these Indians by the mid-1600s nearly emptied the Western Country of its native inhabitants and gave the Iroquois almost exclusive hunting rights in the West. But the Iroquois' monopoly was shortlived. By 1700, Iroquois strength had been smashed by the Twenty Years' War. The Iroquois' loss of power, along with the Iroquois–western Indian Peace Settlement of 1701, provided the western tribes with the opportunity to move back to their lands in the Great Lakes region. The migrations of tribes such as the Wyandots (Hurons), Miamis, Ottawas, Illinois, Potawatomis, and Missisaugas were further motivated by the encouragement of the French to settle around their new posts recently built in the area and the desire of some Indians to move closer to New York and Pennsylvania, where they hoped to establish trade with the English. By 1718, tribes of the Western Country accounted for over 3,500 warriors. Three years later the figure was 6,600. These great numbers awed the Iroquois, whose own armies had dwindled due to the Twenty Years' War, and contributed to a feeling of deep respect, if not outright fear, on the part of the Five Nations toward the western tribes.[1]

130

After 1700, the Five Nations found themselves in a predicament. The western tribes' strength plus their own weakened position convinced the Iroquois that they could not obtain control of the Western Country by force. Yet the Five Nations also knew that their economic well-being, and perhaps their very existence, depended on their being able to hunt safely in the Western Country, which provided them with the beaver furs needed for the valuable Albany trade. Furthermore, the Five Nations were aware that they would suffer many casualties in the event of renewed hostilities with the numerous and powerful western tribes. These realizations set the stage for the shift in Iroquois policy toward the western Indians in the early eighteenth century. The Iroquois hoped that where a policy of war had failed to provide them with a source of furs from the Western Country, a policy of peace would succeed. They also hoped that, whereas warfare had failed to give them dominance and influence over the western Indians, diplomacy would succeed. From these attitudes evolved the Iroquois' policy of rapprochement toward the western tribes. Originally, the Iroquois sought rapprochement solely as a means of obtaining peace and hunting privileges. Before long, however, the Iroquois realized that they could obtain additional benefits from a policy of peace toward western Indians. At that point choice replaced necessity as the mother of the Iroquois' rapprochement policy.

The first step toward improved relations with western Indians came in 1701, when Iroquois deputies journeyed to Montreal to treat with the French and their Indian allies. The Iroquois were hoping that French mediation and protection would improve their relations with the western tribes. Representatives from western tribes were summoned by the French to take part in the negotiations with the Iroquois. The Grand Settlement of 1701 established the Five Nations' neutrality in any future wars between England and France, a peace between the Iroquois and New France's

131

northern and western Indian allies, and the right of all Indians to hunt safely in the Western Country. At the conference, New France's Governor Callieres stated confidently to all the Indian nations that now there would be peace and all could hunt in safety. He added that should the peace be broken, the aggrieved party should not take revenge, but should go to him for justice.[2]

Callieres' words were exactly what the Iroquois wanted to hear. From then on, whenever western Indians violated the peace agreement, the Iroquois would seek justice and protection from the French governor.[3] Even though skirmishes occurred from time to time between Iroquois and western Indians, the Iroquois had good reason not to be disillusioned with the failure of the Settlement of 1701 to establish an absolute peace among all Indians in the Western Country. After all, the settlement did provide the Five Nations with a French ally who had promised to punish any Indians who violated the cease-fire. Furthermore, the settlement brought about a period of relative peace between the Iroquois and the western tribes. Not only did it allow the Iroquois to hunt and travel throughout the West in relative safety, but it provided the Iroquois with the opening needed to visit the villages of the western tribes and peddle their most important ware—the opportunity for the western Indians to obtain English trade goods.

The Five Nations realized that they could use their political and geographical proximity to the English to promote their interests in the Western Country. Since the 1680s, New York officials and traders had been trying to convince the Iroquois that trade with the tribes of the Great Lakes country would benefit the Five Nations and the English. The great losses suffered in the Twenty Years' War forced the Five Nations to seriously consider the New Yorkers' proposal. The Iroquois listened carefully to Governor Bellomont in 1700 when he told them, "You must needs be sensible that the Dowagenhaes, Miami, Ottawas, and Tobaccos and the other remote Indians are vastly more numerous than you Five Nations and that by their continued warring upon you they will in a few years totally destroy you." Bellomont suggested that the Iroquois "try all possible means to fix a trade and correspondence with all those nations, by which you would retain them to yourselves." He added, "with my assistance I am in hopes in a short time they might be brought to be united with us in the Covenant Chain, and then you might at all times go a hunting into their country without any sort of hazzard, which I understand is much the best for beaver hunting."[4]

The Five Nations apparently agreed with Bellomont, for soon thereafter they moved to establish better economic and political ties with those Indians. They offered the western Indians the opportunity to obtain English manufactured goods, which were better yet cheaper than French products. The western Indians, recognizing value, eagerly made arrangements with the Iroquois.[5]

The Iroquois, whose homelands stood between the western tribes and the trade city of Albany, hoped to establish a "geographic" middleman position that would enable them to obtain diplomatic and economic concessions from the western Indians. The Iroquois offered the western tribes free and safe passage through Iroquoia to the English posts at Albany and later Oswego. In return those Indians had to remain at peace with the Iroquois and not molest Iroquois hunters in the West. Many western Indians, wanting English trade goods, quickly accepted the Iroquois' proposal. As a result the Iroquois soon established themselves as geographic middlemen. This significant development greatly contributed to the Iroquois' economic and political success during the first half of the eighteenth century.[6]

English observers were able to record the proceedings of a conference in 1710 between the Iroquois and one western tribe. Cadwallader Colden reported that the Iroquois prepared for their talks with the Waganhas (Ottawas) by solicit-

133

ing English support. Colden noted that the Iroquois sent messengers to Albany "to tell that they designed to meet some Waganha sachems in the general meeting to be held at Onondaga and therefore desired their Brethren to send some persons of note . . . to represent their Brother Corlaer [the New York governor] and to bring some of the River Indian sachems along with them. Captain Evert Banker and Mr. David Schuyler were sent." The conference between the Waganhas, Iroquois, River Indians (i.e., remnant bands of Algonquian-speaking Indians living along the Hudson River), and the English convened during the first week in June. According to Colden, the Senecas first met privately with the rest of the Iroquois and told them, "that when the Waganha ambassadors came this last time to them they spoke to the ambassadors as follows: 'We take you by the hand to conduct you to our Brother Corlaer and Quider. The doors stand everywhere open for you. Your lodgings are prepared from the Seneca's country to that of our Brother Corlaer and Quider, the path is made plain and easy and there is no evil in our country.' "

On June 7, the Iroquois, in conjunction with the New York government and the River Indians, presented the following wampum belts to the Waganhas:

> 1st Belt. Brethren, I desire a firm and everlasting peace to be kept inviolably not only by us but by our children likewise. If you shall preserve this peace our children will grow up in joy, but if you do the contrary, either you or I will repent it.
>
> 2nd Belt. Brethren, by this we cleanse your minds and wash away all evil thoughts.
>
> 3rd Belt. By this we reconsile the young men our soldiers to yours that if any nation should after this attack either of us, we may jointly defend ourselves and destroy our enemies. Brethren, If any of our people fall into your country naked and hungry supply them with victuals and clothing.
>
> 4th Belt. Brethren. If any difficulty should hereafter happen between any of your people and any of this house [i.e.

134

the Iroquois, River Indians, or English], let no revenge be taken till enquiry made of the occasion of such injury. Come first to us here if any harm happen to be done by any of our people before you take revenge, for you may safely do it and we shall do in like manner with you.

5th Belt. Brethren. I desire that we may walk and travel safely and trade freely.

6th Belt. Brethren. Corlaer and Quider and the River Indians speak to you by this belt as well as the Five Nations who altogether make one house here. The path from the place where you live to Albany is beaten and made plain by this belt and all molestation or trouble removed out of the way. If any other nation would walk in this path who is not acquainted with it, help him forward. You have a free and safe passage to my Brother Corlaer to walk in it as you please without molestation.

7th Belt. Brethren. We hear that one [of] your great sachems who always inclined to our Brother Corlaer and Quider is dead. We desire you may put another good man in his room.

As soon as the sachem completed his speech, Albany agents presented two strowd blankets and other gifts to clothe the new Waganha sachem. The following day the Waganhas gave their reply:

[Belt] 1. Brethren Corlaer and Quider. You have accepted me for your child. I have last summer sucked one of your breasts, but now I am come to suck them both. Have compassion on us as a Father hath on his children. Father, I take the hatchet out of your hands because you have spoken of peace that you may have peace everywhere.

[Belt] 2. Father you have taken me into your Covenant Chain which shall be preserved so firmly that no ax shall be able to cut it asunder.

[Belt] 3. Father Corlaer and Quider. I am resolved to go to your house to see how the trade is there, and if you use us well we will return next Spring.

[Belt] 4. Now Father and Brethren. We accept of the peace as it is offered to us and thank the whole house for it. We promise to observe it forever in token . . . we give these two calumets.[7]

These negotiations probably were typical of the treaty settlements that occurred between the Iroquois and the western tribes. The Iroquois gave wampum belts to show off their close English alliance to the Waganhas (belts 6 and 7); to establish peace and an alliance with the Waganhas (belts 1, 2, 3, and 4); to obtain the right to travel and hunt safely in the Western Country (belts 3 and 5); and to offer, in exchange, a free and safe passage to the Albany trade to the Waganhas (belt 6). The Waganhas accepted the Iroquois' proposals and presented their own wampum belts to show that they would uphold peace and the Covenant Chain (belts 1 and 2), and that they looked forward to trading at Albany (belt 3).

After 1710, the Iroquois continued their strategy of offering the western tribes free and safe passage to the Albany trade in return for peace and the right to hunt and travel in the West, and throughout the 1720s, the Albany trade with the western tribes continued to grow.[8]

Governor William Burnet of New York was partially responsible for the increase in the number of western Indians taking part in the Albany trade. Burnet gave New York's western fur trade a boost when he secured a prohibition of the Montreal-Albany trade, which had been carried on between the merchants of those two cities since the turn of the century. This made many western tribes even more eager to obtain Iroquois permission to pass through their homelands to reach the Albany trade. On July 12, 1721, Governor Burnet reported that the Montreal-Albany trade had been stopped, and, as a result, many far Indians were now trading at Albany. Burnet sought to increase trade with the western tribes in another way. In 1722, he instructed Major Abraham Schuyler to lead a party of traders to a location on Lake Ontario (perhaps Oswego), where they were to reside for one year. Burnet ordered them "to trade with the far Indians that are come from the upper lakes, and endeavor by all suitable means to persuade them to come and trade at

Albany or with this new settlement." Burnet told Schuyler, "You are also to acquaint all the far Indians that I have an absolute promise and engagement from the Five Nations that they will not only suffer them to pass freely and peaceably through their country, but will give them all due encouragement, and sweep and keep the path open and clean whenever they intend to come and trade with this province." Between them, Burnet and the Iroquois succeeded in bringing many western Indians to trade at Albany and at the new establishment on Lake Ontario. The arrangement was advantageous for everyone involved: the English and western Indians conducted a mutually beneficial trade, while the Iroquois developed their "geographic" middleman position. As a result, right up until mid-century western Indians regularly traveled through Iroquoia to trade at Albany and Oswego.[9]

Not all Iroquois were eager to have the western Indians passing through their country. Some were afraid of the great numbers of far Indians passing through Iroquoia en route to Albany. On occasion, some Iroquois even tried to prevent western Indians from trading in New York. In 1710, several Iroquois men nearly disrupted negotiations with the Ottawas, when they became drunk and threatened to kill the Ottawas whom they disliked. In 1715, a group of pro-French Onondagas attacked some western Indians in order to stop them from trading at Albany.[10]

Most Iroquois, however, were glad that western Indians were traveling through Iroquoia and trading at Albany. By granting the western Indians a safe and free passage through their homelands, the weakened Iroquois, who could not afford continued warfare, obtained peace from those tribes and the right to hunt and travel safely in the Western Country. Furthermore, some Iroquois were able to develop a lucrative trade with the western Indians passing through Iroquoia. Iroquois provided the Indian travelers with the goods and services they needed for their journey between Albany and the Western Country. In return the Iroquois obtained furs which they resold to English traders for a substantial profit.[11] Many Iroquois believed that granting the western Indians a passage to Albany would benefit the Five Nations in another way. They were convinced that the increase in business at Albany would result in better trade values. New York officials and businessmen, who were eager to trade with western tribes, constantly urged the Iroquois to give the far Indians permission to travel through Iroquoia. The New Yorkers assured the Iroquois that they too would benefit from the increased trade at Albany and Oswego, since goods would become more plentiful and less expensive.[12]

The Five Nations were so convinced that the English-western Indian trade was beneficial to them that they frequently asked the English to improve trade conditions so that even more western Indians would be drawn to Albany. The Iroquois argued that they could be more successful in building good relations with the western tribes if the British would lower retail prices at Albany, because cheaper goods would be more of an inducement to draw the western Indians to Albany. The Iroquois were even willing to pay higher prices than the western Indians if it meant an increase in trade and better relations with those tribes. One Iroquois sachem told Governor Hunter, "We shall always be willing to encourage their [the western Indians'] coming [to Albany], but the Brethren can do more to promote this trade than we can, that is by selling goods cheap. Yea, we would have you for this purpose sell cheaper to them than you do to us, and this will infallibly draw them [western Indians] to you." Similar comments were made to Governor Burnet in 1722.[13] These requests show that the Iroquois wanted to get western tribes trading at Albany, even if it meant offering better prices to those tribes than to the Iroquois. The only logical explanation for this position is that the Iroquois realized they had much to gain by drawing western Indians to

138

the Albany trade. Specifically, such an arrangement would allow the Iroquois to obtain peace with the western Indians, to hunt in the Western Country, and to trade with the western Indians as they traveled through Iroquoia.

The Iroquois also asked the English to curb unfair trade practices. Sachems pointed out that the far Indians came to trade once, but after being cheated, they never came back again. Apparently, the Iroquois told the western Indians that they could find cheap prices for manufactured goods and quality rum, if they journeyed through Iroquoia and traded at Albany or Oswego. The use of such a sales pitch by the Iroquois would explain their comments made to Governor Cosby at a conference in 1735. They complained that at Oswego the prices were too high and the rum was diluted, conditions which made the Iroquois look like liars in the eyes of the western Indians.[14]

Along with asking for better prices and trade practices, the Iroquois frequently sought prohibition of the Montreal-Albany trade, which they felt was undermining their efforts to draw the western tribes to Albany. The Iroquois argued that if the English outlawed the Montreal-Albany trade, the western tribes, desirous of English goods, would have to bring their business to Albany and Oswego.[15]

In the early 1720s, Governor Burnet shut down the Montreal-Albany trade, and, as the Iroquois predicted, many far Indians began coming to Albany to obtain goods no longer available from the French. The Iroquois' satisfaction was short-lived though. On June 16, 1725, the Board of Trade, spurred on by merchant interests, repealed the acts banning the Montreal-Albany trade, on the grounds that they violated New York traders' civil rights. Soon thereafter, the Iroquois were again complaining about New York's trade with Canada.[16]

While some of the Five Nations concentrated on developing their role as geographic middlemen, others sought to become economic middlemen in the trade between the En-

139

glish and the western tribes. The idea was not a new one.
During the previous century, the Iroquois had tried repeatedly to establish themselves as economic middlemen by carrying English goods to the villages of the far tribes. Their
efforts usually failed. After 1700, however, Iroquois sometimes were able to succeed as economic middlemen. Western tribes, depending on the Iroquois for English trade
goods, were then less likely to attack any of the Five Nations, including Iroquois hunters in the Western Country.
In this way, the Iroquois' role as economic middlemen, although not as developed nor as important as their role as
geographic middlemen, did provide some of the Five Nations with economic benefits and better diplomatic relations
with western Indians.[17]

The Iroquois' close ties to the English helped them to establish better relations with the western tribes in several
other ways. The Iroquois had the advantage of being New
York's foremost Indian ally. As such, they could be of use to
western Indians who desired improved relations with the
English. Those tribes knew that the Iroquois' friendship
could facilitate the development of an English-western Indian trade. The Iroquois gladly served as the vehicle to carry
western tribes into the Covenant Chain and repeatedly
helped western tribes establish diplomatic and economic relations with the English. Both the English and Iroquois made
it clear to western tribes that peace was a prerequisite of
trade. For example, in 1715, the New York governor welcomed a group of western Indians to the Albany trade and
reminded them that "all that are friends to the Five Nations
shall be looked upon as friends to this government and shall
be welcome to come hither, as on the other hand, all that are
enemies to the Five Nations shall be looked on as enemies to
us."[18]

British support of the Iroquois was manifested in other
ways. The English often sent agents to attend Iroquois conferences with the western tribes. The Iroquois realized that

the presence of English agents showed the western Indians that the English took an interest in the Confederacy's affairs. At times the Five Nations even asked the English to send representatives to these meetings. English use of the Iroquois as messengers or wampum belt carriers also demonstrated to the western tribes the closeness of their relationship. These actions provided additional reasons for those western Indians, who desired English trade, to maintain peaceful relations with the Iroquois. The Iroquois were aware that English support was quite helpful—if not absolutely necessary—in maintaining friendly relations with the western tribes. As a result, whenever English support for the Iroquois in the West seemed to waver, the Five Nations requested it be made strong again.[19]

The Iroquois' quest for better relations with the western Indians was aided by the arrival of English traders in the Western Country. Every tribe that began trading with the English usually had to agree to remain at peace with the Iroquois, who were English allies. Therefore, Iroquois influence and security in the Western Country rose according to the amount of English trade done in the West. English traders penetrated the West during the 1720s, and by the 1730s traders from New York, Pennsylvania, Virginia, and the Carolinas were trading throughout the Western Country. The amount of business done by the English in the West continued to grow during the 1740s. To facilitate this trade the Miamis established the Indian trading village of Pickawillany in 1748. By 1750, Englishmen were scattered as far as the Illinois Country. These English traders brought more and more tribes into the Covenant Chain, and every tribe that became friendly toward the English became one less enemy for the Iroquois. By 1745, this new alignment in trade relations allowed the Iroquois to hunt and trade in the Western Country, with little fear of being attacked.[20]

The Iroquois also relied on English military power and arms and ammunition to ensure their position in the West-

141

ern Country. For example, in 1701, the Iroquois ceded to the English all their western lands, which they no longer controlled anyway because of their weakened state. In return, the English promised to protect the Iroquois' right to hunt out west. Some of the Five Nations signed a similar deed in 1726 in order to obtain English military support. In autumn of that year Governor Burnet convinced the Senecas, Onondagas, and Cayugas that New York would protect them from their enemies if they deeded their western hunting lands to the English. The Iroquois, also wanting protection for their homes, asked the governor to include their castles in the deed. Burnet was only too happy to comply with their request, and the deed was signed.[21] As the 1700s progressed and the English became more influential in the Western Country, the promise of British protection for the Iroquois, combined with the opportunity for trade, undoubtedly convinced many western tribes not to make war on the Iroquois.

Along with using the French and English to control the western tribes, the Five Nations employed a third tool to forge a policy of peace with the Indians of the Western Country. After 1701, the Iroquois negotiated directly with the western tribes to develop closer social, political, and military relations with the far Indians.

Many Iroquois hunted, traveled, and lived in the Western Country. Some Iroquois even married Indians from western tribes. By mid-century large numbers of Iroquois were living on lands watered by the rivers and streams running into the Great Lakes and the Ohio River. In 1742, Iroquois sachems informed the governor of Pennsylvania that numerous Iroquois men were "out amongst the Nations to the Westward." Other accounts show that Iroquois commonly resided in villages of western tribes. Therefore, friendly social contact between Iroquois and far Indians became the norm.[22]

Iroquois often learned western Indian languages. The similarity between the Iroquois and Huron languages (both

142

stem from the same Iroquoian-language stock) facilitated communication between Iroquois and western Indians, many of whom spoke or understood the Huron tongue. Some Iroquois learned the Ottawa-Algonquian language, which was the other major language used by western Indians. A sign language also may have been used for communication among different Indian groups.[23]

The Iroquois sometimes consolidated social ties by inviting western Indians to come and live in Iroquoia. In this way, the Five Nations strengthened themselves while they developed better social ties to western tribes who were relatives or friends of those who moved to Iroquoia.[24]

The Iroquois Confederacy also worked diligently to establish military and political relations with the far Indians. The Iroquois' rapprochement with the western tribes not only neutralized a potentially dangerous enemy—the western tribes—but it transformed that enemy into an ally. The Iroquois' military position improved with every mutual-defense pact negotiated between the Five Nations and the western tribes. Every time the Iroquois added a "link" to the Iroquois-English Covenant Chain, they were subtracting a potential ally from New France. Throughout the first half of the eighteenth century, the Five Nations did everything they could to ally themselves with the far Indians. On numerous occasions the Iroquois joined western Indians to war on the tribes of Virginia and the Carolinas. The Five Nations also offered aid and assistance to western tribes in trouble. For example, when the Fox Indians became embroiled in a conflict with the French in the early 1700s, the Iroquois provided them with supplies, advice, and other support. By the 1740s, the Five Nations had formed alliances with most of the important tribes of the Western Country. One Iroquois sachem proudly announced to the New York governor that "all the Indians which were formerly our enemies are now entered into the Covenant with us almost as far as the River Mississippi." In 1742, Pennsylvania officials described the vast Iroquois network of western Indian alliances and concluded that the Five Nations were allied to at least eight major Indian nations numbering well over 6,000 warriors.[25]

The Iroquois saw King George's War (1744–48) as an opportunity to make further inroads among the tribes of the Western Country. The fighting between the English and French prevented New France from obtaining the trade goods needed to supply her Indian allies. The Iroquois took advantage of the situation by using their geographic middleman position to the utmost. The Five Nations offered the western tribes access to English trade goods, which could be obtained either by passage through Iroquoia to Albany or to Oswego or by trade in pro-English Indian villages along the Ohio River. In return the Iroquois insisted on continued friendship between the Five Nations and the western tribes, and military assistance in case the Iroquois had to fight the French. The western Indians were in no position to dicker. They needed manufactured goods, and the Five Nations controlled the means to the only available source. Most far tribes quickly accepted the Iroquois demands, and throughout King George's War, large numbers of western Indians traded with the English in New York or along the Ohio River, and numerous far Indians joined Iroquois war parties against the French.[26]

After the war ended the Five Nations used their English connection and the lure of English trade goods to keep the western tribes in the Covenant Chain. The Iroquois were extremely successful, and by 1754, they had numerous alliances with tribes of the Western Country, much to the dismay of the French who believed they were losing all their Indian allies to the Iroquois and English.[27]

Throughout the first half of the eighteenth century, the Iroquois Confederacy was committed to a policy of rapprochement toward the tribes of the West. The political, military, and economic success of the Five Nations de-

144

pended upon maintaining peace with the far Indians and promoting coexistence for all Indians in the Western Country. Occasionally disagreements and skirmishes occurred. But the reasons and framework for establishing and keeping peace were firmly fixed in all the participants' minds by the mid-1700s, so peace among the tribes usually prevailed.

Living to the north of Iroquoia were the tribes that the French called the "domiciliated" Indians of Canada. These northern tribes lived in several villages located near the cities of Montreal and Quebec. In 1711, the Jesuit Joseph Germain wrote a letter to his superior indicating the locations of the domiciliated Indians. According to Germain, over 1,200 Ottawas, Hurons, Algonquins, and Abenakis lived in missions near Quebec. Father Germain proudly noted that the Huron mission at Laurette, near Quebec, was quite successful, because the Hurons were fervent Christians. He added that the Abenakis also had a mission near Quebec at St. Francis. The Jesuit pointed out that another important mission village was located near Montreal at Sault St. Louis (also called Caugnawaga). The Caugnawaga settlement, which dated back to 1669, had a population of nearly 600 Praying Iroquois, making it "one of the oldest and largest [French missions]." By mid-century there were two other domiciliated villages. Becancour, near Trois Rivieres on the St. Lawrence River, was an Abenakis mission, and Oka (also called Lake of the Two Mountains), near Montreal, was made up of Praying Iroquois, Algonquins, and Nipissings. A sixth domiciliated village of Abenakis and Loups was in the process of being established at Missikoui, at the entrance of Lake Champlain. Jesuits were in charge of all these missions with the exception of the Lake of the Two Mountains, which was served by the Seminary of Saint Sulpice.[28]

The domiciliated Indians had fought alongside the French and against the Iroquois during the Twenty Years' War. In 1701, these northern tribes, along with New France's other

145

Indian allies, ratified the Grand Peace Settlement with the Iroquois. From then on the Iroquois Confederacy was determined to keep peace with the domiciliated Indians of Canada. Between 1701 and 1708, Iroquois deputies frequently met with northern Indians to renew the peace and "consult about matters for the good of the country." Occasionally, the Iroquois tried to influence the behavior of various domiciliated Indians, but usually the independent-minded northern Indians did as they pleased. For example, in 1706, the Albany Commissioners of Indian Affairs observed that the Five Nations had tried to convince the northern Indians not to make war on New England, but they had "had little or no effect." The following year Iroquois sachems tried to talk the Caugnawagas into making peace with New England and moving back to Iroquoia, but again they were unsuccessful.[29]

The Iroquois peace with the Indians of Canada almost came to an end in 1709, when New York officials convinced many Iroquois to join the English invasion of New France. Yet, even though these Iroquois were willing to declare war against the French, they still did not want to fight the northern Indians. In July, 1709, the Onondagas sent a warning to the Indians living near Montreal, informing them about the coming invasion and cautioning them not to fight alongside the French. The Mohawks sent a similar warning to the Caugnawagas. According to New France's Governor Vaudreuil, the Mohawks told the Praying Iroquois that "It was with great regret they [the Mohawks] had consented to [war on New France]; that the hatchet which had been placed in their hands did not afford them any pleasure, but that it was impossible for them to refuse it . . . considering the large military force that was at [Albany]." The Mohawks then advised the Caugnawagas "as good brothers, that the French never could resist the English army; that it was still time for those at Sault St. Louis to take their choice and to retire, but if they did not do so, they might consider themselves dead men."[30]

The way things turned out, the Iroquois did not have to fight either the French or the domiciliated Indians. The English colonies' planned invasion of Canada never occurred, so the Iroquois were able to maintain their peace with the Caugnawagas and other Indians allied to New France.

Several English colonies made a second attempt to invade New France in 1711. Once again, they solicited the Iroquois' help. Once again, the Iroquois warned the Praying Iroquois not to get involved. And then once again, the plans for the invasion were abandoned. So in the end, the Iroquois peace with the domiciliated Indians remained unbroken.

After 1711, the Iroquois Confederacy returned to its policy of neutrality in regard to the English and French, and it generally adhered to a policy of peace toward the northern tribes. The Iroquois wanted peace with the northern Indians even if hostilities broke out between the English and French. In 1712, the Iroquois reminded the Caugnawagas that they were at peace and asked them "to remain passive on their mats, and not to take any sides [in the event of renewed Iroquois-French hostilities]." The Iroquois' worries never materialized and peace continued. The Iroquois' close ties to the domiciliated Indians were apparent during a conference between Iroquois deputies and Governor Vaudreuil in 1717. The Iroquois had gone to Montreal in order to express condolences over the death of King Louis XIV. The deputies told Vaudreuil that the Iroquois Confederacy hoped that the new French king would "protect us from any attacks that may be made against us. We ask the same favors for all those [Indians] of the Sault St. Louis, and of Sault an Recollet, for the Abenakis, the Outauois, the Nepissings, and all others who belong to us and are our brethren."[31]

The Iroquois paid close attention to relations with the Abenakis, one of the more powerful domiciliated tribes. In

1718, a French official noted that the Five Nations were secretly trying to enlist the Abenakis as allies against New France. Iroquois-Abenaki relations continued to be close. On several occasions the Abenakis even asked the Iroquois to join them in a war against the New England colonies. Luckily for the English, the Iroquois refused.[32]

Actually, the war between the Abenakis and the New England colonists could have brought an end to the Iroquois-Abenaki peace. In the spring of 1723, English officials pressured the Iroquois into ordering the Abenakis to cease hostilities with the English or else face a war with the Iroquois Confederacy. By October it was evident that the Abenakis would not halt their activities, so the Confederacy was forced to declare war. Yet the Iroquois were not eager to fight, particularly since the Caugnawagas and other domiciliated Indians had promised to back the Abenakis in case of an Iroquois attack. So, the Iroquois reneged on their promise to aid the New England colonists. Throughout 1724, the Iroquois repeatedly refused to help the English make war on the Abenakis. Governor Burnet wrote to the Board of Trade, "I have not been able to effect any thing material that way [i.e., to secure Iroquois aid for Massachusetts] except some messages from the Six Nations to the Eastern Indians to persuade them to desist, which the Eastern [Indians] have answered evasively; and their answers have furnished an excuse to the Six Nations for their declining to go to war with them."[33]

The Iroquois were reluctant to fight against the Abenakis, who were being aided by the Caugnawagas, Micmacs, and other northern Indians. On November 28, 1724, Governor Vaudreuil wrote to a French minister, "Deputies from the Five Nations came this summer to assure me that they will not take up the hatchet in favor of the English against the Abenakis; and in order to retain them in these favorable dispositions, I thought I could not do better than to send Sieur de Joncaire to winter at Niagara and among

148

the Senecas."[34] Vaudreuil had no reason to be alarmed, for the Iroquois had no intention of fighting the Abenakis or any other French Indians.

Throughout the 1730s, the Iroquois and domiciliated Indians remained on good terms. Iroquois visitors were constantly among Canada's mission Indians. Communication between Iroquoia and the villages of the northern tribes was common. And Iroquois warriors frequently joined northern Indian war parties against southern tribes. The Iroquois were satisfied with their friendly relations with the domiciliated Indians. In 1740, Iroquois deputies proudly told New York's lieutenant governor that the Five Nations were allied to all the northern Indians and western tribes. The following year the Iroquois renewed their peace treaty with the northern tribes to ensure neutrality in case war broke out between the French and English.[35]

In 1742, the Iroquois made another effort to preserve peace with the domiciliated Indians. An Onondaga deputy was sent to Montreal to apologize for the murder of a Sault St. Louis Indian by an Iroquois warrior. The Onondaga messenger told Governor Beauharnois that the murder had "stained a leaf [of the Great Tree of Peace] with blood; we bury this affair by this belt; Father, we request you to prevail on your nations to forget it." Beauharnois accepted the apology and assured them that the peace that had long been in effect between the Iroquois and the French and their Indian allies would remain unbroken. In 1744, an Iroquois spokesman at the Lancaster Conference assured English officials that the Iroquois Confederacy had great influence with many tribes, "particularly over the Praying Indians . . . who stand in the very gates of the French."[36] Before long the Iroquois would have the chance to test their friendship with the Praying Indians.

The War of the Austrian Succession, known in the colonies as King George's War, broke out in North America in March, 1744. At first the northern Indian allies of New

149

France aimed their attacks only at New England, so the Iroquois stalled and refused to take up the English hatchet against the tribes of Canada. But in the fall of 1745, French and northern Indian war parties began raiding the New York frontier. Thereafter, more and more English pressure was placed on the Five Nations to honor the Covenant Chain and declare war against the French and Indians. The Iroquois Confederacy succumbed to English demands in 1746 by agreeing to join the English in the war against New France. Yet even then the Five Nations promised to fight only the French, not the Indians of Canada.[37]

Relations between the Iroquois and northern Indians grew tense in 1746. In July, a delegation from the Five Nations visited Canada and asked the Caugnawagas to remain neutral, but the Praying Iroquois refused. Later that month Caugnawaga Indians traveled to Iroquoia, where they spread the alarm that a French army would soon be attacking the English and the Mohawks, who were aiding the English. The implied threat was clear: if the Five Nations carried out their promise to go to war, as the Mohawks had already done, Iroquois villages would be sacked by French and Indian forces. The Confederacy began to reconsider the decision to fight alongside the English. Most Iroquois, skeptical about the amount of help and protection they could expect from their English allies, did not want to risk an all-out war against the French and Indians. They made their new position clear to the French. The four upper Iroquois nations insisted that they had accepted the hatchet from the English "only to get rid of them," but the Confederacy had no intention of actually joining the English in King George's War. The French and domiciliated Indians responded by declaring war on the Mohawks only.[38]

The warfare continued along the Canadian and New York frontiers throughout 1747. Of the Five Nations, only the Mohawks, who were closest to the English and the most loyal, officially aided the English in the war against New

150

France. The other four nations refused to admit publicly that they had taken up the English hatchet, even though individual warriors from each tribe were taking part in Mohawk and English raids into Canada. Leaders of the Senecas, Cayugas, Onondagas, Oneidas, and Tuscaroras were counting on diplomacy to shield their people from French and northern Indian attacks. Iroquois representatives met secretly with the domiciliated Indians and reached an agreement not to fight them in any war between European powers. Once friendship was assured the Iroquois sought to weaken the French and northern Indian alliance through another tactic. The Iroquois, realizing that New France was short on supplies, tried to lure the northern Indians away from the French by offering them the opportunity to trade with the English. Some tribes, desperate for trade goods, took the bait and joined the English against the French. But most northern Indians did not abandon the French alliance. Some even continued their attacks on the Mohawks. For the most part, however, the Iroquois Confederacy was successful in preserving friendly relations with the tribes of Canada. Even the Mohawks benefited from the Confederacy's negotiations with the northern tribes. One French official admitted that the Caugnawagas favored the Mohawks and "are suspected of giving the [Mohawks] notice when we are in pursuit of them, by firing three shots when the detachments are approaching their camp." King George's War strained, but did not shatter, the Iroquois-northern Indian peace.[39]

The Treaty of Aix-la-Chapelle officially brought King George's War to a close in October, 1748, and allowed the tribes of Canada and the Five Nations to resume normal relations. The peace between the Iroquois and the northern Indians was threatened in 1750 when the French, in an effort to convince the Confederacy to surrender its claims to the Ohio Country, tried to unleash the Missisaugas and other tribes against the Five Nations. The Iroquois side-

151

stepped the French machinations by negotiating a new treaty with the Missisaugas. After 1750, the Five Nations and northern tribes remained on good terms. Iroquois and northern Indian warriors once again joined together to raid Indians in Virginia and the Carolinas, and Caugnawagas and other northern Indians regularly visited the Five Nations and traded at Oswego and Albany.[40] Yet despite the outward appearances of peace, the Iroquois and domiciliated Indians had cause for concern. They knew the British-French competition for the Ohio Country was beginning to heat up. What they did not know was that the rivalry would boil over into a new war in 1754. At that point peace between the Five Nations and the tribes of Canada would again be tested.

The Iroquois had several reasons for following a policy of peace toward the domiciliated Indians. The Iroquois realized that the northern Indians' numbers, strength, and proximity made them a potentially dangerous foe. Various census reports between 1711 and 1738 show that the domiciliated Indians had about the same number of warriors as the Iroquois. The Abenakis alone were strong enough to worry the Five Nations. In 1718, a French officer noted, "This [Abenaki] Nation is the only support of the colony against the English or the Iroquois." Father Loyard, a French Jesuit, also believed that the Abenakis were a capable fighting force. In 1722, Loyard wrote, "Of all the savages of New France, those who have rendered and who are in a condition to render the greatest services are the Abenakis. This nation is composed of five villages, which in all make 500 men bearing arms. Two of these villages are situated along the River St. Lawrence near Three Rivers. . . . The three others are in the region of Acadia."[41]

The Iroquois had another military reason for wanting to maintain friendship with the northern tribes. The Iroquois and the domiciliated Indians were allies in the war against the Catawbas and other southern tribes. After 1701, warri-

152

ors from the northern tribes regularly joined the Iroquois for raids on the Flatheads, Cherokees, and other southern Indians. The Iroquois also realized that the northern tribes were a potential ally against the French or western Indians. Even an Iroquois–northern Indian neutrality would deprive New France of numerous Indian allies in the event of renewed French-Iroquois hostilities.[42]

The domiciliated Indians' powerful allies were another reason why the Iroquois wanted to remain at peace with the northern tribes. The domiciliated Indians were allied to New France and western nations like the Miami, Ottawa, and Huron. After 1701, the weakened Iroquois wanted to remain at peace with the French and the strong western tribes, so they had no alternative but to keep the peace with the domiciliated Indians too.

The Iroquois Confederacy had political reasons for maintaining a policy of peace toward the tribes of Canada. Factionalism in Iroquois politics made it difficult, if not impossible, for the League Council to declare war on the northern Indians. Many Iroquois were pro-French and thus sympathetic toward the domiciliated Indians. The policy of peace mitigated political divisions within the Confederacy by placating those Iroquois who were members of the pro-French faction or who had relatives or friends living in Canada.[43]

The Iroquois also realized that their importance to the English increased according to the number of tribes that were allies or friends of the Iroquois Confederacy. The more tribes with whom the Iroquois had influence, the more useful were the Iroquois to the English. Therefore, the Iroquois did their best to maintain good relations with the northern tribes, while the English frequently tried to make use of the Iroquois' connections. For instance, in 1704, the New York governor asked the Iroquois to use their influence to prevent the Abenakis from attacking New England colonists. Two years later, the Albany commissioners again asked the Iroquois to "exert their influence with the Indians in Canada and elsewhere not to make war on New England." Throughout the early 1720s, the English continued to use the Iroquois to mediate a peace between the Abenakis and New England colonists.[44]

Economics provided the Iroquois with an additional reason for keeping peace with the domiciliated Indians of Canada. After 1700, the Iroquois frequently bartered valuable furs for French arms, ammunition, blankets, and other manufactured goods. The trade with the French depended in part upon continued peace between the northern tribes and the Iroquois. The French would have been unwilling to trade with the Iroquois if the latter were at war with the domiciliated Indians, who were allies of New France. And even if the French had been willing, they would have been unable to trade with the Iroquois, since the domiciliated Indians-Iroquois warfare would have made travel unsafe for Indian and white traders. If the Iroquois wanted to trade with the French, they had to remain at peace with the Indians of Canada.

Good relations with the Canadian Indians affected the Iroquois' economy in other ways. Peace allowed the domiciliated Indians to travel through Iroquoia and to serve as middlemen in the Montreal-Albany trade. The safe passage to Albany also enabled many northern Indians to take advantage of the inexpensive trade goods offered by the English. The Iroquois probably had mixed feelings about the northern Indians' travel through Iroquoia. The Montreal-Albany trade enabled the French to obtain English goods for trade with western Indians, thereby undermining the Iroquois' geographic middleman position with the western tribes. Yet the northern Indians' passage to Albany was not a total loss. Since the Iroquois stood between the Albany trade and the northern tribes, they were in a position to sell northern Indian travelers some of the provisions and services they needed for the trip between Albany and Canada. Some Iroquois even served as carriers in the Montreal-

Albany trade. In either case, the Iroquois profited by remaining at peace with the domiciliated Indians and by allowing them a free passage to Albany.[45]

The Iroquois had important social reasons for maintaining peace with the domiciliated Indians of Canada. Many Iroquois were reluctant to fight against relatives and friends living in Canada. Iroquois began moving to Canada during the 1670s. By 1684, about 650 Iroquois were living there. The Iroquois exodus northward continued throughout the first half of the eighteenth century. On October 2, 1735, Father Nau of the Sault St. Louis mission wrote to a fellow priest, "The Five Iroquois Nations . . . are visibly on the decrease, on account of their incessant quarrels and the use of intoxicants supplied by the English. It is for this reason that the more provident abandon a country where they cannot live peaceably, and come to settle among us. Others, who are accused of witchcraft, are also obliged to take refuge at Sault St. Louis." By 1736, 363 Iroquois men, plus their families, lived at the Lake of Two Mountains and the Sault St. Louis missions.[46]

The northern tribes were neither as numerous nor as powerful as the tribes of the Western Country. Yet the Iroquois still could not afford to alienate the northern Indians due to their proximity and potential importance. After 1701, the political, military, and economic success of the Five Nations depended in part upon maintaining peace with the domiciliated Indians of Canada, as well as the far Indians of the Western Country.

The Pennsylvania Strategy

After 1701, the Five Nations, in conjunction with the Pennsylvania government, developed a strategy aimed at controlling the nearby Indians and lands of Pennsylvania. The Iroquois sometimes led and other times followed the Pennsylvania government in the creation of the new strategy. The Five Nations, confident that they could extend their authority over remnant and individualistic tribes like the Delawares, Shawnees, Conestogas, and Ganawese, were particularly interested in the Susquehanna and Delaware river valleys, located just south of Iroquoia.

By establishing hegemony over Pennsylvania Indians and lands, the Iroquois hoped to gain various economic, political, and military advantages. They could obtain economic and military aid from the Pennsylvania government in return for their friendship and cooperation. They could profit by selling the Indians' land to the English. And they could improve their strength by enlisting the Pennsylvania tribes as military allies. With all this to gain, the Iroquois took advantage of every opportunity during the first half of the eighteenth century to establish control over the Indians and lands of Pennsylvania.

Iroquois relations with Pennsylvania Indians can be traced back to the 1600s. In 1687, Governor Thomas Don-

156

gan of New York wrote to the Lords of Trade, "The Five Nations are the most warlike people in America . . . all the Indians in these parts of America are tributaries to them." In 1712, a New York official reported, "There are above 2000 Indians to the southward and westward who are tributaries of the Five Nations and under their command."[1] Such accounts gave rise to notions that Pennsylvania Indians were tributaries who were dependent upon the Iroquois, or that the Iroquois held suzerainty over Pennsylvania Indians. These descriptions are inaccurate and misleading.

The Indian concept of a tributary was quite different from the European concept. For the Indian, tributary status implied neither inferiority nor opprobrium. It did not make the tributary submissive to, or dependent upon, the nation that received the tribute. Tributary status simply meant that one tribe accepted the protection of another and then acknowledged that relationship by token gifts of wampum. The so-called tributary tribes of Pennsylvania were not under the Five Nations' authority prior to 1700. These tribes that lived in the Susquehanna and Delaware river valleys (i.e., the Delawares or Lenapes, Conestogas, Shawnees, and Ganawese) governed themselves, owned and sold their own land, sometimes skipped tribute payments to the Iroquois Confederacy, and did not always comply with Iroquois requests or directives.[2] In effect, the Pennsylvania tribes were autonomous during the last years of the seventeenth century. It would be more accurate, therefore, to refer to Pennsylvania Indians as props, tributary allies, or junior partners of the Iroquois Confederacy, rather than as tributaries, since the term when used by itself, implies an inferior status.

After 1701, instead of honoring the traditional relations between the Iroquois Confederacy and the tributary allies, the Iroquois slowly moved toward establishing complete control and authority over their tributary allies. The Iroquois, weakened by the Twenty Years' War, wanted to use

157

the Pennsylvania tribes to help reestablish the economic, political, and military strength of the Five Nations.

The first phase in the development of the Iroquois' strategy to gain hegemony over the Pennsylvania Indians and their lands lasted from 1701 until 1718. During those years the Iroquois, perhaps more by circumstance than by design, began to make their presence felt in Pennsylvania. Between 1701 and 1718, the Five Nations increased their interaction with Pennsylvania Indians. After 1701, The Iroquois escalated their war on southern tribes in Virginia and the Carolinas. Since Iroquois warriors either had to travel through central or western Pennsylvania to reach the South, the Iroquois were in frequent contact with Pennsylvania Indians. Sometimes Pennsylvania Indians even joined Iroquois war parties for raids on southern tribes.

The Iroquois and Pennsylvania Indians interacted in other ways. Indians of the Confederacy and Pennsylvania met regularly to discuss trade, defense, and intertribal relations. On almost a yearly basis from 1701 until 1718, the tributary allies presented wampum belts to the Iroquois to acknowledge their relationship. During Queen Anne's War, the Iroquois called on their Pennsylvania Indian allies to help them against the French.[3]

The Pennsylvania government, aware of the Iroquois' rising importance in the colony, took an active role in developing better relations with the Five Nations. Government officials repeatedly offered friendship and trade to the Iroquois Confederacy. In 1711, Lieutenant Governor Charles Gookin went out of his way to show the Five Nations that his colony wanted their friendship. When he learned that Iroquois representatives were at Conestoga, he immediately set out for that Pennsylvania Indian town. On June 18, he arrived there and presented five belts of wampum to the Five Nations and one to the Conestoga Indians in order to renew the bonds of alliance between those Indians and the Pennsylvania government. On another occasion Gookin commissioned a party of

158

Delawares to deliver two wampum belts to the Five Nations "as tokens of a firm and real friendship between them and us." When the Delawares returned from their mission, they reported that the Five Nations had received the gifts "very kindly and thankfully." The Delawares then gave a wampum belt to the lieutenant governor on behalf of the Senecas, who were requesting trade. The Senecas also asked for a lasting friendship and open road between Pennsylvania and the Seneca country. The governor was glad to accept the Senecas as friends and trading partners.[4]

Yet despite the increase in Iroquois' contacts with Pennsylvania Indians and whites that occurred between 1701 and 1718, the Iroquois' relationship to Pennsylvania tribes remained basically unaltered. The Pennsylvania Indians were still independent allies of the Five Nations. Throughout these years the Pennsylvania tribes continued to rule themselves and did not always back the Iroquois. The Pennsylvania tribes repeatedly negotiated treaties with the English, without Iroquois interference. Sometimes Pennsylvania Indians showed their independence by refusing to honor their obligations as tributary allies of the Iroquois Confederacy. In 1709, the Delawares, when they learned that the Confederacy was preparing for war with the French, decided not to deliver tribute wampum to the Five Nations. The Delawares also declined to send warriors to aid the Iroquois, even though they were obligated to do so. In each case the Confederacy neither interfered with, nor protested the actions of, the Pennsylvania tribes. The Confederacy realized it had no right to meddle in the internal affairs of the Pennsylvania Indians.[5]

The second stage in the development of the Iroquois' plan to gain control over the Pennsylvania Indians and their lands lasted from 1719 until 1727. During those years the Iroquois Confederacy gained the recognition and friendship of the Pennsylvania government.

159

Between 1719 and 1727, the Iroquois became an increasing concern for the Pennsylvania government. The Iroquois' war against the tribes of Virginia and the Carolinas posed a threat to Indian and white settlers in Pennsylvania. Iroquois warriors passing through Pennsylvania en route to the southern battlefields sometimes harassed settlers and stole supplies from their farms. The Iroquois, by enlisting Pennsylvania Indians for their war parties, also involved Pennsylvania tribes in the southern war. To make matters worse, the Pennsylvania Indians, whose settlements stood like a buffer between the southern tribes and the Iroquois, absorbed most of the retaliatory blows by southern Indian war parties.

Pennsylvania's Governor Keith was troubled by Iroquois actions threatening the security of Indians and whites in his colony. In 1721, the governor, hoping to put an end to the fighting, made a trip southward. With the help of Governor Spotswood of Virginia, he worked out a peace settlement between the Pennsylvania and southern Indians. Shortly thereafter, Governor Keith met with an Iroquois representative at Philadelphia and encouraged him and his Confederacy to accept the treaty settlement also. The governor knew that peace with the southern tribes could not be retained without the Iroquois' cooperation.[6]

Pennsylvania officials also had to deal with Iroquois pretensions to Susquehanna lands. The Pennsylvania government believed that William Penn's purchase of an Iroquois deed for the Susquehanna lands from Thomas Dongan, the former governor of New York, negated any claims the Five Nations might have to those lands. Some Iroquois, however, thought otherwise. In 1719, Cayuga sachems offered to sell lands in the Susquehanna Valley to the New York government. Pennsylvania officials learned about the Cayugas' claim to the Susquehanna lands the following year, when a Conestoga chief named Civility came to Philadelphia for a private conference with James Logan, secretary of the

160

Pennsylvania Council. Civility informed Logan that some of the Five Nations, especially the Cayugas, were displeased with the numerous Pennsylvania colonists settling on the Susquehanna lands. Civility added that the Iroquois were claiming ownership of those lands. Logan replied that Civility and all the Indians "were sensible of the contrary, and that the Five Nations had long since made over all their right to Sasquehanna to the government of New York, and that Governor Penn had purchased that right." Civility agreed, but then added he was merely warning the secretary to "better prevent all misunderstanding."[7]

Governor Keith was astounded by the Cayugas' claims, and he immediately sent off a letter of protest to the governor of New York, condemning the Cayugas' boldness. Keith explained that the Iroquois had sold their rights to the Susquehanna lands to Dongan, who, in turn, had sold them to William Penn. He pointed out that the Iroquois had always acknowledged that transaction. Governor Keith concluded that "neither the whole Five Nations together, nor any one of them separately, have the least appearance of a just right to any of these lands they would now claim."[8]

The Cayugas, however, were not about to give up their claims to the Susquehanna lands. On June 15, 1722, Governor Keith met with the Conestogas, Shawnees, and Ganawese at Conestoga. He reminded the Indians that many years ago they had consented to William Penn's purchase of the lands on both sides of the Susquehanna River. Now settlers from other colonies were trying to settle those lands, without any consent from the Pennsylvania government or from the tribes living there. The governor suggested that the Indians cede the lands to Pennsylvania, so no one else could settle on them. The Indians replied that they agreed with the governor and wanted to prevent the Marylanders from settling on the Susquehanna, but they did not wish to discuss "the business of land lest the Five Nations may reproach or blame" them. According to Pennsylvania officials,

161

the Indians said that they "know that the Five Nations have not any right to these lands, and that four of the towns do not pretend to any, yet the fifth town, viz. the Cayugoes are always claiming some right to lands on Sasquehanna, even where they themselves now live; wherefore, they think it will be a very proper time when the governor goes to Albany to settle that matter with the Cayugoes, and then all parties will be satisfied."[9]

The significance of the Indians' reply was clear to Govenor Keith. The Susquehanna tribes refused to acknowledge the Cayugas' claim to the Susquehanna lands. Yet, they did not wish to offend any of the Five Nations by selling those lands to Pennsylvania. In effect, the Pennsylvania government could no longer purchase land in the Susquehanna Valley without first obtaining consent from the Iroquois.

The Pennsylvania government had another reason to be concerned with the Iroquois Confederacy. In March, 1722, a Seneca man was murdered at Manakassy, a branch of the Potomac River, by some whites during an argument over rum. The Pennsylvania government, wanting to avoid ill feelings between the Iroquois and the colonists, decided to send a messenger to the Five Nations to condole them for the Seneca's murder. James Logan and the Pennsylvania Indians chose to send Skatcheetchoo, a Cayuga who had been living with the Pennsylvania Indians for several years.

The murder provided the Pennsylvania government with the opportunity to expand its communications and relations with the Confederacy. On May 4, 1722, Skatcheetchoo returned from Iroquoia with a reply: the Iroquois were willing to accept Pennsylvania's apology for the Seneca's death, if the governor came to Iroquoia to express condolences to the Senecas. The Five Nations hinted that if the governor came to their country they might even make peace with the southern tribes. The governor was pleased. He knew that the governor of Virginia would soon be trav-

162

eling to Albany to meet with the Five Nations. That would be the perfect occasion for a joint conference with the Iroquois. Governor Keith quickly dispatched Skatcheetchoo back to the Iroquois with his answer: he would gladly visit Iroquoia when the governors of New York and Virginia would also be there.

The stage was set for a meeting between the Pennsylvania governor and the Iroquois Confederacy. On June 15, Governor Keith told the Shawnees, Conestogas, and Ganawese that he had accepted the Five Nations' invitation to meet with them in Albany and that he would be leaving shortly for the conference to make the alliance chain "as bright as the sun." Keith hoped to accomplish several things. He wanted to settle the matter involving the murdered Seneca. He wanted to ratify a treaty of friendship between the Iroquois and Pennsylvania. He hoped to work out a peace settlement between the Iroquois, Pennsylvania Indians, and southern tribes. And he wished to extinguish Iroquois land claims in the Susquehanna Valley.[10]

The conference between Governor Keith, representatives from New York and Virginia, and the Iroquois Confederacy occurred in early September, 1722. The Pennsylvania governor spoke first to the Iroquois. After explaining how the Seneca man was killed during a drunken brawl over a trade disagreement, Keith presented gifts to the Iroquois and said, "I desire you may receive them [gifts] as a pledge of our firm friendship with the Five Nations; that you will ever remember us as your brethren, and not suffer your young men, when they travel, to hurt any of our inhabitants, no more than they would their own, or to kill their cattle and stock; and that this visit and the Covenant Chain which is hereby brightened may be recorded in everlasting remembrance."

The Iroquois thanked the governor for his good will and then renewed the Covenant Chain between the Confederacy and the Pennsylvania colony. The Iroquois said they

163

would forgive the murder of the Seneca in Pennsylvania. Later, the Iroquois added, "We here now freely surrender to you all those lands about Conestoga which the Five Nations have claimed, and it is our desire that the same may be settled with Christians." The Iroquois also asked for the right to trade at Philadelphia.[11]

The Pennsylvania governor did not fall into the Iroquois' trap. He realized that by accepting the Iroquois' free surrender of "those lands about Conestoga," he would be recognizing later Iroquois claims to the rest of the Susquehanna Valley. Keith therefore shrewdly replied, "Brethren, you know very well that the lands about Conestoga upon the River Susquehanna belong to your old friend and kind brother William Penn; nevertheless I do here, in his name, kindly accept of the offer and surrender which you have now made to me, because it will put an end to all other claims and disputes if any should be made hereafter." Regarding trade, Keith said, "Considering how well you are provided with goods at Albany, I think Philadelphia will be far out of your way to trade, but as often as any of your people come to us in love and friendship, they shall be treated like brethren."[12]

Deputies from Virginia then met with the Iroquois and worked out a settlement to stop the warfare between the northern and southern tribes. Governor Spotswood guaranteed that southeastern tribes would not go north of the Potomac River or west of the Appalachian Mountains. Iroquois deputies, who claimed to speak for the Conestogas, Shawnees, and Susquehanna River Indians as well as for their own Confederacy, pledged that they would not go south or east of the said boundaries.

The Virginia and Pennsylvania governors later agreed that the Pennsylvania tribes, who had been included in the Virginia-Iroquois Treaty, should ratify the treaty to ensure their adherence to its provisions. Upon his return to Pennsylvania, Governor Keith met with the Susquehanna River Indians to obtain their agreement to the treaty. He pointed out that the treaty "concerns you for they [the Iroquois] have included you in it." He then reminded them that any Indian who crossed the Spotswood Boundary without a passport from his colonial governor would either be put to death or sold into slavery. Realizing the futility of disagreeing with both the Iroquois Confederacy and the English, the Indians replied that they would "take care to observe . . . the treaty which is engaged on our parts."[13]

The September, 1722, negotations between the Iroquois and the governments of New York, Pennsylvania, and Virginia elevated the prestige and position of the Iroquois Confederacy. Virginia and Pennsylvania representatives had been forced, by necessity, to travel hundreds of miles to negotiate with the Iroquois. Both colonial governments needed the Iroquois' cooperation to settle problems plaguing their colonies. Virginia and Pennsylvania wanted Iroquois warriors to stop raiding southern Indians and harassing colonial settlers, and Pennsylvania wanted the Iroquois to give up their claims to Susquehanna lands.

By 1727, the Iroquois had greatly advanced their position in Pennsylvania. The Pennsylvania government recognized that it had to deal with the Confederacy. Pennsylvania leaders knew that Iroquois land claims in the Susquehanna Valley had to be settled. They were also aware that Iroquois relations with tribes of Pennsylvania and the South could affect the colony's security. Pennsylvania Indians often joined Iroquois war parties against southern tribes, because they were awed by Iroquois power. The Conestogas, Shawnees, and Ganawese were all afraid that the Senecas would attack them if they made peace with the southern tribes. Governor Keith noted that Pennsylvania Indians did not want to offend the Iroquois and were "cautious of even mentioning them but with respect."[14]

Yet despite the fact that Iroquois power had grown in Pennsylvania during the early 1720s, the Pennsylvania tribes still showed signs that they ruled themselves and were not mere satellites of the Iroquois Confederacy. The Pennsylvania tribes did not always back the Five Nations' official positions regarding relations with southern tribes or land claims in the Susquehanna Valley. They also publicly criticized the Spotswood Boundary negotiated for them by the Iroquois in 1722. From 1719 to 1727, Pennsylvania tribes negotiated directly with Pennsylvania officials with no interference from the Five Nations. And when Pennsylvania Indians did conduct official business with the Iroquois Confederacy, they did so on an equal basis. Pennsylvania officials were aware that the tribes of Pennsylvania were friends and allies of the Five Nations, but were not under their domination. For example, Governor Keith publicly told the Conestoga Indians that the Iroquois were "great friends and allies" of the English and Indians of Pennsylvania, but he never referred to the Iroquois as masters of the Conestogas or of any other Pennsylvania tribe. Even the Iroquois did not claim authority over all Pennsylvania tribes. The Five Nations ratified the Spotswood Treaty "in behalf of the Tuscaroras, the Conestogas, the Shawanese, the Octatiguanannkroons, and the Ostagues." No other tribes were mentioned.[15] Apparently, the Iroquois did not feel they had the authority to speak for the other Susquehanna River tribes or for any Indians living along the Delaware River. Although Iroquois power was on the increase in Pennsylvania during the 1720s, the Five Nations still did not control the Pennsylvania tribes.

The third phase in the development of the Iroquois' plan to gain hegemony over the Pennsylvania Indians and their lands lasted from 1728 until 1746. During those years the Confederacy collaborated with the Pennsylvania government to gain complete control over Pennsylvania tribes.

Pennsylvania officials decided to help the Iroquois establish authority over Pennsylvania Indians because they believed that the Confederacy could help them control the

166

Pennsylvania tribes. Between 1728 and 1732, the government was having problems with the Indians of the Susquehanna and Delaware river valleys. The Shawnees in particular were a major source of conflict. Two incidents occurred in 1728 that branded the Shawnees as troublemakers. In early May, a white resident at Conestoga informed Governor Gordon that war might break out among "Indians of these parts" because Shawnees had recently murdered two Conestogas. Shortly thereafter, the governor learned that the Shawnees were also threatening white settlers. Gordon received reports that the area around Mahanatawny (about a day's journey from Philadelphia) was in turmoil, because Shawnees, attempting to steal provisions, had exchanged gunfire with settlers.

The government feared—with good reason—that Shawnees and other Pennsylvania Indians were becoming too friendly with the French. On August 4, 1731, Governor Gordon informed the Pennsylvania House of Representatives that the French were trying to win over Shawnees who lived in the upper Allegheny River valley. The following month the Albany commissioners noted that Joncaire had gone out to bring the Shawnees into the French interest. The expert French frontiersman apparently was successful, for, by the end of 1731, two Pennsylvania traders reported that the Shawnees and other Indians on the upper Allegheny were dealing with the French. One trader insisted that several Shawnees had even gone to visit the French governor at Montreal and "ever since that time there has been a great appearance of friendship and goodwill between the French and them."[16]

Other incidents contributed to Pennsylvania's growing concern with Indian affairs. In the spring of 1728, Thomas Wright, an Indian trader, was murdered by several Indians. When the governor demanded justice from the Conestogas living in the area where the crime was committed, he was given an evasive response. The Indians claimed that the

167

Minisinks (a Delaware tribe) were to blame. The governor, having no recourse, reluctantly accepted their dubious story, and said that he would have to obtain satisfaction from the Minisinks. The Delawares provided another source of friction when they began protesting about land sales in 1728. Sasoonan (alias Alumapees), an important chief of one Lenape band, complained to James Logan that whites were settling on lands that had never been purchased from his tribe. When Logan produced a ten-year-old deed, signed by Sasoonan and the Lenapes, to prove that the land had been fairly purchased by the government, Sasoonan replied that he remembered the treaty, but that the treaty and deed did not include the lands that were now being settled by the German Palatines.[17]

Pennsylvania's white settlers became increasingly concerned about the Indian problems. Before long, rumors of coming Indian attacks were circulating through white settlements. At one point a trader at Conestoga notified Governor Gordon that many frontier settlers feared Indian attacks, and that some settlers had even abandoned their farms. Other reports were soon reaching the Pennsylvania governor. In the fall of 1728, several traders informed the governor that Shawnees had hanged Timothy Higgins, a servant who worked for a trader named Henry Smith. Governor Gordon was concerned that other whites might also be in danger, because the Indians considered many traders to be dishonest. Gordon, however, refused to believe that Indians would actually hang a white man. He said he wanted to get to the cause of the rumors and restlessness among the Indians. The governor's hunch later proved correct when it was learned that Higgins was alive.[18]

Pennsylvania settlers sometimes lashed out at any Indians they could find. After a small Shawnee raiding party attacked whites in the spring of 1728, some settlers retaliated by murdering three friendly Indians. Tensions remained so high that Governor Gordon ordered the people of Pennsyl-

168

vania not to "abuse any Indian native around us, vist; the Delawares, Conestogas, Ganawese, Shawanese, Mingoes, or those of the Five Nations, or any other coming and demeaning themselves peaceably amongst us, but that on all occasions they treat all the said Indians with the same civil regard that they would an English subject."[19]

In the midst of these difficulties, Governor Gordon and other officials decided that the Iroquois could help them control the Pennsylvania tribes. In the spring of 1728, the governor received word that the chiefs of the Five Nations would soon be arriving at Philadelphia to renew the Covenant Chain. Gordon quickly informed the House of Representatives about the upcoming visit, hinting that the Iroquois might be of use to the government, since all Pennsylvania tribes "have an entire dependence on those [five Iroquois] Nations."[20]

Whether the tribes were really dependent upon the Five Nations was of little concern to Governor Gordon. He proceeded on the assumption that they were. In June, Gordon and his council met with Sasoonan and his Delawares. An Iroquois named Shickellamy, who was sent to Pennsylvania by the League Council to keep an eye on the troublesome Shawnees, was also present at the meeting. If Shickellamy had any authority over the Delawares, it certainly was not evident. The Iroquois representative merely sat there while Sasoonan put forth Delaware views on land sales and other issues which affected Pennsylvania Indians and whites. But Governor Gordon and his advisers were not deterred by Shickellamy's silence. They decided that Shikellamy and the Iroquois could provide the solution to the government's growing problems with the Shawnees, Delawares, and other tribes.

In September, 1728, the Pennsylvania Council recommended to Governor Gordon that he send the following message to Shickellamy: "That as he [Shickellamy] is appointed (as 'tis said) by the Five Nations to preside over the

169

Shawanese, it's expected he will give a good account of them; That they came into this government as strangers and had leave to settle amongst us, the Conestoga Indians becoming their security, and that 'tis to be hoped they have behaved themselves well." The secretary of the Pennsylvania Council added, "It was further considered by the Board that as the Five Nations have an absolute authority over all our Indians, and may command them as they please, it is of great importance to remove any impressions that have been made upon them [Iroquois] to the prejudice of the English, and that by all means it is necessary they should be spoke with." The council then sent a message, delivered by the Conestogas, inviting the Iroquois to visit the governor at Philadelphia.

Governor Gordon agreed with James Logan and the rest of his advisers. He immediately dispatched two deputies to inform Shickellamy that the government wanted him to watch the Shawnees very closely. Gordon noted, "He [Shickellamy] is a good man, and I hope will give a good account of them [Shawnees]."[21] Gordon and his council had taken two significant steps: they decided to recognize the Iroquois' absolute authority over all Pennsylvania Indians, and they proposed to utilize that authority to control the actions of the Pennsylvania tribes. It was a bold plan, and they quickly put it into effect.

The Iroquois were eager to cooperate. In October, 1728, Governor Gordon met with Sasoonan and several Delawares at Philadelphia. Once again Shickellamy attended the conference. This time, however, his contribution was evident. Sasoonan renewed friendship on behalf of all Pennsylvania Indians. The Delaware chief then said that the Iroquois had often told the Delawares to "mind their own private business" and let the Iroquois "take care of what related to peace and war." As a result, the Delawares "have ever had good and peaceful thoughts" toward the English. Sasoonan added that he hoped friendship between the Pennsylvania Indians and the English would continue, as the Iroquois requested. Governor Gordon responded by renewing the Covenant Chain between his colony and all the Indians. The governor then distributed presents to all the chiefs. One official noted that a special gift was given to Shickellamy, "whose services had been and may yet further be of great advantage to this government."[22] No doubt the Iroquois envoy was pleased. Soon Shickellamy would show that he was willing to assist the Pennsylvania government in numerous ways.

The Pennsylvania tribes quickly perceived the government's interest in the Iroquois Confederacy. On May 26, 1729, representatives of the Conestogas, Ganawese, Shawnees, and Delawares met with Governor Gordon and promised to keep open the communications between the Pennsylvania government, the Pennsylvania Indians, and the Five Nations.[23]

Pennsylvania officials had their own plans for communicating with the Iroquois. In 1731, Governor Gordon informed the House of Representatives about James Logan's scheme to prevent the French from winning over the Shawnees. Logan proposed that Pennsylvania make a treaty with the Iroquois, because "by their means the Shawanese may not only be kept firm to the English interest, but likewise be induced to remove from Allegheny nearer to the English settlements." Logan believed "that such a treaty becomes now the more necessary, because 'tis several years since any of those [Five] Nations have visited us, and no opportunity ought to be lost of cultivating and improving the friendship which has always subsisted between this government and them."[24]

Three days later the House of Representatives gave the governor the financial backing to make a treaty with the Iroquois. Governor Gordon immediately informed his council that "an opportunity now favorably presented itself of sending a message to the Six (formerly called the Five) Nations by Shekallamy, who is willing to undertake it, and is a trusty good man and a great lover of the English." The governor and the Council members agreed that Shickellamy should be given a reward for his help. They also decided that a gift of £10 was to be presented to the Five Nations when they were issued the invitation to come to Philadelphia.

Governor Gordon met with Shickellamy on August 16, 1731, and explained his proposition for the Iroquois. He told him to inform the Five Nations "that from the first settlement of this province by William Penn, there has subsisted a firm friendship between this government and them, that accordingly they have frequently visited us as their friends, that it is several years since we have seen any of them at Philadelphia, that we sent them a message about two years since, but would now willingly see some of their old wise men of authority amongst them, to discourse of some affairs concerning their own security and the peace of these countries."[25]

Shickellamy understood the implications of Gordon's request. He realized that the Pennsylvania government wanted a close working relationship with the Iroquois Confederacy and that both parties could profit from it. He carried that message to Iroquoia.

Shickellamy returned from his mission in early December and requested an audience with the governor. Conrad Weiser, who was employed as Pennsylvania's official Indian interpreter and who was Shickellamy's close friend, served as interpreter. Shickellamy announced that he had delivered the message to the Five Nations' chiefs, who were pleased to hear from the governor. He added that the Five Nations had gladly received the governor's presents and promised to come to Philadelphia in the spring. The governor was satisfied and gave Shickellamy £10 worth of goods for his help.[26]

Everything was set: Iroquois sachems would be arriving in Philadelphia in the spring to ratify the new treaty. Both the Confederacy and the Pennsylvania government stood to benefit by the new relationship. The former would gain power over Pennsylvania Indians and would profit by aiding the government of Pennsylvania, while the latter would have the Five Nations to police the Pennsylvania tribes and facilitate the implementation of government policy within the colony.

Governor Gordon also realized that he could use the Iroquois to check the expansion of the other colonies. On April 18, 1732, he informed Governor Ogle of Maryland that the Iroquois "have been acknowledged by all the natives of these parts as their masters." He added that "since their conquest of the Sasquehanna Indians, [the Iroquois] have always claimed that river and all the lands upon it or its branches as their property, and this claim has constantly been acknowledged by all the other Indians in these parts."[27] Governor Gordon was probably trying to establish Iroquois ownership to the Susquehanna lands in order to block Marylanders from settling in the Susquehanna Valley. Later he could tell the Maryland governor that the Iroquois had sold those lands to Pennsylvania. In that way Pennsylvania would have clear title to all Susquehanna lands and Maryland would be legally excluded from the area. It was, therefore, in Pennsylvania's best interests to back Iroquois claims in the Susquehanna Valley.

The fiction about the Iroquois' absolute authority over Pennsylvania Indians and lands was quickly becoming a reality, but it was not yet fact. Between 1728 and 1732, Pennsylvania tribes clung to their indepedence. They continued to negotiate on their own behalf with the government and received little interference from the Iroquois. Shickellamy's presence in the Susquehanna Valley may have been the Confederacy's sole attempt to influence Pennsylvania Indian affairs. Yet even Shickellamy did not appear to have any authority over the Delawares, Conestogas, or Ganawese, as evidenced by his lack of participation in conferences be-

173

tween those tribes and colonial officials.[28] Shickellamy's initial duties seem to have been only to watch over the Shawnees. The Iroquois were probably displeased because the Shawnees were threatening the Conestogas and Pennsylvania whites, and making overtures to the French. The League, therefore, may have sent Shickellamy to gather intelligence and keep an eye on the troublesome Shawnees. It is even possible that some of the Pennsylvania tribes may have asked the Confederacy to send an ambassador (i.e., Shickellamy) to mediate the difficulties between the Shawnees and Conestogas, both of whom were Iroquois allies.

On August 18, 1732, Iroquois sachems arrived in Philadelphia for their scheduled conference with the governor. For five days they rested and enjoyed the hospitality of their hosts. Then, on August 23, the treaty negotiations that would forever alter the Iroquois' relationships with the Pennsylvania tribes began. Representing the government were Thomas Penn, the proprietor, Patrick Gordon, the governor, and the members of the governor's council. Representing the Iroquois Confederacy were Shickellamy and three other Oneida chiefs, along with two Seneca chiefs, one Cayuga chief, and fifteen other Iroquois.

Thomas Penn spoke first, through the interpreter Conrad Weiser. He renewed friendship with the Iroquois and stated that he wished to make the Covenant Chain "stronger and brighter." He added, "As proof of this we would now enter into a close discourse with you on affairs that nearly concern your own peace and safety; for as true brothers that are as one body and have the same interest, we lay to our hearts whatever may effect and touch you. But this requires plainness and freedom; we should open our hearts, conceal nothing."

The proprietor asked the Iroquois about their relations with the French and the Indian tribes to the north and west. Penn told them to consider the questions carefully and that they could speak freely the next day. He concluded by say-

174

ing, "and when we have finished this friendly treaty, we shall have a present for you to return with home that will confirm all we shall say to you."

Hetaquantagechty, a Seneca, immediately replied that he and the other deputies were glad to meet with the proprietor and governor. He explained that although the chiefs who were present came only from the Senecas, Oneidas, and Cayugas, they were commissioned to act for the entire Confederacy. He promised that they would be open and truthful about all matters to be discussed. The conference then adjourned for the night.[29]

The tone for the conference was set during that first day. Pennsylvania officials had made it clear that their government and the Iroquois Confederacy had similar interests and that both could profit through cooperation. Iroquois deputies showed that they were interested in the proposition and willing to cooperate.

The next morning Governor Gordon told his council members that since the Indians wanted additional time to consider their reply, the meeting would not reconvene until the following day. The governor and his council then discussed whether it would be better to hold the conference outdoors or inside the council chamber. Some council members expressed fears that the Iroquois would not speak freely if the conference were held out in public. So it was decided to let the Iroquois choose the setting. To no one's surprise, the Iroquois asked to meet in the privacy of the governor's house. The Iroquois, realizing that Pennsylvania Indians would not appreciate the Iroquois-Pennsylvania machinations, wanted closed-door sessions.

Shortly thereafter, the conference resumed, this time in the secrecy of the governor's chambers. Hetaquantagechty, the Iroquois spokesman, informed the Pennsylvania officials that the Iroquois were presently at peace with the French, as well as with the northern and western tribes. He added that the Iroquois were trying to prevent the French

175

from winning over the Shawnees and other Indians living on the Ohio River.

Hetaquantagechty noted that the Iroquois were pleased to conduct such friendly talks with the proprietor, whom they called "Brother Onas." He said that the Confederacy was willing and eager to have more frequent talks with the Pennsylvania government and that "these may be managed by means of Shickellamy and Conrad Weiser." Thomas Penn approved of all that was said and then presented the Iroquois with gifts, adding that they would discuss several subjects more closely later. The council then adjourned for the night.[30]

The meeting reconvened the next day. The Iroquois, responding to several specific questions, assured Pennsylvania officials that the Confederacy held great sway over many powerful western tribes, who always did whatever the Iroquois "ordered or directed." The Iroquois' exaggerated account of their influence with the western tribes was taken at face value by the Pennsylvania officials, who were quite satisfied with the Iroquois' response.

The officials then explained the problem that Pennsylvania was having with the Shawnees. According to council minutes, officials told the Iroquois that:

> The Shawnees who were settled to the southward, being made uneasy by their neighbors, about sixty families of them came up to Conestoga, about 35 years since and desired leave of the Sasquehanna Indians who were planted there, to settle on that river; that those Sasquehanna Indians applied to this government that they might accordingly settle, and they would become answerable for their good behavior. . . . the proprietor agreed to their settlement, and the Shawanese thereupon came under the protection of this government; that from that time greater numbers of the same Indians followed them, and settled on Sasquehanna and Delaware; that as they had joined themselves to the Sasquehanna Indians who were dependent on the Five Nations, they thereby fell also under their protection. That we had held several

176

treaties with those Shawanese, and from their first coming were accounted and treated as our own Indians; but that some of their young men having between four and five years since committed some disorders, though we had fully made it up with them yet being afraid of the Six Nations they had removed themselves to Ohio, and there had lately put themselves under the protection of the French, who had received them as their children. That we had sent a message to them to return, and to encourage them had laid out a large tract of land on the west side of the Sasquehanna, round the principal town where they had been settled, and we desired by all means that they would return thither.[31]

The Iroquois were then told "that as they were the chiefs of all the northern Indians in these parts, and the Shawanese had been under their protection, they should oblige them to return." The Iroquois deputies asked whether the Confederacy alone had to bring back the Shawnees. The officials replied that they wanted the Iroquois to join with them to get the Shawnees to return. The Iroquois deputies said they needed time to think, so the conference adjourned for the day.[32]

At last the proposition had been officially presented. The Pennsylvania government was willing to form a close alliance with the Iroquois Confederacy, to recognize Iroquois sovereignty over Pennsylvania Indians, and to provide gifts to the Five Nations. In return, the Iroquois had to help the government control the unruly tribes of Pennsylvania.

The Iroquois gave their reply on August 28. Hetaquantagechty, on behalf of the Confederacy, thanked the officials for advising them to strengthen themselves through alliances with neighboring Indians. Laying down some strings of wampum, the Iroquois spokesman announced that his people were willing to intervene with the Shawnees, but that they wanted the government to join them in calling back the Shawnees from Ohio. Hetaquantagechty argued that if Pennsylvania traders stopped supplying the Shawnees in Ohio, the Shawnees would have to move closer to Philadelphia.[33] In effect, the Iroquois were accepting the government's offer, but at the same time they were admitting that the Shawnees would not obey Iroquois orders that they return to Pennsylvania. The Iroquois realized that only a trade boycott could force the Shawnees to leave the Ohio River.

Thomas Penn replied on August 29. He thanked the Iroquois for their willingness to join Pennsylvania against the Shawnees and said that he hoped to put the plan into effect as soon as possible, but, with winter approaching, the traders and Shawnees could not be recalled until spring. Penn agreed that Shickellamy and Weiser would be ideal intermediaries between the government and the Confederacy. The Iroquois then expressed their satisfaction with all that was said and the conference adjourned.

On August 31, Pennsylvania officials met again with the Iroquois deputies. The proprietor reiterated the major points that were to be included in the treaty. First, a close friendship was to be established between the government and the Confederacy. A council fire was to be established for the Iroquois at Philadelphia, and Shickellamy and Conrad Weiser were to be the go-betweens. Secondly, the Iroquois were supposed to bring more tribes into the Covenant Chain and inform those new allies that, by joining the Iroquois, they were also becoming friends of the English. Finally, the Iroquois were to establish control over the Shawnees and remove them and the Delawares from the Ohio River back to Pennsylvania. The proprietor confirmed the new arrangements by presenting guns, powder, lead, clothing, tobacco, and other gifts to the Iroquois.

The Iroquois gave their response to Thomas Penn's speech on September 2. Hetaquantagechty assured the officials that the League Council would approve of all that was said by Penn, and that the sachems would ratify the treaty as soon as possible. The Iroquois added that they would be leaving within two days and would need supplies and horses

178

to carry their many presents back to Iroquoia. Penn promised to provide everything needed for the trip home. Governor Gordon then made arrangements for the Iroquois' entertainment for the rest of their stay in Philadelphia. One official observed, "The Indians, taking the proprietor, governor, and members of council by the hand, departed, and thus the treaty ended."[34]

The Treaty of 1732 marked the beginning of a new relationship between the Pennsylvania government and the Iroquois Confederacy. From that point on they shared a symbiotic relationship. The Iroquois, due to the government's support, were able to extend their authority over the lands and tribes of Pennsylvania, while the government, because of the Iroquois' executive authority, was able to control the Indians and lands of Pennsylvania. After 1732, Pennsylvania Indians realized that the Confederacy had the authority and backing of the government. At the same time the settlement elevated the status of Shickellamy. He became the ambassador of the Confederacy and the Iroquois viceregent in charge of Pennsylvania Indian affairs. And finally, the Treaty of 1732 marked the beginning of the end of the traditional Iroquois–Pennsylvania Indian relationship. After 1732, the Iroquois rapidly became the preeminent partner in the Covenant Chain, and the Pennsylvania tribes became dependencies rather than allies of the Iroquois Confederacy. In effect, the negotiations and Treaty of 1732 constituted a self-fulfilling prophecy. Because the Pennsylvania government recognized the Iroquois' absolute authority over the Pennsylvania tribes, the Iroquois were able to establish hegemony over those tribes.

Over the next few years the Iroquois Confederacy and the Pennsylvania government worked to improve their partnership. Each side protected its own interests, but whenever one side heard any rumors or news that might threaten the arrangement, it informed the other. Pennsylvania officials made good use of the Iroquois. In 1733,

Thomas Penn complained to Shickellamy and Hetaquanta-gechty that some Indians had recently passed near English settlements at Pextan in a disorderly and wanton manner. Penn pointed out, "As the Six Nations have the command over all the Indians, it is in their power to prevent abuses of this sort, and we hope they will give orders accordingly." The two Iroquois representatives got the message: the Pennsylvania government, recognizing Iroquois authority over Pennsylvania Indians, expected the Iroquois to exercise a police function over those tribes. Usually the Five Nations did their job well. They watched over the Shawnees and kept most Pennsylvania Indians in line. Thomas Penn was particularly pleased with Shickellamy's performance. Shickellamy not only served as an intermediary between the Five Nations and the Pennsylvania government, but he also acted as an ombudsman to promote better relations between Indians and whites in Pennsylvania. He made officials aware of the Indians' complaints and kept the government informed about events in the villages of various tribes. When a problem did occur, Shickellamy quickly helped the government solve it. A grateful Penn assured the Iroquois, "Shickellamy is our good friend, and we expect he will endeavor to live in good understanding with all our people, and care shall be taken on our parts that no person shall offend him without feeling our displeasure."[35]

The Iroquois-Pennsylvania relationship was strengthened in 1736, when sachems met with Pennsylvania officials to ratify the landmark Treaty of 1732. The two parties renewed the promises made four years earlier. Significantly, for the first time, the Five Nations renewed the Covenant Chain not only for themselves, but also for the Delawares, Conoys, and the Indians living on the Susquehanna, as well as for all the other Indians allied to the Five Nations.

The sachems expressed hope that the government would recall its traders from the Ohio River valley, thereby forcing the Shawnees to return to Pennsylvania. They also requested that traders not be allowed to bring rum to Iroquois warriors passing through Allegheny. They asked for cheaper prices and better trade values at Philadelphia. And finally, they gave their views on land sales in Pennsylvania. The sachems signed a deed releasing all land in Pennsylvania's Susquehanna Valley to the Pennsylvania government. They recognized the government's sole authority to buy more lands in Pennsylvania. And they reminded Pennsylvania officials that Civility and the Conestogas had "no power" to sell land; only the Iroquois could sell lands to the Pennsylvania government. The sachems then asked officials to help them obtain satisfaction for their land claims in Virginia and Maryland. The Iroquois maintained that they owned "all the lands of Susquehanna and at Shenandowa."[36]

The officials replied to each of the points. James Logan pointed out that it would be senseless for Pennsylvania to recall its traders from the Ohio Country, since traders from other colonies would only replace them. Logan told the Iroquois that the government could not help them with rum problems or trade regulations: they would have to look out for themselves. He added, "As to the claim [the Iroquois] make on the lands of Maryland and Virginia, we know not how this is supported; the lands on Susquehanna, we believe, belong to the Six Nations by the conquest of the Indians of that river; but how their pretensions are also made good to the lands to the southward we know not, and we ought to be better informed before we can write on this head." Logan then presented the Iroquois with numerous gifts and provided them "with horses and carriages to make their journey home as easy as possible." Shortly thereafter the conference adjourned.[37] Most likely, the sachems were pleased as they made their way back to Iroquoia. They had received valuable gifts from the Pennsylvania government. The Pennsylvania-Iroquois partnership was reaffirmed. And the Pennsylvania government, while not recognizing

181

the Five Nations' claims to lands in Virginia and Maryland, had accepted Iroquois claims to Pennsylvania lands also claimed by Susquehanna River tribes.

In the next few years there were other indications that the Iroquois and the Pennsylvania government were developing a close working relationship. In 1737, the Pennsylvania Council expressed concern that Iroquois warriors were being killed in raids on southern tribes and advised the Iroquois to make peace with the southern Indians, for continued warfare would only weaken the Iroquois and make it harder for them to defend their villages. In 1740, Delawares complained that Pennsylvania traders gave better prices and values to the Iroquois than to other Indians. At a conference in 1740, Governor George Thomas explained to Shickellamy that a Mohican had recently attacked a settler named Henry Webb. The governor said that the Mohicans were not cooperating and had refused to give up the guilty man. Thomas added, "This conduct in a King who is one of the tributaries of the Five Nations, is a direct violation of the treaties subsisting between them and us. . . . We therefore desire the Five Nations . . . interpose their authority, and not only take notice of the failure of duty in the Mohican King, one of their tributaries, but order [the Indian guilty of assault] to be severely punished."

The Pennsylvania government also used the Iroquois to counter land claims filed by Pennsylvania Indians. In March, 1741, a band of Delawares complained that their lands in Bucks County had been taken from them without payment. The Pennsylvania Council brought forth deeds, signed by the Five Nations, and statements from the Iroquois that the Delawares "have no lands to dispose of, and praying the proprietor not to buy or accept of any grant of lands from them." The Pennsylvania Council then disallowed the Delaware claims and upheld the right of the Iroquois to sell those lands.[38]

Many Pennsylvania tribes were unhappy with the machi-

182

nations of the Iroquois–Pennsylvania government alliance. Between 1732 and 1742, these Indians did all they could to retain their independence. The Shawnees proved to be the most intractable of the Iroquois' Pennsylvania Indian allies. Time after time the Shawnees refused to adhere to Iroquois orders that they return to their former homes on the Susquehanna from the Ohio River valley. In 1736, the Frenchman Joncaire visited the Shawnees and reported that they "continued to reject the evil advice of the Iroquois, and were disposed to follow their [French] Father's pleasure." Joncaire's report was an understatement. In the past year the Shawnees had repeatedly ignored Iroquois and Pennsylvania directives. On one occasion some Shawnees even murdered an Iroquois deputy. Both actions underscored the Shawnees' sovereignty. Other tribes, to a lesser extent, also showed that they were independent of the Iroquois Confederacy. During the 1730s, the Conestogas, Ganawese, and Delawares continued to negotiate directly with the Pennsylvania government.[39] But their days of independence were numbered. Those Indians who remained in Pennsylvania came increasingly under the control of the Iroquois Confederacy.

The alliance between the Iroquois Confederacy and the Pennsylvania government was further strengthened in 1742. In July of that year Iroquois sachems arrived in Philadelphia for a conference that proved to be beneficial for both the Pennsylvania government and the Confederacy. The Iroquois advanced their interests in several ways. They received additional gifts from the government for the Susquehanna lands. They officially voiced their opposition against Maryland settlers squatting on Susquehanna lands. And they conspired with the government to tighten their control over the Delaware Indians.

Pennsylvania officials were pleased with the talks. The Iroquois informed the governor that many western tribes were allied to the Confederacy. The Iroquois promised that

183

in case war broke out between France and England, the Confederacy would help the latter. And finally, the Iroquois acted decisively to help Pennsylvania counter Delaware land claims. The Pennsylvania government was claiming ownership of lands in the Delaware Water Gap based on a 1686 deed allegedly negotiated between William Penn and resident Delawares. In fact, the document produced by Penn's sons was probably just a rough draft, never fully approved by either party. In 1737, the Delawares were tricked into accepting the dubious 1686 deed through the notorious Walking Purchase, in which the Delawares were misled into thinking that the lands in question were at the fork of Tohickon Creek and the Delaware River. Later, to the Delawares' dismay, Pennsylvania officials walked off the purchase from a starting point on the Lehigh River, instead of on Tohickon Creek. This procedure gave Pennsylvania control of vast territory at the fork of the Delaware and Lehigh rivers. The resentful Delawares protested the fraudulent land grab, and then refused to move off the lands. It was at this point that Pennsylvania officials asked the Iroquois to intervene on their behalf. After consideration, the Iroquois decided to aid the Pennsylvanians. On July 12, Canassatego, the Iroquois' spokesman, told the governor, "The other day you informed us of the misbehavior of our cousins the Delawares with respect to their continuing to claim and refusing to remove from some land on the River Delaware." He added, "Then you requested us to remove them. . . . We see with our own eyes that they have been a very unruly people and are altogether in the wrong with their dealings with you. We have concluded to remove them, and oblige them to go over the River Delaware, and to quit all claim to any lands on this side for the future."[40] In effect, the Iroquois were agreeing to help the government remove the Delaware Indians from lands which the Delawares traditionally had owned and refused to sell. Prior to 1742, the Iroquois had no pretensions to lands in the Delaware Valley.

184

Now, however, the Iroquois were ready to claim those lands in order to aid the Pennsylvania government.

Canassatego then turned to Sasoonan and the other Delawares who were present at the meeting. In a haughty tone, the Iroquois speaker said:

> Let this belt of wampum serve to chastize you; You ought to be taken by the hair of the head and shaked severely till you recover your senses and become sober. . . . Our Brother Onas' case is very just and plain. . . . We have seen with our eyes a deed signed by nine of your ancestors above 50 years ago for this very land. . . . But how come you to take upon you to sell land at all? We conquered you, we made women of you, you know you are women, and can no more sell land than women. Nor is it fit you should have the power of selling lands since you would abuse it. . . . Did you ever tell us that you had sold this land? Did we ever receive any part, even the value of a pipe shank, from you for it? You have told us a blind story that you sent a messenger to us to inform us of the sale but he never came among us, nor we never heard any thing about it. This is acting in the dark, and very different from the conduct our Six Nations observe in their sales of land. On such occasions they give public notice and invite all the Indians of their united nations, and give them a share of the present they receive for their lands. . . . We . . . assign you two places to go—either to Wyoming or Shamokin. You may go to either of these places, and then we shall have you more under our eye. . . . Don't deliberate, but remove away [immediately]. . . . Neither you nor any who shall descend from you ever hereafter to presume to sell any land. . . . depart the council and consider what has been said to you.[41]

Canassatego's words undoubtedly did severe damage to the Delaware's pride. Though the Iroquois had been referring to the Delawares as "women" since the late 1600s, the designation was never meant as an insult. Most likely, it signified the Delawares' position as one of the Iroquois' most important tributary allies. The term "woman" certainly did not imply Delaware inferiority. But Canassatego's

185

use of the term was anything but complimentary. He squeezed new meaning out of the word, putting the Delawares in their new place as Iroquois subjects. Yet despite the Iroquois' insulting remarks, the Delawares could not strike back. They knew that they could not defeat the Iroquois-Pennsylvania government partnership. So they withdrew from the council. On that day the Delawares lost much of their land and part of their sovereignty.[42]

During the next year the Pennsylvania government made further use of the Iroquois' growing executive authority over the Pennsylvania tribes and lands. On November 20, a group of Christian Delawares petitioned the governor for permission to remain living on the Delaware River. The Christian Delawares assured the governor that they had had nothing to do with the earlier problems caused by Sasoonan's Delaware band. The governor denied them permission on the grounds that "it might not only be resented by the Six Nations, but . . . by the [other] Delawares." He told them that if the Iroquois granted them permission, they could stay on the Delaware River. This reply further reinforced the Iroquois' authority in Pennsylvania. The Iroquois eagerly accepted the executive authority thrust upon them by the government. When three Delawares murdered a trader in 1744, the Iroquois quickly carried out their police function. Governor Thomas told the Pennsylvania Assembly that "Shickellamy and the Indians settled at Shamokin . . . apprehended two of the murderers."[43]

Yet, just when the Iroquois-Pennsylvania partnership seemed to be going so well, an incident occurred that threatened to break the alliance apart. On January 24, 1743, an Indian trader named Thomas McKee informed the Pennsylvania Council that Iroquois warriors had been involved in a skirmish with white settlers in Virginia. Two days later, Governor Thomas sent off an urgent letter to Conrad Weiser: "I hoped that our last treaty with the Six Nations would have made us easy for some time to come as

186

to all Indian affairs, but you will see by the enclosed deposition . . . by Thomas McKee, that if things are not prudently managed we may chance to be involved in the consequences of their [the Iroquois'] resentment against the people of Virginia." He explained, "although the [Iroquois] Indians behaved very peaceably in their journey through Pennsylvania, so soon as they got into Virginia, they fell to killing the inhabitants' cattle and hogs, and shot one man's mare, and by that means were themselves the occasion of the misfortune that followed. . . . the Virginia captain upon his approach to the Indians hung out a white flag . . . but they fired and killed him and some of his men before one shot was fired by his party." The governor asked Weiser to persuade the Iroquois to settle this affair peacefully with the Virginia governor. He warned that if the Iroquois decided to make war on the Virginia colonists, the Pennsylvania government would have to stop Iroquois warriors from passing through Pennsylvania to reach Virginia, and this would undoubtedly cause an Iroquois-Pennsylvania war.[44]

Conrad Weiser reported to the governor on April 5 that the Iroquois at Shamokin had given him a different account of the incident, insisting that the Virginians had fired first. Weiser added that he had asked the Iroquois to settle the matter peacefully. He said that, according to Shickellamy, the Iroquois were willing to discuss the affair with the Pennsylvania governor, and for the time being, the Iroquois had asked their allies not to attack the people of Virginia. Weiser warned that unless the matter were resolved quickly, war would break out between the Five Nations and Virginia. Soon thereafter, Governor Thomas made arrangements for a conference to settle the Iroquois-Virginia controversy.[45]

On June 25, 1744, representatives from Pennsylvania, Virginia, and Maryland arrived at Lancaster, Pennsylvania, to meet with deputies from the Iroquois Confederacy. Before the conference began, Governor Thomas met privately with the Virginia and Maryland commissioners and stressed to them the importance of the Iroquois' friendship. Thomas explained, "The [Iroquois] Indians by their situation are a frontier to some of them [i.e., English colonies], and from thence, if friends are capable of defending the settlements; if enemies of making cruel ravages upon them; if neuters, they may deny the French a passage through their country and give us timely notice of their designs." Thomas pointed out that these were only some of many reasons for maintaining good relations with the Iroquois and cautioned, "Every advantage you gain over them in war will be a weakening of the barrier of those colonies, and consequently will be in effect victories over yourselves and your fellow subjects."[46]

Governor Thomas opened the Lancaster Conference by stating that the goal of both the Iroquois and English should be to establish a lasting peace. The Iroquois replied that they were willing to make peace, but first they wanted to settle the Iroquois-Virginia incident, as well as several disputes over land.

Based upon the right of conquest, the Iroquois went on to establish their claims to certain tracts of land in Virginia and Maryland. They maintained that since they had defeated the Conestogas, Conoys, and other tribes of Virginia and Maryland, they had the right to sell the lands once inhabited by those Indians. The Iroquois then complained that their right to travel in Virginia was being hampered by settlers. On several occasions, they had already moved their road to Virginia farther to the west, but whites always settled in the way of any new trails. The Iroquois, arguing that they could no longer move the road farther westward because of the mountain barrier, warned, "Either the Virginia people must be obliged to remove more easternly or . . . warriors marching that way to the southward shall go sharers with them in what they plant."

The commissioners of Maryland and Virginia reluctantly

accepted what the Iroquois said. Maryland representatives told the Iroquois, "Although we cannot admit your right [to land ownership in Maryland], yet we are so resolved to live in brotherly love and affection with the Six Nations that upon giving us a release in writing of all your claim to any lands in Maryland, we shall make you a compensation to the value of £300 currency." The Virginia commissioners also reluctantly accepted the Iroquois' demands. The Virginians began by denying Iroquois land ownership in Virginia. They then granted the Iroquois the right to travel in Virginia according to guidelines specified in the Spotswood Treaty of 1722. The Virginia representatives added, "We may proceed to settle what we are to give you for any right you may have or have had to all the lands to the southward and westward of . . . Maryland . . . and [Pennsylvania], though we are informed the southern Indians claim these very lands you do."[47]

The positions taken by both the Virginia and Maryland commissioners show that both those colonies apparently decided to deny the Iroquois' title to any southern lands in order to avoid establishing a precedent that could later be used by the Iroquois to claim additional lands. At the same time, though, Virginia and Maryland were willing to pay the Iroquois for their release of claims in order to establish goodwill with the Confederacy.

After a brief consultation, the Iroquois deputies responded to the offers made by the colonial governments. The Iroquois agreed to sign a release for all Maryland lands in exchange for the compensation offered by Maryland. Next they replied to the Virginia commissioners. The Iroquois denied that they were to blame for the renewal of hostilities with the Catawba Indians, maintaining that the governor of New York had given them belts on behalf of the Cherokees and Catawbas. They said that the Catawbas had later reneged on their promise of peace and had insulted the Iroquois' honor. Therefore, the Iroquois be-

189

lieved, "the war must continue till one of us is destroyed." The Iroquois then replied to the offer of compensation for the Five Nations' claims in Virginia. They wanted to know the amount of compensation they would receive before they agreed to any release of claims. When the Virginians showed the Iroquois deputies the goods the Confederacy would receive as compensation, the Iroquois quickly approved the deal.[48]

Next, the representatives of Pennsylvania, Virginia, and Maryland turned to other matters. Governor Thomas informed the Iroquois that France and England had recently declared war on each other. He reminded them that the Iroquois Confederacy and the English colonies were allied through the Covenant Chain, adding "We therefore expect that you will not suffer the French or any of the Indians in alliance with them to march through your country to disturb any of our settlements. And that you will give us the earliest and best intelligence of any designs that may be formed by them to our disadvantage, as we promise to do of any that may be to your's." The Virginia commissioners also reminded the Iroquois about their treaty of friendship, and they implored the Iroquois to make peace with the Catawbas. The commissioners from Maryland then reiterated the peace settlements agreed to by the Iroquois and English colonies.[49]

Canassetego, serving as the Iroquois' spokesman, promised the Pennsylvania governor that the Five Nations would not allow the French to march through Iroquoia to attack English settlements. Next, Canassetego made several remarks which were probably designed to impress the English with the Confederacy's great importance. Although his statement exaggerated the Iroquois' power, it was a successful piece of propaganda. He said that the Five Nations had "great authority and influence" over numerous tribes allied to New France and guaranteed that those Indians would "not join the French against you." Canassetego added, "Our

190

interest is very considerable with them [French Indians]. . . . we shall use it for your service." He also promised that the Iroquois would help the Pennsylvania government find the Indians who had recently murdered a Pennsylvania trader and two of his assistants.

The Iroquois then thanked the Maryland and Virginia commissioners for renewing the Covenant Chain and settling the land disputes. In regard to the Catawbas, Canassetego said, "We shall not be against a peace on reasonable terms provided they will come northward to treat about it." The Iroquois added that there were still some Tuscaroras living in Virginia, and they wanted to be free to send messengers to them. Also, there were Conoy Indians in Virginia who wanted to move north to Iroquoia, and the Iroquois asked that they be given free and safe passage out of Virginia. The Virginia commissioners consented to the Iroquois' requests.

Finally, the Iroquois used the conference forum to expand the image of the Confederacy further. Canassetego proudly told the colonial representatives, "We heartily recommend union and good agreement between you our [English] Brethren. Never disagree but preserve a strict friendship for one another, and thereby you as well as we will become stronger. Our wise forefathers established union and amity between the Five Nations; this has made us formidable, this has given us great weight and authority with our neighboring Nations. We are a powerful Confederacy, and by your observing the same methods our wise forefathers have taken, you will acquire fresh strength and power."[50] Actually, the Iroquois were neither as united nor as powerful as Canassetego bragged they were. But the colonial representatives were willing to accept the Iroquois claims, because they believed it was to their own advantage to build up the Iroquois' power and retain them as a friendly Indian nation. The English colonies realized that the Iroquois, because of their numbers and geographic lo-

191

cation, could serve as a buffer against French attack. They also knew that the Confederacy could be used to manipulate other tribes who were more loosely organized and thus more difficult to deal with than the Five Nations. Furthermore, the English understood that by recognizing Iroquois sovereignty over various Indian tribes, the English colonial governments could secure title to the lands possessed by those tribes by simply making one purchase from the cooperative Iroquois Confederacy. These realizations help explain why the English colonies recognized, and even aided, Iroquois efforts to establish control over neighboring tribes and lands. The English believed that the Five Nations, as suzerains and buffers, would be valuable assets for the English colonies.

The Lancaster Treaty was significant for both the English and the Iroquois. The English received an Iroquois pledge of friendship and peace. The Iroquois also promised they would remain neutral in the English-French war, and that they would not allow French armies to pass through Iroquoia to attack English settlements. Furthermore, the Iroquois assured the English that they would consider making peace with the Catawbas. At the same time the Iroquois promised to aid the Pennsylvania government in capturing Delaware Indians who had murdered a Pennsylvania trader and his two assistants. And finally, Virginia and Maryland obtained releases for all lands that the Iroquois claimed in those colonies.

The Iroquois likewise benefited from the treaty agreements. The Iroquois received the right of travel in Virginia. They received compensation for their land claims in Virginia and Maryland. Also, Iroquois authority over other tribes was reinforced by English acceptance of the Iroquois' claims that they had conquered, and now controlled, tribes like the Conestogas and Conoys. Finally, peace between the Iroquois and the southern English colonies was guaranteed. The Iroquois-Virigina incident was settled, and the Cove-

192

nant Chain was brightened between the Iroquois Confederacy and all the English colonies.

With the signing of the Lancaster Treaty in 1744, the Iroquois completed their quest for hegemony over nearby Indians and lands. The Five Nations' preeminent status had been won at the negotiating table, and not on the battlefield. English cooperation and recognition, and not Indian warfare, had given the Iroquois control over the tribes and lands located near Iroquoia. Certainly not all Pennsylvania Indians welcomed the Iroquois. Some Indians, particularly among the Shawnees and Delawares, resented Iroquois interference and settlement. But in the end Pennsylvania Indians either submitted to the power of the Iroquois and Pennsylvania government alliance, or they fled to new homes on the Ohio River where they would be free to govern themselves. The Iroquois had succeeded in winning control over the Indians and tribal lands of Pennsylvania. Before long, however, the Five Nations would realize that their victory was only temporary.

The Iroquois Confederacy and the Pennsylvania government maintained their symbiotic relationship throughout 1745 and 1746. When King George's War began heating up, Pennsylvania officials used the Iroquois to control Pennsylvania Indians. Governor Thomas was especially concerned about the Shawnees, who were trying to lure the Delawares away from Shamokin to Ohio. Thomas realized that the Shawnees and Iroquois had no love for each other, yet, despite the potential for trouble, he was not about to let the Iroquois Confederacy forget its commitment to police the Pennsylvania tribes. In 1745 and 1746, officials repeatedly called on the Five Nations to counter threats by Shawnees and other enemies.[51]

After 1746, the Five Nations rapidly lost their status as Pennsylvania's number one Indian ally. Ironically, the totality of the Iroquois' success in Pennsylvania contributed to

193

their demise. The Five Nations simply put themselves out of business. Once they had facilitated the transfer of Indian lands over to the Pennsylvania government and drove out intransigent tribes from Pennsylvania's borders, the Five Nations had very little else to offer the Pennsylvanians. To make matters worse for the Iroquois, Pennsylvania officials were beginning to focus their attention on the Ohio Country, an area where the Confederacy had little influence.

By 1747, the Five Nations also had to contend with a new political rival. Indians living on the Ohio River and its tributaries were emerging as a power bloc. Pennsylvania officials realized that the Iroquois Confederacy had no control over the Ohio Indians, a conglomeration of individuals from various tribes. Shawnees and Delawares had moved to Ohio to escape the Five Nations' authority. There they were joined by Miamis, Wyandots, and other upper Great Lakes Indians, who were hoping to establish trade with the English, and by Iroquois expatriates, who were searching for better economic opportunities or trying to escape from troubles and smallpox in Iroquoia. As their numbers grew, the Ohio Indians became increasingly more important to the Pennsylvania government. Pennsylvanians did not want to see the Ohio tribes join the French alliance. Instead, they hoped to trade with the Ohio Indians and enlist them in the war against New France.

In November, 1747, ten Iroquois warriors living on the Ohio River came to Philadelphia to meet Pennsylvania officials. The Ohio Iroquois (who were also known as "Mingos") told the Pennsylvania Council that if they and other Ohio Indians had better weapons, they would fight the French. President Palmer and the council learned from Conrad Weiser that the Ohio Indians—boasting 500 warriors and numerous allies—were establishing their own council fire on the Ohio River, independent of the Iroquois Confederacy. As a result, the Pennsylvania officials decided to open direct relations with the Ohio tribes. Speaking for the government,

194

Palmer thanked the Mingos for their visit and distributed presents to them, promising that Weiser would bring additional gifts to all the Ohio Indians in the spring. Other actions further showed that Pennsylvania was focusing its attention on the Ohio tribes. In January, 1748, the Pennsylvania Assembly, while refusing to appropriate money to secure the Iroquois Confederacy's friendship, approved funds to purchase presents for Ohio tribes. The following month President Palmer announced a new proclamation regulating the rum trade with Ohio Indians.[52]

The Five Nations, fearing that the Ohio Indians would take their place as Pennsylvania's most favored Indian nation, moved quickly to prevent a separate alliance between the Pennsylvania government and Ohio tribes. In April, Shickellamy assured Pennsylvania officials that the Ohio Indians were "altogether subject to the Six Nations"; and he persuaded them not to send Weiser and the promised supplies to the Ohio tribes until after Iroquois representatives arrived in Philadelphia to discuss the matter. Officials soon realized that they were being misled by Shickellamy and the Iroquois. A report made in June by Pennsylvania Indian trader George Croghan indicated that the Ohio Indians were operating independently of the Confederacy and were in desperate need of supplies. The following month, Conrad Weiser admitted to the Pennsylvania Council that the Ohio Indians disliked Shickellamy. Actually, the Ohio Indians not only disliked Shickellamy, they refused to listen to him.[53]

The Pennsylvania government met with Ohio Indians in July and learned firsthand about the Indians' autonomy and significance. A party of fifty-five Indians, including Ohio Iroquois, Shawnees, Delawares, Nanticokes, and Twightwees (Miamis), had come to Lancaster requesting an audience with Pennsylvania officials. When the conference began on July 19, the Pennsylvania representatives learned that the Ohio Iroquois had brought the other Indians to Lancaster and were serving as their spokesmen. The Indians explained that Scarooyady, "a chief of the Oneida Nation, living at Ohio, was appointed Speaker for the Indians." This occasion marked Scarooyady's emergence as a chief of the Ohio tribes. Over the next few years, Scarooyady would put together a reputation and a power base rivaling those of any League sachems at Onondaga.

The Ohio Iroquois reminded the Pennsylvania commissioners that the English had often asked the Iroquois League Council to bring more Indian tribes into the Covenant Chain, adding "these messages [the sachems] have transmitted to us . . . in consequence whereof we have now the pleasure to present to you some of the chiefs of the Twightwee Nation . . . with a request that you would be pleased to admit them into your amity." The Mingos explained that the Twightwees, wanting English friendship and trade, had asked them for help in opening relations with the Pennsylvania government.

The Ohio Iroquois then turned to another matter. They asked the Pennsylvania government to forgive the Shawnees, "who have given you just cause of complaint." The Mingos promised to act as "intercessors for the Shawanese," thereby guaranteeing their future conduct.

Scarooyady and the Ohio Iroquois were taking a chapter right out of the Iroquois Confederacy's Pennsylvania Strategy: the Ohio Iroquois were offering to play the same role on the Ohio River that the League Council became famous for in Pennsylvania. The Mingos wanted to serve as the intermediary between the Pennsylvania government and the Ohio Indians. The rest of the Ohio Indians were willing to accept the Ohio Iroquois as their mediators. They knew that the Ohio Iroquois' tribal affiliation carried great weight with the Pennsylvania government. The Indians, aware that the Mingos were not controlled by the League Council at Onondaga, realized that they could use the Ohio Iroquois as their mouthpiece without surrendering their indepen-

196

dence to the Iroquois Confederacy. The arrangement was ideal. The Ohio Indians could negotiate through the Ohio Iroquois to obtain English friendship and trade, while the Ohio Iroquois could establish themselves as influential go-betweens.

Pennsylvania officials, knowing how successful the Iroquois Confederacy had been in Pennsylvania, eagerly recognized the Ohio Iroquois' position among the Ohio tribes. The Pennsylvania commissioners thanked all the Indians for coming to Lancaster and for strengthening the Covenant Chain. The commissioners told the Twightwees, "we are always ready to receive favorably the applications of all those whom our Brethren of the Six Nations shall recommend as worthy of our friendship and regard." They then spoke to the Ohio Iroquois about the Shawnees, "As you [Iroquois] have taken upon the office of intercessors, take this string of wampum and therewith chastize [the Shawnees] in such terms as shall a proper severity with them, tho' the expressions are left to your discretions, and then tell the delinquent Shawanese that we will forget what is past and expect a more punctual regard to their encouragements hereafter." The message was clear to all the Indians present. The Pennsylvania government was accepting friendship with the Twightwees and Shawnees, because the Ohio Iroquois had vouched for them. Scarooyady and the Ohio Iroquois were now the official contacts between the Pennsylvania government and the Indians living on the Ohio River.[54]

The Pennsylvania government followed up the July conference by dispatching Conrad Weiser on an official visit to the Ohio tribes in late summer. Weiser found Indians from various tribes living together in villages along the Ohio River and its tributaries. He met with the tribes' deputies at Logstown, where the Ohio Indians had established their council fire. Weiser learned that 789 warriors lived in the area, including 163 Senecas, 162 Shawnees, 100 Hu-

rons, 40 Neutrals, 74 Mohawks, 15 Mohicans, 35 Onondagas, 20 Cayugas, 15 Oneidas, and 165 Delawares. The non-
Iroquois, though in the majority, relied on the Ohio Iroquois in dealings with the Pennsylvania government. The
Mingos eagerly accepted the responsibility given to them.
Weiser noted that on one occasion the Ohio Iroquois told
some Hurons who were recent arrivals in the area, "We
the Six Nations and all our Indian allies with our Brethren
the English, look upon you as our children, tho' you are
our Brethren." The Mingos added, "We . . . receive you to
our council fire and make you members thereof, and we
will secure your dwelling place to you against all manner
of danger." The Ohio Iroquois realized that their leadership depended upon the backing of other tribes and the
Pennsylvania government. Weiser reported that Scarooyady begged him for supplies, since the Ohio Indians "often
must send messengers to Indian towns and nations, and
had nothing in their council bag, as they were new begin-
ners, either to recompense a messenger or to get wampum
to do the business." Weiser reinforced the Ohio Iroquois'
leadership position by providing them with the needed
supplies.

As an experienced hand in Indian affairs, Conrad Weiser
fully understood the potential importance of the Ohio River
tribes. On September 17, he delivered a speech to the various tribal deputies on behalf of President Palmer and the
Pennsylvania Council. Weiser explained that the Ohio Indians had recently been to Philadelphia asking for weapons to
fight the French, adding that although a British-French
cease-fire was now in effect, he would give them presents
anyway to show Pennsylvania's good faith. Weiser then encouraged the Indians to become better organized and cautioned them not to rob English traders. He pointed out,
"You are now become a people of note and are grown very
numerous of late years, and there is no doubt some wise
men among you, it therefore becomes you to act the part of

wise men and for the future be more regular than you have been for some years past, when only a few hunters lived here." When he was finished speaking, Weiser distributed Pennsylvania's gifts to the Indians. Significantly, the Ohio Iroquois received no more gifts than anyone else. The Ohio tribes were willing to defer to the Ohio Iroquois politically, but when it came to dividing up profits, all Ohio Indians were equals.[55]

Weiser's expedition was Pennsylvania's first official visit to the Indians living west of the Allegheny Mountains. Weiser strengthened relations between the government and the Ohio tribes, and he opened up relations with the Ohio Indians independently of the Iroquois League Council at Onondaga. In the process, Weiser reinforced the leadership of Scarooyady and the Ohio Iroquois.

Pennsylvania officials dealt directly with Ohio tribes throughout 1749 and 1750. The Ohio Iroquois, playing a valuable role as intermediaries in the negotiations between the Pennsylvania government and Ohio Indians, gained great influence and prestige. They improved relations and trading conditions between Pennsylvanians and Ohio Indians, complained to the Pennsylvania government about whites settling west of the Alleghenies on Indian lands, and asked Pennsylvania to protect the Ohio tribes from French threats. The government was impressed with the Ohio tribes. In September, 1750, Governor Hamilton explained to Governor Clinton of New York that Iroquois, Shawnees, Delawares, Miamis, and other Indians living on the Ohio River totaled 1,500–2,000 warriors, making them even more important than the Five Nations. Hamilton was, therefore, concerned when he learned that the French were trying to win over the Ohio tribes. In October, he reported to the Pennsylvania Assembly, "the Indians at Ohio are in great danger of being corrupted by [French] presents or subdued by their arms, unless some proper and speedy measures are taken to prevent it."[56]

In early 1751, the Pennsylvania government began making plans to secure friendly relations with the Ohio tribes. The Assembly asked Conrad Weiser to distribute gifts to the Ohio Indians at Logstown on May 15, and then to represent Pennsylvania at an intercolonial congress being held with the Iroquois Confederacy at Albany. Weiser, making it clear that he could not attend both conferences, recommended that he be sent to Albany. Weiser explained, "my presence at the ensuing treaty at Albany will be of more consequence than the journey to Ohio . . . since there is no particular treaty to be held at Ohio." He added, "It is well known that the Indians on Ohio take their measure from the Six Nations, who are to be fixed for the English at Albany." This statement should not be interpreted as meaning the Confederacy governed the Ohio tribes. Weiser meant that either the Ohio Indians followed the lead of the Ohio Iroquois, whose Confederacy would be "fixed for the English at Albany," or he simply meant that the Iroquois Confederacy's actions influenced all tribes, including the Ohio Indians. It is also possible that Weiser, believing his own career could best be advanced by attending the intercolonial conference at Albany, exaggerated the importance of the Five Nations. In any event, Weiser was trying to make the point that he could be more useful negotiating a treaty with the Five Nations at Albany than merely distributing presents at Logstown. Governor Hamilton accepted Weiser's argument, and, at Weiser's suggestion, appointed George Croghan and the mixed-blood interpreter Andrew Montour to make the Logstown trip.

Hamilton gave Croghan specific instructions: meet with the Ohio Iroquois first and then use them to develop better communications with the other Ohio tribes. Croghan carried out his orders to the letter. On May 18, he and Montour arrived at Logstown, where they were greeted by Indians "firing guns and hoisting the English colors." Over the next few days Croghan met with the Ohio Iroquois. He gave them presents, suggested they strengthen their alliance with the other Ohio Indians, and asked them for help in preparing a joint speech that would illustrate the government's recognition of the Ohio Iroquois as leaders of the Ohio tribes. Croghan also asked the Mingos to assist him in delivering the speech and distributing gifts to the Ohio tribes. Croghan also had orders to discuss land sales with the Ohio Iroquois, who had complained to the Pennsylvania government that they deserved some compensation whenever the Iroquois Confederacy at Onondaga sold land to Pennsylvania. Governor Hamilton instructed Croghan to tell the Iroquois, "We sent your belt to the Six Nations Council at Onondaga, being under an engagement to treat with none but them about lands, and they have your Belt now under consideration."

Croghan's preliminary talks with the Ohio Iroquois went extremely well, so on May 28, he met with representatives from all the Ohio tribes, including the Ohio Iroquois, Delawares, Shawnees, Wyandots, and Miamis. Croghan began by saying he spoke on behalf of the Pennsylvania government and the Ohio Iroquois. He renewed friendship with the Ohio tribes, exhorting them not to cooperate with the French. He then reminded the individual tribes that the Mingos were their intercessors with the Pennsylvania government. Turning to the Ohio Iroquois chiefs, Croghan said, "We have [long] lived in true brotherly love and friendship together. Since that there are several nations joined in friendship with you and us, and of late our Brethren the Twightwees: Now Brethren, as you are the head of all nations of Indians, I warmly recommend it to you to give our Brethren the Twightwees your best advice . . . and likewise I give . . . the Owendatts [Wyandots] in charge to you." Croghan then told all the Indians that the French were interfering with English traders in the Ohio Country; and he encouraged them not to allow French forts in Ohio.

The next day each tribe endorsed Croghan's remarks.

The Ohio Iroquois, speaking last, obviously intended to live up to the Pennsylvania government's expectations. The Mingo spokesman proclaimed, "We, your Brethren the Six Nations . . . thank you for your good advice, and you may depend on our giving our new Brethren the Twightwees our best advice; and we will have them and the Owendatts always under our eyes as well as the Delawares and Shawanese, that we may all become as one people, which is the way to be as strong on Ohio as that mountain . . . which is the Onondaga Country." The Ohio Iroquois then promised that the Ohio tribes would prevent the French from taking over the Ohio Country if they received the Pennsylvania government's support.[57]

Croghan's Logstown Conference with the Ohio tribes established the Ohio Iroquois as Pennsylvania's most-favored Indian nation in the Ohio Country. Croghan had delivered the governor's speech and presents, in conjunction with the Ohio Iroquois, to the other Ohio Indians gathered. He had told the Ohio Indians to listen to the Mingos' advice. And he had listened with approval as the Ohio Iroquois promised to provide good advice and leadership to the Delawares, Shawnees, Twightwees, and Wyandots. No doubt the Ohio tribes were impressed by the Pennsylvania government–Ohio Iroquois relationship. The Ohio Iroquois, fully established as Pennsylvania's right arm in the Ohio Country, were now guaranteed a leadership position among the Ohio tribes. And the Pennsylvania government was assured that the Ohio Indians would not cooperate with the French.

While Pennsylvania officials were working to develop closer ties to the Ohio Indians, they were not completely ignoring the Iroquois Confederacy. Between 1749 and 1754, the Five Nations watched over their tributary allies in Pennsylvania, and Pennsylvania officials continued to conduct business with League sachems. Pennsylvania officials purchased land from the Confederacy and used the Five Nations to block Connecticut's claims in the Susquehanna Valley. Pennsylvania leaders conducted frequent diplomatic talks with the Iroquois. And they listened sympathetically when League spokesmen complained about Pennsylvania's separate dealings with the Ohio tribes. The Five Nations insisted that all of Pennsylvania's transactions with Ohio Indians take place through the League Council at Onondaga.[58]

Yet despite Iroquois complaints, the Pennsylvania government, worried that French advances would disrupt English influence and trade with the Ohio Indians, was not about to stop negotiating directly with Ohio tribes. In 1753, Pennsylvania officials met with Ohio Indians who were returning from Winchester, Virginia. The Indians had been with Virginia officials discussing a possible end to the Catawba War. The Pennsylvanians distributed gifts to condole the Indians for recent losses at the hands of the French and encouraged the Indians to oppose French encroachments in Ohio. Pennsylvania officials were particularly interested in maintaining the support of Scarooyady and three other Ohio Iroquois chiefs: Broken Kettle, Tanacharisson (or the Half-King), and Kachshwuchdanionty. The Pennsylvania government later called upon the Ohio Iroquois leaders to use their influence to stop the fighting between Ohio Indians and Catawbas. Pennsylvania officials, believing that the Ohio tribes were autonomous, also negotiated aid and lands sales with the Ohio Indians. The Pennsylvania government considered the Ohio tribes important trading partners and military allies and used the Mingos to deal with the Five Nations and various tribes of the Ohio Country. Ohio Iroquois leaders like Scarooyady and the Half-King provided the Ohio tribes with loose, informal ties to the Iroquois Confederacy, yet neither they nor the other Ohio Indians blindly obeyed the Five Nations' wishes. The Ohio tribes considered the advice of the prestigious League Council at Onondaga, but they made their own decisions.[59]

By the end of 1754, the Iroquois Confederacy clearly was

no longer Pennsylvania's number one Indian ally. At best the Five Nations shared that honor with the Ohio tribes. The Confederacy was still doing business with the Pennsylvania government, but the Ohio tribes were getting a large share of the Pennsylvanians' attention. The unique symbiotic relationship between the Iroquois Confederacy and the Pennsylvania government began unraveling after 1745. With the emergence of the Ohio tribes as a power bloc and English-French attention riveted on the Ohio Country, the Five Nations were jilted by fickle Pennsylvania leaders no longer needing their help. At that point, the Iroquois' Pennsylvania strategy fell apart.

7

The Southern Wars

Throughout the first half of the eighteenth century, the Iroquois Confederacy made war on the Indians who lived in what is now the southeastern United States. Most Iroquois attacks were aimed at the Catawbas, and, to a lesser extent, at the Cherokees, Choctaws, and Chickasaws.

The Iroquois' eighteenth-century wars on the southern tribes began shortly after 1701. However, Iroquois men had taken the warriors' paths southward for many decades. A lull occurred in the fighting between 1692 and 1701, when the Five Nations found themselves on the defensive against the French and northern Indians during the Twenty Years' War. Iroquois warriors, understandably, were more concerned with protecting their families and homes than they were with traveling hundreds of miles to raid southern Indians who were no threat to Iroquoia. In 1701, the Iroquois Confederacy signed a peace treaty with the French and northern Indians. Shortly thereafter Iroquois warriors resumed their attacks on the southern tribes. The Iroquois hostilities against the southern Indians, and, in particular, against the Catawbas and the Choctaws (both of whom were also referred to as "Flatheads"), continued for the next fifty years. Despite numerous attempts by the English to mediate a peace between their Iroquois and southern Indian allies, or repeated Iroquois pledges to honor cease-fires, the Iroquois war against the Catawbas and other southern tribes dragged on into the second half of the eighteenth century.[1]

Early historians and observers believed that the Iroquois' seventeenth century wars against the southern Indians were fought for individual glory and revenge. Modern historians, accepting these explanations for the seventeenth century warfare, have generally assumed that the Iroquois wars against the southern tribes in the eighteenth century were waged for the same reasons.[2] This, however, was not the case. Whereas the Iroquois of the 1600s fought by choice for glory and revenge, the Iroquois of the 1700s fought by necessity for a variety of reasons. Although glory and revenge were still important motivating factors, external pressures from the French and their Indian allies, as well as from the English, provided the Iroquois with additional reasons to attack the southern tribes during the eighteenth century.

The Iroquois' involvement in the eighteenth-century wars on the southern tribes can be traced back to 1700. In that year, the French decided to use their Indian allies to block the expansion of English traders and to force southern tribes like the Catawbas and Choctaws into abandoning the English and joining the French cause. The governor of New France instructed Longueuil to implement the new French strategy against the southern Indians. In 1700, Longueuil met with the Ottawas, Hurons, Potawatomis, and Missisaugas at Detroit and told them that the king wanted them to war against the Indians and English of Virginia and Carolina. When the French officer promised the Indians that they could keep all goods that they took from English traders, they unanimously agreed to take up the hatchet against the English and Flatheads of Virginia and Carolina. On June 19, 1700, Longueuil traveled to the White River and repeated his message to other Indians allied to New France. After receiving powder and ball from the French

206

officer, the Indians on White River agreed to raid the Virginians and their Flathead allies.[3]

The French made similar requests of the Iroquois, and between 1701 and 1708, warriors from the Five Nations fought alongside western Indians against southern tribes. The Iroquois received French powder and shot for their raids on the Flatheads, but there were other dividends too. Many Iroquois realized that a sure way to guarantee their peace and friendship with the French and western Indians, which they needed so they could hunt in the Western Country without having to fear for their own lives or those of their relatives back home, was by joining the French and western Indians in the attacks on the southern tribes.[4]

The Iroquois continued their attacks on the Flatheads during the early months of 1708, but by summer they were ready to halt their hostilities against the Indians of Virginia, Maryland, and Carolina. In August, several sachems promised the Albany commissioners that their warriors would stop fighting the Catawbas. The following month some Iroquois even asked the New York governor to help them make peace with the Indians of Maryland. The sudden turnabout in the Iroquois position was due to the fact that the Iroquois believed that the French, who were largely responsible for their war on southern Indians, were about to be conquered by the English. Many of the Five Nations were even preparing to join an English expedition aimed at expelling the French from Canada. After the failure of the English scheme to defeat New France, the Iroquois resumed their war on the southern tribes. The fighting continued for the next two years.[5]

In 1710, the Iroquois once again considered making peace with the southern Indians. Governor Robert Hunter of New York met with the Five Nations in August. After renewing the Covenant Chain, Hunter asked the Iroquois to stop fighting the Catawbas. To his surprise and satisfaction, the Iroquois promised they would. In January, 1711, the Albany commissioners gave the Iroquois good reason to comply with Hunter's request. They informed the Five Nations that an English fleet was coming to invade Canada and that Port Royal had already been captured.[6]

For the next year and a half, the Five Nations honored their pledge not to war on the southern tribes. Several considerations explain their willingness to suspend hostilities against the Flatheads. The Iroquois were being threatened in 1710 and 1711 by various enemies. During those years the Five Nations heard rumors of English and French plots to destroy them. At the same time the Iroquois actually suffered from attacks by some western tribes like the Potawatomies, Sauteurs, and Ottawas. As a result, Iroquois men may have been reluctant to go on extended war parties down South, since it would mean leaving their families and homes vulnerable to attack by the western tribes or other enemies.

Many Iroquois were also disenchanted with the French, whom they felt were the instigators of the western Indians' attacks. Therefore, they were probably less willing to aid the French against the Flatheads. At the same time, the Iroquois were thoroughly convinced that the English would soon defeat the French. Chief Hendrick and three other Mohawks had recently returned from a visit to London, where they had been royally received, and they spread the word of the great power of the English. The recent capture of Port Royal and the news of the British fleet's approach also may have been interpreted by the Iroquois as signs that the French could not possibly withstand the coming joint colonial invasion. When the Iroquois added the New Yorkers' promises of protection, supplies, and cheaper goods to the near certainty of English victory, the reasons to listen to the English were overwhelming. Therefore, when the English told the Iroquois not to attack the Flatheads, but to concentrate on extending their alliances to all tribes friendly to the English, the Iroquois obeyed. Besides, the Five Nations probably real-

208

ized that it would be senseless for them to attack the Catawbas in order to improve relations with the French, since it appeared inevitable that the French were going to be expelled from Canada anyway.

Finally, after June, 1711, many of the Five Nations were involved with preparations for the upcoming expedition against Canada, so they had no opportunity to take part in any raids on the southern tribes. In any event, the Five Nations, for the second time in two years, called off their war on the southern Indians after they became convinced that the English would drive the French out of Canada. Unfortunately for the Iroquois, the second English attempt to take Canada, like the first, ended in failure. Once again the Five Nations were forced to ask the governor of New France to pardon them for their role in the English invasion of Canada. Shortly thereafter, the Iroquois resumed their hostilities with the Flatheads, hoping that their participation in the war on the Catawbas could reinstate them to favor with the government of New France.[7]

In the early months of 1712, the Iroquois got an additional impetus to attack the Flatheads of Carolina. During the spring, the Iroquois received wampum belts from the Tuscaroras, an Iroquoian-speaking tribe, who were allies living in the Carolinas. The Tuscaroras asked the Five Nations to help them fight the Catawbas and colonists of Virginia and the Carolinas. The governor of New York, after learning about the Tuscaroras' request, sent a message to each of the Five Nations warning them not to get involved in the fighting, "but to use all possible endeavors to make an accomodation and to oblige those [Tuscarora] Indians to desist from making war on the people of Carolina." The Iroquois promised that they would ask the Tuscaroras to stop fighting, if the governor requested the Carolinians to put down their arms.

Peace might have been made had it not been for the machinations of the French, who used the Tuscarora War, and the recent defeat of the English expedition, to convince some Iroquois to join the Tuscaroras in their fight against the English colonists and Catawbas. The French told the Five Nations that they had intercepted orders for Francis Nicholson (the commander of the English forces which had recently failed to conquer Canada) that showed that the English intended to defeat the Five Nations as soon as Canada had been subdued. Moreover, the French maintained that the colonies of New York and Carolina wished to destroy the Five Nations because the Iroquois were friends of the Tuscaroras. The French added that the high cost of powder at Albany was proof of English intentions. Believing the French, many Iroquois joined the Tuscaroras' war.[8]

The English were not pleased that one of their Indian allies was warring on another. In September, 1714, Governor Hunter of New York asked Iroquois sachems to stop their young men from making war upon any Indians, like the Catawbas, who were English allies. The sachems maintained that they could not make peace with the Flatheads until they first consulted with the Five Nations' warriors. Whether the sachems were merely stalling for time, or whether the warriors refused to listen to the admonitions of their sachems and the governor, is not certain. What is certain is that Iroquois raids on the Flatheads continued.[9]

In the summer of 1715, the English did a dramatic about face regarding the Iroquois-Catawba war. Governor Hunter met with the Five Nations in August, 1715, and asked them to join the English against the Catawbas, who had recently declared war on Carolina. The governor asked the Iroquois to stop the war against the English colonists by mediation or armed intervention. Governor Hunter said, "The cause of [the Flatheads'] fury against His Majesty's subjects is chiefly this, that when the Flatheads implored [Carolina's] assistance against the Five Nations, they absolutely refused it because you [the Five Nations] were ever in strict alliance with the Crown and good friends to the subjects of Great

210

Britain." The Five Nations were too sophisticated to accept Governor Hunter's simplistic explanation. They insisted that the Catawbas were fighting because the Carolinians had reneged on their agreement to give the Catawbas better prices for trade goods after the Catawbas had helped Carolina defeat the Tuscaroras. The Iroquois offered to destroy the Catawbas if the English provided considerable amounts of arms and ammunition.

Governor Hunter quickly accepted the proposal. By September, Iroquois warriors were raiding the Catawbas. This time the raids occurred with the approval of the English, who were using the Five Nations to convince the southern Indians to keep the peace with the colonies.[10]

On October 3, 1715, the Five Nations informed the Albany commissioners that eight messengers had been sent to ask the Catawbas to cease their hostilities against the Carolina colonists. The Iroquois move was unexpected. In August and September the Iroquois had insisted repeatedly that they would not negotiate with the Catawbas, whom they considered treacherous enemies. As late as September 15, the Five Nations had reiterated to the commissioners that they were going to exterminate the Catawbas and requested large amounts of arms and ammunition to do so. The Iroquois had even asked New York to "keep it a secret that they [the Catawbas] may not know of it, for if they do they shall be on their guards." Considering the Iroquois' earlier statements, it is hard to explain why they sent peace envoys to the Catawbas in early October. There are two likely possibilities: the peace delegation may have been a decoy to catch the Catawbas off guard with a surprise attack; or the Iroquois may actually have been trying to settle the conflict. The Iroquois originally promised that they would destroy the Catawbas in return for large amounts of military supplies from New York. Later, they may have reconsidered the difficulties of a full-scale war, and so decided to try for a peaceful settle-

211

ment. The Iroquois may have felt that everyone could benefit: the English and Catawbas would get peace, while the Five Nations would receive arms and ammunition from the English without having to wage a costly war against the Catawbas.

Whatever were the Iroquois' motivations, the English did not appreciate the move toward a peaceful solution. The Albany commissioners made it clear that the Iroquois would receive the military supplies only after they began fighting the Catawbas. Soon thereafter, the Five Nations resumed their attacks on the southern Indians.[11]

As things turned out, however, the English decided that they did not, after all, want the Five Nations to destroy the Catawbas. By the spring of 1717, when Governor Spotswood of Virginia was negotiating a peace treaty with the Flatheads, he and the other English governors requested that the Iroquois cease their attacks. But the Five Nations were not about to suspend their war simply because the English had changed their minds. Two French envoys, Longueuil and Joncaire, had recently distributed gifts among the Iroquois to ensure their continued hostilities with the Flatheads. Furthermore, ambassadors from several southern tribes allied to New France had just urged the Iroquois to continue attacks on the Flatheads.

Governor Spotswood was furious with the Iroquois' refusal to honor the cease-fire with the Catawbas. On May 30, he wrote a letter to New York's Governor Hunter complaining about Iroquois violations of the truce. According to the governor, he was negotiating a treaty with the Catawbas in April, when a party of Iroquois attacked the Catawba deputies, killing five, and capturing five others. Spotswood recommended that a conference with the Iroquois be scheduled to discuss the matter.[12]

Governor Hunter met with the Five Nations in June. After thanking them for their aid in the recent English war against the Catawbas, he reminded the Iroquois that since the war was now over, they should stop their attacks. The Iroquois at first apologized for attacking the Catawbas, who had made peace with the Virginia government, but then spoke of their hatred for those "treacherous Catawbas." The French were at least partly responsible for the Iroquois' determination to fight the southern tribes. According to Cadwallader Colden, the French were encouraging young Iroquois warriors to raid southern tribes "whether the sachems would [agree] or not." For the next five years, warriors of the Five Nations, despite English disapproval, continued their war.[13]

Throughout 1717 and 1718, the governors of Virginia, Pennsylvania, and New York tried their utmost to bring about a peace. In the summer of 1717, Governor Spotswood dispatched Captain Christopher Smith on a mission to Iroquoia. Smith had orders to meet with the Five Nations at Albany to discuss the Iroquois' April attack on the Catawbas, who were then negotiating a peace treaty at Fort Christiana with Governor Spotswood. Smith got the Senecas to admit that they had attacked the Catawbas at the fort, but could not get them to make reparations. The Senecas maintained that since they were not aware that the Catawbas were at peace with Virginia, they were not to blame for the incident. The Senecas further frustrated Virginia's hopes for peace when they claimed they could not return any Catawba prisoners—as the Catawbas demanded—because they had none. Although far from pleased with the answers, Captain Smith had no alternative but to accept them and warn the Senecas not to attack again.

Before returning to Virginia, Captain Smith stopped at Conestoga, where he met with Pennsylvania's Governor Keith and several leaders of the Pennsylvania tribes. The officials got the Indians to agree not to join the Five Nations in any further attacks on the Catawbas.[14]

Governor Robert Hunter also tried to bring about an Iroquois-Catawba peace. In the autumn of 1718, he met

213

with the Five Nations to renew the Covenant Chain. After the Iroquois expressed concern over rumors that the English planned to conquer the Five Nations and take their lands, as they had taken the Tuscaroras', the governor assured them that the English had no such intentions. He explained that the Tuscaroras had lost their land because they had attacked the Carolinians first. Hunter added, "You say that you believe these rumors more readily because powder is so expensive." He then pointed out that the last time he saw them he gave them powder as a gift for hunting and protection, but that they used it to attack some southern Indians who had never bothered the Five Nations. The governor added, "let them be who they may, what did you gain by it? You have lost a number of your swift young people, one of whom is worth a thousand Flatheads." At the end of his speech, Hunter gave the Iroquois some powder in order to calm their fears of a conspiracy, but he warned them not to use it to attack the southern tribes.

The Five Nations had no intention of listening either to Governor Hunter or to Governor Spotswood. The Iroquois depredations against the Indians and whites along the southern frontier continued throughout 1718 and 1719.[15]

By June, 1719, the governors of Pennsylvania, Maryland, and Virginia had repeatedly complained to the New York governor about Iroquois incursions into their colonies. Yet, the New York governor could not stop the southern raids. When he did question the Five Nations about their attacks, they replied that they raided only southern tribes that were at war with the English colonies. Meanwhile, as the English were trying to halt the Iroquois attacks, the French were doing all they could to encourage them. Of the two powers, the French were far more successful, and, throughout 1720, the Iroquois continued to make war on the southern Indians.[16]

Governor Keith promised the tribes within Pennsylvania that he would try to bring peace between them and the

214

southern tribes, and, perhaps, even the Five Nations. The governor's determination soon brought about an important breakthrough in the efforts to establish a peace between the Iroquois and the Indians of Virginia and Carolina. In the spring of 1721, Keith journeyed to Virginia to mediate a peace between the tribes of Pennsylvania and Virginia. He secured the help of Governor Spotswood. Together they established the conditions for a peace between the southern Indians and those of Pennsylvania. Spotswood proposed that the Potomac River and the mountains extending along the back of Virginia be established as boundaries between the tribes of Pennsylvania and those of the South. He said the southern Indians had promised, on condition that the northern Indians observed the same boundaries, not to go across the river or the mountains. After Keith explained that the Pennsylvania tribes lived east of the mountains and had to cross them in order to hunt, Spotswood agreed to limit the Virginia-Pennsylvania Indian boundary to the Potomac River. But the governors concurred that both the Potomac River and the Allegheny Mountain should be observed by the Five Nations, who lived north of the river and west of the mountains. The arrangements made by the two governors brought peace between the Virginia and Carolina tribes and the Pennsylvania Indians. They were also the first steps toward a treaty between some of the southern tribes and the Iroquois.[17]

On June 17, 1721, Governor Keith met with Iroquois deputies at Conestoga. After discussing several important matters, such as improved trade relations and the rum traffic between Pennsylvania and the Iroquois, the governor announced that peace had been ratified between the southern tribes and the Indians of Pennsylvania. He then ordered the Five Nations to stop pressuring the Pennsylvania Indians to join them on southern raids. He warned the Five Nations that they had to end their war on the southern tribes, who were allied to the English. Keith added that

215

when the French "persuade you to go out to war against others it is only that you may be destroyed yourself." The Iroquois deputies listened carefully to his words, and at least some of the Five Nations were willing to comply with his requests. One Iroquois deputy later told James Logan that Governor Keith would have been more successful had he ordered the Iroquois not to war in the South, for then the Five Nations would have been more apt to listen.[18]

Later that summer Governor Burnet of New York met with the Five Nations, and he, too, urged the Iroquois to stop their war on the Catawbas. On August 7, Burnet told the Iroquois that the Virginia governor wanted "to settle the limits bewixt the Indians of Virginia and them that neither should pass the River Potomac or the high mountains to the westward of Virginia without leave of their respective governments." The Iroquois spokesman agreed to the limits placed on travel so long as the Virginia Indians observed the same limits. For a while it appeared as if the Iroquois war on the southern Indians was over.

Within a month, though, Governor Burnet learned that the Iroquois had broken their promise. On September 7, Burnet met again with the Iroquois. This time he chastized them for reneging on their pledge. Again the Iroquois promised to abide by the boundary established by Governor Spotswood.[19]

The governors of New York, Pennsylvania, and Virginia had high hopes that the delicate peace would not be broken. In September, 1722, the New York governor reminded the Iroquois not to war on the Indians of Virginia and Carolina. The Iroquois assured the governor that, although they were warring on some Catawbas, they had not attacked any Indians protected by the boundary agreement. The next month Governor Keith met with representatives of the Pennsylvania tribes. After informing them of the Five Nations' recent treaties with the colonies, he explained that to ensure peace between southern and northern Indians, Virginia had

216

adopted a new, stringent policy: if any southern Indians "shall come to the northward of Potomac or pass to the westward of the great ridge it shall be lawful to put them to death, and if any of the Five Nations shall pass the said boundaries to the southward or eastward of the same boundaries, they shall be treated as public enemies and be put to death or transported into other countries beyond the seas." Keith pointed out that all Indians had to have passports from their colonial governors if they intended to travel in the restricted zones. He reminded the Indians that when the Five Nations had consented to the new treaty with Virginia, they did so not only for themselves but also for the Pennsylvania tribes who were their allies and tributaries. He added that for their own safety they must notify all their people to abide by the new treaty.[20]

The 1721–22 treaties resulted in a temporary decrease in the number of raids on the southern tribes, but did not, however, end the warfare against these Indians. Not all southern Indians were protected by the agreements—only those tribes living south of the Potomac and east of the Appalachian Mountains. After 1722, therefore, the Five Nations could—and did—make war on southern tribes living west of the mountain boundary. Yet even southern Indians living within the borders of the boundaries were not completely safe, for between 1723 and 1733, warriors often violated the Confederacy's pledge not to make war.[21]

In late 1734 and early 1735, the Five Nations asked the English to help them make peace with the Catawbas. This sudden change of heart was the result of smallpox epidemics that had raged throughout the Five Nations in 1732 and 1733, decimating their warriors and ruining their economy. These epidemics apparently cooled the Iroquois' desire to be involved in war against the Catawbas because throughout 1735 and 1736 attacks against the southern tribes came to a halt.[22]

By 1737 the Five Nations had recovered from their bout

217

with smallpox and were no longer eager for a peace treaty with the southern Indians. Early that year the New York governor informed the Iroquois that arrangements had been made for a peace between them and the southern tribes. In March the governor dispatched Lawrence Claase to Onondaga to explain conditions to the Iroquois. Claase indicated that Governor Gooch of Virginia had prevailed upon the southern Indians to send deputies to Williamsburg in April, where he hoped they could meet and treat with representatives from the Five Nations. In the meantime the Virginia governor requested a cease-fire between the parties.

The Iroquois were evasive, insisting that the peace talks take place in Albany. They were even reluctant to agree to the proposed cease-fire. The sachems claimed that the call had come too late, because a large war party of 300 or 400 warriors was already headed southward. The warriors reached their targets, for on July 3, 1737, Governor Gooch notified James Logan that an Iroquois war party had killed three Catawbas, making a total of eleven killed since last April. Gooch added that the Catawbas "are so exasperated that they will hearken to no terms of accommodation, at least, till they have their revenge. But the Cherokees having fortunately found means to fall into a friendly conversation with a party of the Five Nations, had sent with them deputies to conclude a peace for themselves."[23]

Officials in Pennsylvania and New York were not pleased to learn about the attack. In an attempt to prevent cancellation of the peace talks, which were scheduled for April, the Pennsylvania Council sent the Iroquois a message, which indicated that peace had to be made, for the Iroquois had to "clearly see that by their [southern] wars they only lessen their numbers and weaken themselves and render themselves less able to defend their country." The Albany commissioners were also intent on seeing the Five Nations make peace with the southern tribes. On March 6, 1738, the com-

218

missioners asked Lawrence Claase to remind the Senecas that "they are expected at Albany this spring from the Cherokees and Catawbas to make a firm peace between them and the Six Nations." The commissioners wanted Claase to try to hinder Iroquois warriors from going out on new raids against these nations.[24]

By summer the possibility of an Iroquois treaty with the southern tribes was fading fast. Claase reported in July that several Senecas were out fighting against the Catawbas. According to Claase, the Iroquois claimed that "they had stayed at home from hunting in expectation of the deputies of the Cherokees and Catawbas coming to Albany according to the message they had received from Corlaer, but they found now those nations had cheated them for they had lately murdered a Cayuga." What the Iroquois failed to mention was that those southern Indians probably killed the Cayuga in retaliation for a recent Iroquois raid on the Catawbas. In August, some Mohawk deputies approached the Albany commissioners to talk about the possibility of an Iroquois-Catawba peace, but afterwards the commissioners concluded that the Iroquois' position was "all sham as numbers of their warriors are going out a fighting and the war seems to be carried on with additional vigor."[25]

As 1738 came to a close it became evident to the English that the Five Nations were no longer interested in peace with the southern tribes. On December 6, the Board of Trade informed George Clarke, the lieutenant governor of New York, that Governor Gooch of Virginia had complained about the Five Nations' refusal to make peace. According to Gooch, the Iroquois were still at war with the Catawbas and Cherokees living in the Carolina and Georgia backcountry. Gooch had also complained that after a time and place for treaty negotiations had been named and a cease-fire agreed to, the Five Nations "had broke off the negotiations by a treacherous attack on the Catawba Indians and did afterwards murder 11 English inhabitants dwelling on the back of the Mountains." The members of the Board of Trade were astounded by this news and exclaimed to Lieutenant Governor Clarke, "it seems very extraordinary to us that these Five Nations who are protected by the British government should employ their force to destroy other nations of Indians under the same protection which is effectually doing the work of our common enemy." The Board members urged the lieutenant governor of New York to put pressure on the Iroquois to stop their southern raids. But despite the English protests, the Five Nations continued their attacks throughout 1739.[26]

Lieutenant Governor Clarke was not one to give up easily, and he continued his efforts to work out an Iroquois-Catawba peace settlement. His determination produced results. On January 28, 1740, Clarke wrote to the Board of Trade, explaining that he had convinced the Five Nations to make peace with all southern tribes that were English allies. Clarke added that he had written to "Governor Gooch last spring . . . desiring that deputies may be sent from those Indians next June or July to Albany."

For the next few months, Lieutenant Governor Clarke was constantly reminding the Iroquois not to ruin the chances for peace. He met with Iroquois sachems in August and reprimanded them for the Iroquois' "constant practice" of joining French war parties against southern Indians. Clarke informed them that the king wanted the Five Nations to conclude a general peace with all Indians to the south and west. The Iroquois agreed on the condition that within two years deputies from the southern tribes went to Albany to make a treaty. The sachems then consented to a cease-fire until the Indians ratified a permanent treaty.[27]

Not all Iroquois were ready to accept peace with the southern Indians. Some of the Five Nations plotted with the French to sabotage Clarke's plans to bring the Iroquois and southern tribes together for peace talks. Others refused to abide by the cease-fire, and attacked the southern Indians

220

throughout 1741. While the Iroquois were reluctant to end their attacks, the southern Indians were eager for a cessation of hostilities.

Lieutenant Governor Clarke realized that the Iroquois were the major obstacle to peace. In the winter of 1741–42, Clarke grew increasingly concerned over the probability that in spring Iroquois warriors would resume their attacks on the southern tribes. In January, 1742, the Albany commissioners assured Clarke that they would remind the Iroquois that they promised not to attack the southern tribes. The commissioners later reported that the Iroquois told them "that it is the unanimous resolution of the Six Nations that none of their people shall go out a fighting to the southward for these two years and in token of their sincerity they give a belt."[28]

Clarke knew that Iroquois promises made in the cold of a New York winter might, like the snow and ice, disappear with the arrival of warmer weather. So he moved quickly to transform the temporary cease-fire into a lasting peace. On June 15, 1742, Clarke announced to the Five Nations that the southern tribes had met the Iroquois' demand that they ratify a general peace within two years. With much pomp, he presented the Iroquois with tokens and belts sent by the southern tribes to cement a lasting peace. The Iroquois must have been impressed by Clarke's words, because, at least in public, they overlooked the fact that no Flatheads had actually come to Iroquoia to make the peace. The Iroquois accepted the treaty with the Flatheads.[29]

The following month a group of Senecas and Onondagas met with Governor Beauharnois in Canada. The Senecas carefully tried to prepare the governor for the news that the Iroquois, because of English pressure, were making peace with the southern tribes. The Senecas informed Beauharnois that in the spring they would be having a council with the Flatheads. Feigning innocence, the Senecas added that they "know not what they [the Flatheads] want

221

of us." The French governor was not fooled by the Senecas' act. He told them that he knew about the recent Albany conference. Beauharnois warned the Senecas that all of New France's Indian allies were at war with the southern tribes, and they would be insulted if the Five Nations made peace with their enemies. The implied threat was not lost on the Iroquois. Soon thereafter, Iroquois warriors resumed their attacks on southern tribes.[30]

On January 24, 1743, a Pennsylvania trader named Thomas McKee informed the Pennsylvania Council about a recent skirmish between Virginia settlers and Iroquois warriors. He indicated that the Iroquois had been in the South fighting against Indians in Maryland and Virginia. The news troubled Pennsylvania officials. The governor asked Conrad Weiser to persuade the Iroquois to settle the affair peacefully with the Virginia governor. Pennsylvania officials were concerned that, unless the matter were resolved, Pennsylvania might clash with the Iroquois warriors who had to journey through Pennsylvania en route to war in Virginia.[31]

New York officials also were worried that the Iroquois-Virginia incident might spark an all-out war between the Five Nations and the English. When the Albany commissioners told the Iroquois that Virginia's governor was accusing the Five Nations of unprovoked aggression, the Iroquois haughtily replied that the Virginians had fired first. Lieutenant Governor Clarke quickly wrote to Governor Gooch and asked that the Virginia government "not be hasty to take any steps that may lead to widen a breach that may involve all the colonies in a war. . . . The sachems . . . endeavor all they can to restrain their youth from these [southern] excursions, but it is next to impossible."[32]

Despite the fact that the Iroquois' southern raids had brought them to the brink of war with Virginia, and maybe even Pennsylvania, the Five Nations still were not inclined to end their hostilities with the southern tribes. At Onondaga on August 2, 1743, sachems confided to Conrad Weiser, "We are engaged in a war with the Catawbas which will last to the end of the world, for they molest us and speak contemptuous of us, which our warriors will not bear, and they will soon go to war against them again. It will be in vain for us to dissuade them from it." The sachems added that their warriors, while en route southward, would not bother whites if the whites did not interfere with them.

Even New York's usually optimistic lieutenant governor, George Clarke, appeared reconciled to the Iroquois' determination to war on the southern tribes. In his report on New York, the lieutenant governor explained that because of the martial spirit of Iroquois youth, the French could entice the young warriors to join expeditions against the tribes of Virginia, Georgia, and the Carolinas. Clarke added that these attacks were in violation of the public pledges made by the Five Nations.[33]

Several English colonial governments made a joint effort in 1744 to settle the differences among the colonies, their Indian allies, and the Five Nations. In June, representatives from Virginia, Maryland, and Pennsylvania met with deputies from the Five Nations at Lancaster, Pennsylvania, to discuss issues such as Iroquois-English relations, territorial boundaries, land ownership, Iroquois raids on Virginians, the Iroquois' right of passage through Virginia, and the Iroquois' war on the southern tribes.

By the time the conference ended, some important matters had been resolved. The Five Nations renounced all claims to land in Virginia and Maryland in exchange for compensation from those colonies. The Iroquois also promised to remain close friends of the English and not to side with New France. Other issues, however, such as the Iroquois' war on the Flatheads and the Five Nations' right of passage through Virginia remained unresolved.[34]

In response to the Iroquois' demand that they be allowed to travel through Virginia, the Virginia commissioners sar-

223

castically replied that had the Five Nations respected the peace treaty made in 1721–22 they would have no need to be traveling in Virginia. The commissioners added that the Virginia government would agree to a road based on the terms of the Spotswood Treaty of 1722, on the condition that the Iroquois behave as they passed through the colony.

The Iroquois adamantly denied that they were responsible for breaking the peace. They claimed that the Catawbas reneged on their promise to go to Albany to ratify the peace treaty. Instead, the Catawbas called the Iroquois "women" and said that they, the Catawbas, were "double men for they had two [penises]." The Iroquois condemned the Catawbas' treachery, insisting that "the war must continue until one of us is destroyed." The Iroquois then promised to observe better standards of conduct in their future travels through Virginia.

A Virginia commissioner asked the Five Nations to forgive the rash statements of the Catawbas' young men, adding "In this time of war with our common enemies, the French and Spanish, it will be the wisest way to be at peace between you and them."

The Iroquois gave their same evasive response: "We shall not be against a peace on reasonable terms provided they [the Catawbas] will come northward to treat about it."[35]

When the conference adjourned on July 4, 1744, the English were no closer to bringing a general peace between the Five Nations and the southern tribes than they were before the meeting convened at Lancaster. The Iroquois would not stop fighting until the Catawbas came to Iroquoia for peace talks. The Catawbas, claiming the Iroquois had broken their word too many times in the past, refused to comply with the Iroquois' demands. Catawba chiefs later explained that they were afraid to send deputies to Iroquoia, since the Iroquois would probably kill them. They added, "We have already sent our belt and other tokens of peace to the Six Nations . . . and have never yet received any answer or token from them, otherwise than constant war."[36]

After 1744, Iroquois warfare on the southern Indians continued. The constant harassment eventually convinced the Catawbas that they had to submit to Iroquois demands. In July, 1747, Catawba deputies made the long trip northward to negotiate a peace with the Five Nations. Governor Clinton, serving as the mediator, reminded the Iroquois that since King George's War was threatening the New York frontier, Iroquois warriors ought not to be warring on the Flatheads. The sachems reluctantly agreed to keep their warriors at home.[37]

Unfortunately for the Catawbas, Iroquois warriors did not support the sachems' decision. Between 1747 and 1751, various individuals tried to stop the fighting. In 1749, the Pennsylvania governor attempted to mediate a peace between the Iroquois and Catawbas, but he failed. The following year William Johnson spoke with the Iroquois about the possibility of peace with the Flatheads. In July, 1750, South Carolina's governor, James Glen, warned the Five Nations to end their raids into his colony or else face retaliatory measures. The Catawbas sent an additional message, which said they wanted peace and were willing to go to New York for peace talks. In the fall of 1750, the governors of Virginia and South Carolina asked the Iroquois League Council to make peace with the Flatheads. But again the Iroquois refused, claiming that the Catawbas were the ones to blame for the war and insisting that the Virginia governor and the Catawbas come to Albany before negotiations could take place. The Iroquois were willing to negotiate, but only on their terms and their price.[38]

In 1751, plans were set into motion to meet the Five Nations' demands. Governor Clinton invited all of the colonies, from New Hampshire to South Carolina, to meet with the Five Nations at Albany in July, 1751. Clinton was hoping that his joint conference would secure the Confederacy to the English and would be the foundation for a united front against the French. He was, therefore, disappointed when only Massachusetts, Connecticut, and South Carolina decided to attend. South Carolina, hoping for an Iroquois-Catawba peace, sent a deputy plus six Catawba representatives to Albany. But Clinton did not think the Iroquois would be impressed, since the presents being offered by South Carolina were too small. After the conference was over the New York governor reported to his home government that the Albany conference had accomplished several things: the Covenant Chain was renewed; the Iroquois had been convinced to strengthen themselves "by drawing the neighboring tribes into strict alliances with them, and securing a general liberty of trade"; the Iroquois had been asked to stop the French from building a fort at Niagara; and the Iroquois had agreed to make peace with the Catawbas. Clinton explained that the Iroquois and Catawbas had smoked the peace pipe, but peace would not be firmly established "unless the Catawbas take care to give up their prisoners at Albany within a year, as promised." Clinton was exaggerating the importance of the Iroquois-Catawba talks. The Iroquois' sachems had not made peace. All they had agreed to was to make peace if the Catawbas returned all prisoners of war within a year. Only then would the fighting stop.[39]

The Flatheads tried to meet the Iroquois' timetable. As a sign of good faith, in June, 1752, four Catawba Indians returned one Cayuga prisoner to Albany. But the Five Nations were not satisfied. Although Iroquois sachems were inclined to resume peace talks with the Catawbas, the warriors of the Five Nations would have no part of it. They continued to attack Indians on the southern frontier. In 1753, the governors of Virginia, South Carolina, and Pennsylvania made new attempts to stop the fighting between the Iroquois and Catawbas. The Iroquois still refused to cooperate. As a result, Iroquois warfare on the southern

226

tribes continued through the mid-1750s.[40] The Five Nations would not reconsider their position until after the Seven Years' War began.

Several important considerations were responsible for the Iroquois' determination to war on the southern tribes during the eighteenth century. The Iroquois fought the southern Indians in order to improve political and economic relations with New France. Between 1700 and 1754, the French were constantly asking their Indian allies to attack various southern tribes friendly toward the English. The French hoped that the attacks would block English expansion by forcing the southern tribes into abandoning the English and adopting a pro-French position. The French were particularly interested in securing Iroquois support against the southern tribes. An Iroquois-southern Indian war would force the Iroquois to focus their military efforts on southern Indians, and not on New France, and it would help check the growth of Iroquois power, since a number of Iroquois warriors would be killed in the fighting. Furthermore, the Iroquois-southern Indian war would interfere with England's plans to unite all of her Indian allies.[41]

The Iroquois eagerly joined the French against the southern Indians. The great losses sustained by the Iroquois during the Twenty Years' War convinced them that further resistance to the French was futile. After 1701, the Five Nations generally sought peace with New France. The Iroquois realized that accepting the invitation to war on southern tribes was one way to improve French relations. They also knew that they could obtain ammunition, food, blankets, and other gifts from the French in return for their participation in the southern wars.[42]

The Five Nations hoped that fighting the southern Indians might also improve their relations with New France's northern and western Indian allies, who were at war with the southern tribes. The Iroquois' survival depended upon

227

peace with the French Indians. The Iroquois, having lost one-half of their warriors during the Twenty Years' War, could not afford renewed hostilities with the numerous and powerful western tribes. The Five Nations also needed peace with the French Indians so Iroquois hunters could travel safely in the Ohio Country. And the Iroquois realized peace would allow them to trade with the western tribes.[43] Most likely, many Iroquois joined French Indian war parties against southern tribes in order to strengthen the friendship between the Five Nations and the western and northern Indians.

Actual threats may also have prompted the Iroquois to join the French Indians against the Flatheads. For instance, in 1741, Canada's Governor Beauharnois warned the Iroquois, "You know that all the [Indian] Nations are out at war with the Flatheads, and that . . . a peace [between the Iroquois and the Flatheads] would be a declaration of hostilities against them." The following year Beauharnois issued a similar threat to the Iroquois. He said, "I have given his [the Chickasaws'] flesh for food to all the [Indian] Nations. . . . how dangerous it would be for you, in regard to the other Nations to make peace with them."[44]

Sometimes the English colonial governments asked the Iroquois to war on southern tribes. Between 1715 and 1717, the English encouraged the Iroquois to raid the Catawbas, who were at war with Virginia and the Carolinas. In return for their assistance the Iroquois obtained free arms, powder, and supplies, as well as the friendship of the English, who were greatly indebted to the Iroquois for their help.[45]

The Iroquois probably saw the southern wars as a way to further their political relations with Pennsylvania tribes, who were tributary allies of the Iroquois Confederacy. Throughout the first half of the eighteenth century, the Iroquois repeatedly asked the Indians living on the Susquehanna and Delaware rivers to join them in the war on the southern tribes. The Five Nations may have been using the

228

Flatheads as a common enemy in order to cement the Iroquois-Pennsylvania Indian alliance. The war on the Flatheads also provided the Iroquois with the opportunity to expand their social and political contacts with Pennsylvania Indians. Camaraderie was likely to develop between Iroquois and Pennsylvania warriors who joined to raid in the South. Furthermore, the southern wars enabled the Iroquois to offer protection to the weaker Pennsylvania tribes, who in turn became more dependent on the Five Nations. When these political gains are added to the military assistance that the Pennsylvania Indians could provide, it is easy to understand why the Iroquois were so eager to involve the Pennsylvania tribes in the war against the Flatheads.[46]

On occasion, the Iroquois used the southern wars to improve their political position with the southern colonies. The southern warfare gave the Five Nations valuable political leverage against the colonies of Virginia, Pennsylvania, Carolina, and Maryland. Southern colonial officials were upset that the Five Nations were fighting other pro-English Indian tribes, and they were angry that Iroquois warriors, while en route southward, frequently stole livestock and foodstuffs from the colonists, and even attacked colonists themselves. The officials demanded that the Iroquois stop raiding and looting in the South. The Five Nations were willing to listen—for a price. The Iroquois wanted the governments of those colonies to recognize Iroquois rights of passage and land ownership in the South. The colonial officials, wanting to stop the Iroquois incursions in the South, had no choice but to accept the Iroquois demands.[47] In effect, the Five Nations' southern warfare enabled the Iroquois to extract concessions from the southern colonies. Without the southern wars, the Iroquois would have had no presence in the South, and thus no political leverage against the southern colonial governments.

The Iroquois gained other political advantages by fighting in the South. They increased their population through

229

the adoption of prisoners of war. They strengthened themselves further through alliances with southern tribes that were enemies of the Catawbas. For example, between 1712 and 1715, the Iroquois aided the Tuscaroras in their fight against the Flatheads and the southern colonies. The Tuscaroras, after their defeat, fled to Iroquoia, where they were accepted as the sixth Iroquois nation. This Tuscarora migration increased the Iroquois' military and political power. Had the Iroquois chosen not to aid the Tuscaroras in the war on the Catawbas, the Tuscaroras might not have moved to Iroquoia, and Iroquois political and military power would not have increased.[48]

In addition to being politically motivated, the Iroquois' southern wars were economically motivated. The supplies, arms, and ammunition that the French and English provided are examples of how the Five Nations profited from the southern wars. By plundering Indian and white settlements on the southern frontier or by occasionally kidnapping southern slaves for resale in northern markets, the Iroquois also "gained" economically. In addition, Iroquois hunting and trading rights on the Ohio, Potomac, and lower Susquehanna rivers were being defended. The fewer southern Indians there were, the less competition Iroquois hunters and traders would have. One way or another, victories over the southern tribes meant economic profits for the Five Nations.[49]

Social and cultural motivations also help to explain why the Iroquois waged war against the southern tribes throughout the first half of the eighteenth century. Prestige, social position, and political advancement were just some rewards available to warriors achieving great success in battle. The warfare also gave the Iroquois the chance to strike their traditional southern enemies. The Iroquois and Flatheads had been at war since the 1600s, so by the 1700s Iroquois warriors felt honor bound to avenge the blood feud and bad blood between their people and the hated southern

230

Indians. The warfare allowed the Iroquois to satisfy certain emotional needs, such as the desire to obtain revenge or emotional release. Governor Beauharnois of Canada understood the importance of war and revenge in Iroquois society. During a 1741 conference, Beauharnois made the following argument to convince the Senecas to attack the southern tribes: "Children . . . I have heard that the Onondagas desired to . . . get you to make peace with the Flatheads . . . but what would become of your young men, and where could they go to divert themselves? Besides, your blood has been repeatedly shed in the country of that nation."[50]

If social and cultural reasons made war an important and positive aspect of Iroquois life, pragmatic reasons dictated that the war be waged against southern tribes. To begin with, the Iroquois had no one else to fight. In 1701, the Five Nations had ratified a peace treaty with most tribes living to the north, northeast, and west of Iroquoia. And the war-weakened Iroquois were in no position to renew hostilities with New France's powerful Indian allies. Not being able to war on the Indians to their west, north, or northeast, the Iroquois had only one option left. They had to follow the warriors' past southward. Actually, the "choice" was wise for a number of reasons. The Iroquois could count on assistance from the western tribes who were fighting the southern Indians at French instigation. Also, the southern war was a low-risk war for the Five Nations. Iroquois warriors could raid southern Indian villages, but the Flatheads found it difficult to retaliate, because Iroquois allies protected Iroquoia from attacks. Pro-Iroquois Indian villages on the Susquehanna and Allegheny rivers stood between the homelands of the Iroquois and those of the Flatheads. Iroquois warriors could freely pass down the Susquehanna Trail and along the southern and western warriors' paths to raid the southern Indians, while the Flatheads found it nearly impossible to strike back. The route northward was

231

blocked by pro-Iroquois villages on the Susquehanna River. The warriors' path through the Cumberland Gap was also extremely hazardous. This pass had numerous hiding places which were ideal for ambuscades and was frequently traveled by the Iroquois and other northern Indian enemies of the southern tribes.[51] The arrangement was ideal for the Five Nations, since it allowed them to attack the southern Indians with near impunity. This low-risk situation enabled the Five Nations to wage war, as their society and culture required, but yet within Iroquoia have peace, a condition which was essential to the growth of the Iroquois economy.

The eighteenth-century Iroquois wars against the southern tribes differed greatly from those of the previous century. During the 1600s, the Iroquois fought southern Indians primarily for revenge or glory, although economics was a contributing factor. By the 1700s, Iroquois motives for waging war on southern tribes were more complex. By then the Iroquois were fighting for a variety of significant reasons. They had economic, political, and military motives, as well as the more traditional motives of revenge and glory. After 1701, warfare against southern Indians became an important means to help restore the power and prosperity of the Five Nations.

Conclusion: Results of the Restoration Policy

The Restoration Policy was the result of both conscious Iroquois actions and timely Iroquois reactions. Sometimes the Iroquois generated the moves. Other times the Iroquois reacted to moves of their Indian and white neighbors. For example, the Iroquois followed a policy of neutrality toward the English and French in response to their own internal needs and politics, as well as to external pressures from the English and French. The Iroquois actively sought rapprochement with the western and northern tribes for economic, political, social, and military reasons. The Iroquois alternately led and followed the Pennsylvania government in the creation of the Pennsylvania strategy, which gave the Five Nations hegemony over tribes and lands in Pennsylvania. And the Iroquois consciously advanced their own goals by waging war against southern tribes. In its entirety, the Restoration Policy was shaped by necessity, fortuitous circumstances, timely moves, chance, rational geopolitical decisions, internal conditions among the Five Nations, and external initiatives by the Iroquois' white and Indian neighbors. Ultimately preplanned Iroquois actions and wise Iroquois reactions determined the development of Restoration strategies.

For almost fifty years the Iroquois benefited from their Restoration Policy. The policy aided the recovery of the economy after the devastating Twenty Years' War. The resulting peace enabled the Iroquois to trade and farm without having to worry about being attacked by the French and Indians. The rapprochement with western tribes and warfare on southern Indians guaranteed Iroquois hunting rights in the West and on the lower Susquehanna River. The Restoration Policy gave the Iroquois the chance to develop a geographic middleman position between Albany and the Western Country. In this capacity they profited by supplying western and northern Indians with goods and services as they passed through Iroquoia to and from the Albany trade. As an added dividend, the Five Nations, by providing a free and safe passage through Iroquoia, received the western Indians' guarantee of peace and safety for Iroquois hunters in the Western Country. The Restoration Policy also allowed the Iroquois to gain hegemony over Pennsylvania Indians and lands. The Five Nations then profited by selling these lands to the Pennsylvania government. Furthermore, the Restoration Policy enabled the Iroquois to gain economic benefits from both their European neighbors. The Five Nations traded with the English or the French, depending upon whoever offered the best prices and values. Iroquois were employed by the English and French as messengers, scouts, mercenaries, and porters. The Confederacy sold land to the English in Pennsylvania, Virginia, Maryland, New York, and Ohio. And the Five Nations received French and English economic assistance, including ammunition, presents, smiths, and emergency aid during times of disease or famine. In effect, the Restoration Policy helped the Iroquois develop and maintain the types of relations with the English, French, and Indians that were most beneficial to the Iroquois economy.

The Restoration Policy also aided the military recovery of the Five Nations. Through the policy the borders of Iroquoia were secured from attack and peace was guaranteed. As a result, the Five Nations' population was. given the chance to recover from the many casualties it had incurred during the Twenty Years' War. The Restoration Policy provided the Iroquois with many new Indian and white allies. The Iroquois' tributary allies in Pennsylvania served as buffers, insulating Iroquoia from attack and contributing warriors and scouts to aid the Five Nations in times of war. Treaties with northern and western tribes further strengthened the Iroquois. Through these alliances, the Iroquois not only neutralized a potentially dangerous enemy, but they transformed that enemy into a friend. The Iroquois' military position, therefore, improved with every mutual-defense pact negotiated between the Five Nations and French Indians. The Iroquois' policy of neutrality furnished additional military aid by allowing the Five Nations to secure military backing, supplies, and assistance from both the English and French.

The Restoration Policy advanced the political prestige and influence of the Iroquois Confederacy. The policy enabled the Iroquois to use the English and French to further their own political needs. The Iroquois' symbiotic relationship with the English was especially important. The English, believing that they could utilize the Confederacy to deal with other Indians, made the Iroquois their primary Indian ally. Such a designation guaranteed the results. By recognizing the Iroquois Confederacy as most important, the Confederacy did indeed become that. As the first link in England's Covenant Chain, the Iroquois gained stature and influence among other Indians. The English were then able to employ the Iroquois to achieve their goals. At the same time, the Iroquois were able to use their English connection to advance their own interests with other tribes.

Good relations with New France further contributed to the rise of the Confederacy's political power and influence. The western and northern tribes realized that the Five Nations had French backing, so they had to recognize the Confederacy's status as a political ally of New France and deal with them accordingly. Iroquois relations with the French and English were two important keys to Iroquois greatness.

235

The Five Nations' connections to the European powers were largely responsible for their political influence over other Indian tribes during the first half of the eighteenth century.

The Restoration Policy gave the Iroquois the means to retain their own sovereignty. The neutrality that resulted from the policy helped the Iroquois establish a balance of power position. Since neither the French nor the English wished to lose the Iroquois to the other side, both were forced to solicit the Iroquois' favor in order to keep their friendship. This gave the Iroquois leverage, which other tribes lacked against the whites, and allowed the Five Nations to preserve their independence by playing the two European powers off against each other. The Iroquois used each side to check the advances and abuses of the other.

The Restoration Policy enabled the Iroquois to establish relations that were beneficial to the Confederacy. The Five Nations were able to secure a lasting friendship with powerful tribes in Canada and the West. They were able to gain control over nearby tribes of Pennsylvania and manipulate them to their advantage. And the Iroquois were able to wage war against southern Indians without endangering the security of Iroquoia. These far-reaching Indian relations enhanced the Iroquois' political reputation. The more contacts the Five Nations had, the more important they were to the English and the French. And the more important they were to the English and the French, the more Indian allies they could obtain. For the Iroquois, it was a seemingly never-ending spiral toward political success.

Iroquois society was also affected by the Restoration Policy. The policy helped mitigate social division by offering accommodation for all groups. Pro-French and pro-English factions thrived under the Restoration Policy, since each had its function and place of importance. Political differences between warriors and sachems were, likewise, accommodated by the Restoration Policy. Social and political crises

236

were thus avoided by the development of a society which adhered to the Restoration Policy's pluralistic goals. The policy affected Iroquois society in other ways. It allowed Iroquois to maintain close ties with relatives and friends living in Canada. It enabled the Five Nations to increase social contacts with the numerous tribes living around them. Some Iroquois intermarried with Indians in the Western Country, Canada, and Pennsylvania. Others traveled extensively or settled down in regions inhabited by western and northern Indians. As a result, by 1750, the Iroquois population was dispersed and, to an extent, integrated with other Indians of the Eastern Woodlands.

The Iroquois' Restoration Policy worked remarkably well until 1745; then it began to unravel. There were several reasons for its success. Until the mid-1740s, the Five Nations were the most important Indian group on the northern colonial frontier, so both Indians and whites had to cooperate with them. The Five Nations' location in central New York gave them control of major trade and travel routes to the Great Lakes and Western Country. Iroquoia also served as a buffer between New France and English colonies like New York and Pennsylvania. The Iroquois' proximity and numbers made them a potentially strong friend—or enemy—for both Indians and whites. The Five Nations, with their numerous alliances, were ideal intermediaries. Whites used them to negotiate with Indians, and Indians used them to deal with whites. The Iroquois were particularly useful in establishing trade relationships between Indians and whites. The League Council also made the Five Nations unique. Unlike the decentralized, band leadership found among most tribes of the Eastern Woodlands, the confederacy provided a centralized government with which whites could work.

Until 1745, the Iroquois' goals were compatible with those of Indian and white neighbors. Both the French and English wanted the Five Nations' friendship and cooperation, while western Indians needed the Iroquois as inter-mediaries and geographic middlemen. Since the Restoration Policy also sought these ends, Indians and whites were, therefore, more than willing to cooperate with the Five Nations.

Furthermore, the Iroquois were able to implement their Restoration Policy because, prior to 1745, they received little interference from the French or English. Despite the participation of some Iroquois in the attempted English invasions of Canada in 1709 and 1711, the Iroquois Confederacy maintained a neutral position between the English and French throughout most of the first half of the eighteenth century. The Iroquois' stance was facilitated by the fact that the two European powers remained at peace for over thirty years during this period. Thus the Five Nations, not pressured to ally themselves exclusively with either side, were free to pursue their Restoration Policy.

After 1745, the Restoration Policy quickly became inoperative as new conditions arose. King George's War dealt a severe blow to Iroquois neutrality. The Confederacy was in a predicament. Should it join the English war against New France or remain neutral? The League Council teetered back and forth. It declared war, only to back off. Meanwhile individual warriors joined the fight, attacking various French settlements. In the end, the Confederacy maintained its neutrality, but pleased no one. The French were angry that Mohawks and other Iroquois warriors enlisted to fight against Canada. New Yorkers were upset that the League never followed through on its promise to wage war against New France. After the war the New York Assembly, having to repay war debts, felt justified in ignoring Iroquois needs.

With the emergence of the Ohio tribes, whose numbers and powers rivaled the Iroquois', the Five Nations soon lost their status as the most important Indians on the northern frontier. By 1747, the Ohio Indians started their own coun-

238

cil fire and opened relations with the English and French, independent of the Iroquois Confederacy. At that point things began to change. The Iroquois lost their geographic middleman position as English traders began to travel to the Western Country to trade directly with the western tribes. By mid-century, the western tribes no longer needed the Iroquois to trade or deal with the English, so the Iroquois lost the leverage they had with those tribes. The loss of Iroquois influence with the western Indians meant a corresponding decrease in usefulness to the European powers. As France and England increasingly turned their attention to the Western Country, they began to ignore the Iroquois, who no longer had great influence there. Instead, the European powers began to court the friendship of the powerful western tribes, and the Iroquois became less important.

At the same time, Iroquois hegemony over the Pennsylvania tribes began to crumble. Many Pennsylvania Indians, like the Delawares and Shawnees, resented Iroquois interference, so they moved to Ohio, where they were out of reach of the Confederacy's meddling. The Pennsylvania government then began dealing directly with those tribes. As a result, the Iroquois were no longer needed and lost much of their influence in Pennsylvania.

Aside from losing their influence with the English, French, and western tribes, the Iroquois had other worries. Throughout the 1740s, smallpox, famine, and economic disasters plagued the Five Nations. To make matters worse, some Iroquois began an exodus from Iroquoia in search of better opportunities. Plentiful game and rich farmlands drew many Iroquois to the Western Country. By the early 1750s, the Iroquois were again in decline.

After 1754, external pressures and internal divisions delivered fatal blows to the Iroquois Restoration Policy. The French and Indian War (1754–63) snapped Iroquois neutrality, the backbone of the Restoration Policy. In the early years of the fighting, the French won several major victories

239

over the English. In July, 1755, French and Indians decisively defeated General Braddock's regulars, leaving the Ohio Country in French control. The next year the French took Fort Oswego and seized control of Lake Ontario. The French scored additional victories in 1757 at Fort William Henry and German Flats. But then the momentum began to shift. In 1758, Fort Louisbourg fell to Britain's General Amherst. The English then built Fort Stanwix on the New York frontier and conquered Fort Frontenac, giving them control of Lake Ontario and the Oswego region. Before the year was out the English also took possession of Fort Duquesne. British victories and French setbacks remained the pattern in 1759. Sir William Johnson took Fort Niagara in July. The French gave up Forts Ticonderoga and Crown Point in July and August. And General Wolfe seized Quebec in September. In 1760, Montreal fell to the English; at long last the English had conquered Canada.[1]

During the early years of the conflict, the Iroquois clung to their neutrality. But as the war dragged on, the Iroquois were pulled into the fighting. In particular, Seneca warriors joined pro-French war parties, while Mohawks aided the English.[2]

The coming of the French and Indian War and the eventual expulsion of the French from North America by the Treaty of Paris (1763) marked the beginning of a new phase in Iroquois diplomacy. The Iroquois were no longer able to play off their enemies against each other. They could no longer serve as a balance of power between the English and French or between the English colonies and the Western Country. After 1763, the Five Nations' leverage was gone and their strategic importance was rapidly declining.

Instead of being able to play off their enemies, the Iroquois, after 1763, were frequently caught in a squeeze between potentially dangerous adversaries. For example, powerful western tribes sometimes called on the Five Nations to turn against the English. Numerous Senecas sided with

Pontiac and other western Indians in a war against the English in 1763–64. Similarly, Iroquois warriors joined Ohio tribes for raids against the English frontier in Lord Dunmore's War (1774).[3]

The Iroquois also found themselves in the middle of English-American political differences. The coming of the American Revolution smashed any hopes the Iroquois had of recouping power and influence. The Iroquois initially tried to remain neutral in the squabble between the American colonists and the English government, but by September, 1776, cracks began to appear in the Confederacy's solidarity. Within a year the Iroquois nations split over the war issue. Warriors from the Senecas, Cayugas, Onondagas, and Mohawks held fast to the English Covenant Chain, while Oneidas and Tuscaroras, under the influence of "New Light" missionary Samuel Kirkland, sided with the rebel colonists. The American Revolution became an Iroquois civil war. The results were disastrous for the Five Nations. The Iroquois suffered numerous casualties. They were displaced from their homes. Their crops were destroyed. Their political unity was shattered. And, abandoned by the English at war's end, the Iroquois were forced to accept treaties with the United States and New York, thereby giving up much of their homelands.[4] When the war clouds cleared, the Iroquois' position became evident. The Great Tree of Peace, which had shaded the Five Nations for centuries, had been uprooted: the Iroquois Restoration Policy was no more. The Iroquois' days of power, glory, and prestige were now behind them.

In the end, the Iroquois Restoration was only partially successful. It failed to completely restore the Iroquois to the powerful and influential position they had enjoyed prior to 1680. The Iroquois never regained the control they once had exercised over the Western Country. The Restoration Policy also created tensions that hurt the Iroquois in the long run. The policy of neutrality kept alive the fires of factionalism which divided the Iroquois people. The Iroquois' hegemony in Pennsylvania caused bitter resentment among the Shawnees and Delawares, who eventually turned against the Five Nations. And, ironically, even the successes of the Restoration Policy, which had enhanced the Confederacy's influence, undermined the Iroquois, because the Iroquois population became dispersed and weakened as many Indians began moving westward where the Iroquois' reputation was great.

Still, the Iroquois Restoration was more of a success than a failure. The Five Nations did recoup much of their political, military, and economic power. Equally important, the Iroquois Confederacy, through the Restoration Policy, propped itself up and remained a potent political and military force up until mid-century. Only then did the power and prestige of the Iroquois begin to fade.

The Iroquois' success on the colonial frontier from 1650 until almost the mid-1700s had a tremendous impact on other Indians of the Eastern Woodlands. The Five Nations caused numerous Indian migrations. The movement of Indians in and out of the Western Country corresponded with the ebb and flow of Iroquois power. The seventeenth-century Beaver Wars drove tribes out of the Great Lakes region, while the Twenty Years' War and the Restoration Policy allowed them to repopulate Ohio and the West. Many Indians moved to Iroquoia, as Hurons, Eries, Conestogas, Conoys, and others were adopted into Iroquois families. The Tuscaroras moved en masse to central New York, where they became the sixth Iroquois nation. The Confederacy relocated some remnant tribal groups in Pennsylvania, where they became tributary allies protecting Iroquoia from attack. The Iroquois, by establishing hegemony in Pennsylvania, forced some tribes, like the Shawnees and Delawares, westward to escape Iroquois control. And the

Five Nations helped the Miamis, Wyandots, and other western Indians relocate along the Ohio River and its tributaries so they could establish trade with the English.

The Iroquois affected Indian populations in other ways. During the mid-1600s, the Five Nations almost exterminated the Hurons, Tobaccos, Eries, and Susquehannocks. The southern wars of the Iroquois in the following century crushed the Catawbas. By influencing many tribes to stay out of European colonial warfare in the eighteenth century, the Iroquois' quest for neutrality, at the same time, saved Indian lives. The Five Nations served as military allies. They aided the Fox Indians against the French and the Tuscaroras against the English. And they joined with northern and western tribes to fight the Flatheads.

In addition, Iroquois migrations and culture had a pronounced effect on other Indians. Some of the Five Nations moved to Canada, where, as Praying Iroquois, they intermingled with various northern tribes. Iroquois moved into Pennsylvania and had influence over Pennsylvania Indians. Other Iroquois settled along the Ohio River and, as Mingos, assumed leadership among Ohio tribes. The Confederacy itself became a prototype for the Ohio Indians' relations with the English. The Five Nations' vast contacts with the tribes of the Eastern Woodlands affected Indian cultures. The fighting, adoption of prisoners, trade, diplomacy, and introduction to new customs and local habits undoubtedly facilitated interaction and cultural exchange among the various Indians on the colonial frontier.

The Iroquois Confederacy interfered with other Indians' land claims. For example, the English recognized Iroquois title to some Pennsylvania lands based on the right of conquest. Therefore, when the English purchased those lands, they paid the Five Nations and not the Pennsylvania Indians living there. The same was true for lands in the Western Country and, to an extent, in Virginia and Maryland.

As a result, many tribes in Pennsylvania and the West had no legal title to their lands. They had been preempted by the Five Nations.

Iroquois actions greatly affected Indian-white relations throughout the colonial period. The Five Nations influenced Indian relations with the English. By serving as intermediaries, they brought many tribes into the Covenant Chain. They encouraged Indian trade at Albany through their geographic middleman position and contributed to the English-Indian trade in Ohio and the West. They helped the English control various tribes. And they assisted Indians in establishing English contacts. The Five Nations also influenced Indian relations with New France. They aided the French by attacking southern tribes loyal to the English. They weakened the French by luring many tribes away from the French alliance. At times, the Iroquois even instigated and supported Indian wars against New France. Iroquois encouragement of the Foxes, Hurons, and other Indians certainly disrupted French relations with western tribes during the first half of the eighteenth century.

Iroquois actions affected the political, military, and economic development of the French and English colonies. The Five Nations influenced the fur trade and the European contest for empire. The Iroquois had an important impact on westward expansion. During the seventeenth century, the Five Nations prevented the French from taking control of the Western Country. In the 1700s, they aided the English by selling them lands in New York, Pennsylvania, Ohio, Maryland, and Virginia. The Iroquois also advanced the English position by convincing numerous tribes to abandon the French and join the English alliance. This undermined French strength and tipped the balance of power toward the English. The Five Nations' numbers, proximity, and many allies made them important to their European neighbors. Between 1650 and 1754, Iroquois warriors aided, and sometimes terrorized, both English and

French colonists, while the Iroquois' homelands, wedged between Canada and New York, served as a strategic buffer and neutral zone keeping the French and English antagonists apart.

The Five Nations' elliptical connections shaped Indian-Indian and Indian-white relations. Their commerce nurtured colonial growth. Their diplomacy guided westward movement. And their strength determined colonial warfare. The Iroquois' influence began to wane after 1745. English and French attention turned to the Ohio Country, where the Iroquois had little authority. The Ohio tribes emerged as a new power bloc. And the Five Nations' population became dispersed as many Iroquois began moving westward. To make matters worse, the Seven Years' War forced the Confederacy to abandon neutrality. The Five Nations' Restoration Policy became totally inoperative after 1763, when the French were expelled from North America and the Iroquois Confederacy succumbed to civil war during the American Revolution.

But although the Five Nations' significance declined, their imprint on American history lived on. No Indian tribe had a greater impact on the colonial frontier than the Iroquois. The *Ho-de-no-sau-nee* would not be forgotten.

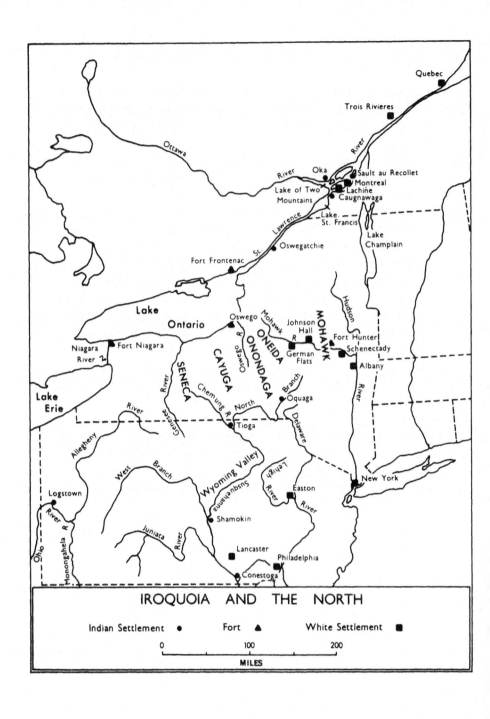

IROQUOIA AND THE NORTH

Indian Settlement ●   Fort ▲   White Settlement ■

0   100   200

MILES

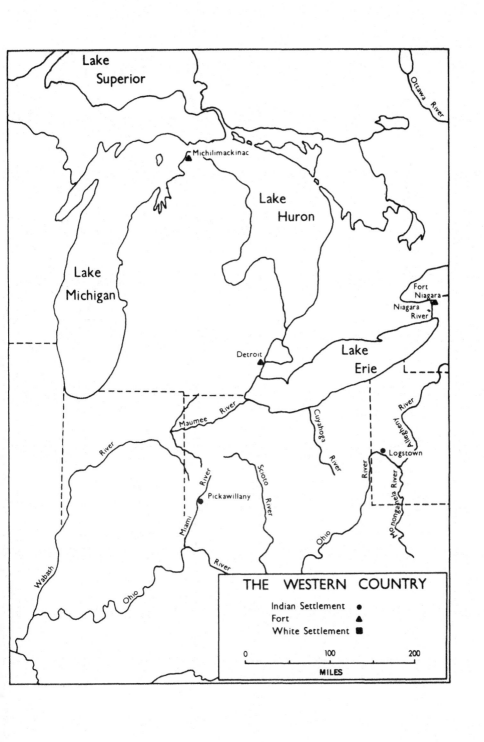

Lake Superior

Lake Huron

Lake Michigan

Lake Erie

▲ Michilimackinac

Ottawa River

Fort Niagara

Niagara River

Detroit ▲

Maumee River

Cuyahoga River

Allegheny River

● Logstown

Miami River

Scioto River

River

Monongahela River

● Pickawillany

Ohio

River

Ohio

Wabash

THE WESTERN COUNTRY

Indian Settlement ●
Fort ▲
White Settlement ■

0   100   200
MILES

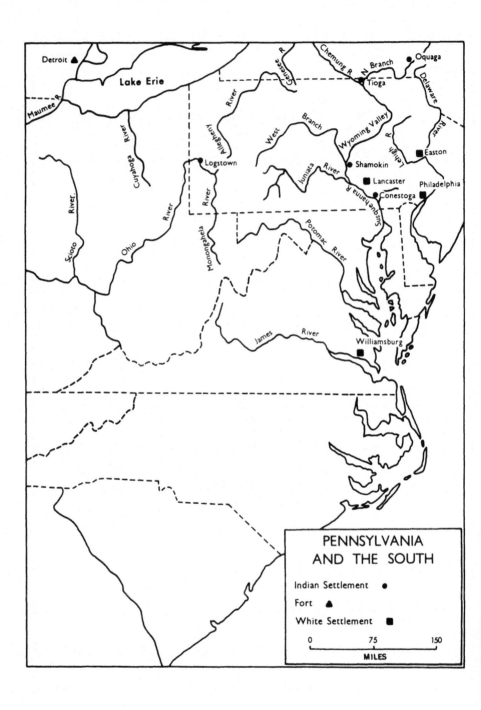

Detroit ▲

Lake Erie

Maumee R

Cuyahoga River

Scioto River.

Ohio River

Allegheny River

Monongahela River

Logstown ●

West Branch

Genesee River

Chemung R

N. Branch

Tioga ●

Oquaga ●

Wyoming Valley

Lehigh R

Delaware River

Easton ■

Juniata River

Shamokin ●

Lancaster ■

Conestoga ●

Philadelphia ■

Susquehanna R

Potomac River

James River

Williamsburg ■

PENNSYLVANIA
AND THE SOUTH

Indian Settlement ●

Fort ▲

White Settlement ■

0   75   150

MILES

Glossary

Abenakis: an Algonquian-speaking confederacy originally located in northern New England. By the early 1700s, many Abenakis had moved to the St. Lawrence region in Canada.

Algonquin (also called *Algonkin*): an Algonquian-speaking tribe that originally inhabited the St. Lawrence region of the Ottawa River. After wars with the Iroquois in the 1600s, Algonquins fled in various directions. Some moved west to Michigan where they joined with Ottawas; others moved north and east, eventually settling at Trois Rivieres and Oka.

Alumapees: see Sasoonan

Cacknawaga: see Caugnawaga

Canassatego: an Onondaga chief who served as the Iroquois' spokesman at a conference in Philadelphia in 1742. On behalf of the Iroquois Confederacy, he ordered the Delawares to abide by the Walking Purchase Treaty and leave the forks of the Delaware River. He also attended Indian conferences at Lancaster in 1744 and Philadelphia in 1749. He died in 1750.

Catawba (also called *Flatheads*): a Siouan-speaking tribe that lived in the Carolina region. Although centered in South Carolina, the tribe frequently traded with Virginians and made war on northern tribes.

Caugnawaga (also called *Cacknawaga, Caughnawaga, Sault St. Louis*): one of the most successful Canadian missions, located near Montreal. By the early 1700s, its population included 500–600 Iroquois who had migrated from central New York.

Caugnawagas (also called *Praying Iroquois*): the name given to the Iroquois living at the Caugnawaga mission.

Cherokee: an Iroquoian-speaking tribe that lived in southwest Virginia, the western Carolinas, northern Georgia, and eastern Tennessee.

Choctaw (also called *Flatheads*): a Muskhogean-speaking tribe that occupied the middle and southern Mississippi region.

Civility: a Conestoga chief who frequently aided Pennsylvania officials in their dealings with Indians during the early decades of the eighteenth century.

Conestoga: an Indian village near the confluence of Conestoga Creek and the Susquehanna River in Pennsylvania. After 1700, its population consisted mostly of Conestogas, although Shawnees, Conoys, Nanticokes, Tutelos and other migrant Indians were also residents.

Conestogas: see Susquehannocks

Conoy (also called *Ganawese*): an Algonquian-speaking tribe which lived along the Potomac River in Maryland. By the early 1700s, many Conoy Indians had relocated to the Susquehanna River region in Pennsylvania.

Corlaer: the term used by the Iroquois to address the governor of New York. An honorary title, it was first used for Arent Van Curler (the trusted friend of the Mohawks and founder of Schenectady), who died in 1667.

Covenant Chain: an economic, political, and military alliance between the English, the Iroquois, and other tribes. Its origins can be traced back to Indian-white relations in colonial New York. By the 1670s, New York emerged as the primary spokesman for the English colonies, while the Iroquois assumed the preeminent position among Indians accepting membership in the Covenant Chain. Through the Covenant Chain, the Iroquois became the number one English ally, promising to bring more tribes into the alliance.

Delawares (also called *Lenni Lenape*): a loose confederacy of Algonquian-speaking Indians who occupied portions of eastern Pennsylvania, New Jersey, and Delaware. By the mid-1700s, many Delawares had moved westward toward the Ohio country.

Detroit (originally called *Fort Ponchartrain*): a French fort and settlement established by Lamothe Cadillac in 1701 on the present site of Detroit.

Dowagenhaes: see Ottawas

Far Indians: the Iroquois' name for various tribes of the upper Great Lakes region.

Five Nations: the five Iroquoian-speaking tribes of central New York—the Mohawks, Oneidas, Onondagas, Cayugas, and Senecas—that comprised the Iroquois Confederacy. After 1712, when the Tuscaroras move from North Carolina to join them, they are also called the Six Nations.

Flatheads: a term used by the Iroquois and other northern tribes to designate the Catawbas and Choctaws, after their custom of using artificial means to flatten their children's heads.

Fox (also called *Reynard, Outagamie*): an Algonquian-speaking tribe of the upper Great Lakes region.

French Indians: any Indians allied to the French.

Fort Cataraqui: see Fort Frontenac

Fort Frontenac (also called *Fort Cataraqui*): a French fort built in 1673 at the northeast end of Lake Ontario, on the present site of Kingston, Ontario.

Fort Niagara: a French post established by Joncaire in 1720 near the location at which the Niagara River empties into Lake Ontario. By 1726, a stone fort had been built at Niagara.

Ganawese: see Conoy

Hendrick: a Mohawk chief and a close political ally of William Johnson and the English. His father was a Mohegan and his mother a Mohawk. He frequently joined English attacks against the French and was killed at the Battle of Lake George in 1755.

Hurons (also called *Wyandots, Owendatts*): a powerful Iroquoian-speaking confederacy of the upper Great Lakes region, originally settled around Lake Simcoe, and south and east of Georgian Bay. After being defeated by the Iroquois in the mid-1600s, the Indians migrated into Michigan and other areas surrounding the upper Great Lakes.

Iroquoia: the New York homelands of the Iroquois.

Iroquois: the Mohawks, Oneidas, Onondagas, Cayugas, and Senecas. *See also Five Nations.*

Johnson, William: a New York trader, politician, and soldier who sometimes served as the official liaison between the English and the Iroquois. He was a trusted friend of the Mohawks.

Joncaire (Louis Thomas de Joncaire, Sieur de Chabert, 1670–1739): a French soldier captured by the Senecas in the late 1690s, he eventually was adopted by them and became their trusted friend and advisor until his death. He also served as a French agent among the Iroquois and other tribes.

Joncaire, Chabert (Daniel Joncaire, Sieur de Chabert et Clausonne, 1716–1771): the son of Joncaire, often called "Chabert." After 1739, he succeeded his father as a French agent among the Iroquois.

Logstown: an Indian village on the Ohio River, about eighteen miles below Pittsburgh. It was originally settled by Delawares and Shawnees, but, by 1749, it had a mixed population of Delawares, Shawnees, Iroquois, Hurons, Mohicans, and Ottawas.

Miami (also called *Twightwee*): an Algonquian-speaking tribe that lived in the region southeast of Lake Michigan.

Michilimackinac: a French outpost built in 1700 on the point of land between Lakes Michigan and Huron.

Mingos: New York Iroquois who settled in Pennsylvania and Ohio.

Missisauga: an Algonquian tribe of the upper Great Lakes region. At one time it may have been a division of the Chippewa, but by the early 1700s, it was a distinct tribe, residing in the area between Lake Huron and Lake Erie.

Minisink: a tribal division of the Munsee.

Munsee: one of the main divisions of the Delawares. The Munsee originally lived on the headwaters of the Delaware River. One of the divisions of the Munsees was the Minisinks.

Nanticoke: an Algonquian-speaking tribe that lived on the eastern shore of Maryland and southern Delaware. By the mid-1700s, many Nanticokes, under Iroquois protection, had moved northward into Pennsylvania and New York.

Nipissing: an Algonquian tribe that originally occupied the area around Lake Nipissing, Ontario. By the late 1600s, many tribal members had migrated to settlements along the St. Lawrence River.

Northern Indians: the Canadian Indians who were allies of New France.

Ohio Country: the lands watered by the Ohio River and its northern tributaries, which now comprise the state of Ohio and portions of Indiana.

Ohio Indians: Indians who migrated to the Ohio Country during the eighteenth century.

Ohio Iroquois (also called *Mingos*): New York Iroquois who settled in the Ohio Country.

Onas (also called *Brother Onas*): the Iroquois' name for the proprietor of Pennsylvania. It was a play on the name for William Penn, meaning quill or feather.

Onontio: the Iroquois' name for their French "father," that is, any governor of Canada. Meaning "great mountain," it originated in the translation for the name of Governor Montmagny (governor of Canada, 1636–48).

253

Oswegatchie (also called *Swegatchy*): a French mission established in 1749 on the present site of Ogdensburg, New York.

Oswego: an English trading post and fort established in 1726 at the southeast end of Lake Ontario, on the present site of Oswego, New York.

Ottawa (also called *Waganha, Dowagenhae*): an Algonquian-speaking tribe originally located on the northern shore of Georgian Bay. The Indians later migrated to Michigan and other regions of the upper Great Lakes.

Outagamie: see Fox

Outauois: see Ottawa

Owendatts: see Hurons

Praying Iroquois: members of the Five Nations who converted to Catholicism and settled in French missions in Canada.

Quider: the Iroquois' name for Peter Schuyler, the trusted mayor of Albany and a commissioner of Indian affairs.

River Indians: the remnant bands of Algonquian-speaking Indians who lived along the Hudson River in New York.

Sasoonan (also called *Alumapees*, "Keeper of the Wampum Records"): the head chief of the Unami, one of the main divisions of the Delawares. He frequently represented his people in negotiations with the Pennsylvania government and the Iroquois. He died at Shamokin in 1747.

Sault St. Louis: see Caugnawaga.

Scarooyady: an Oneida Indian who migrated to the Ohio Country, where he became an important leader and spokesman for the Ohio Indians. He died at Lancaster in 1757.

Shamokin: an Indian village located at the fork of the Susquehanna River, near present-day Sunbury, Pennsylvania. The settlement consisted mostly of Delawares, Shawnees, and Iroquois.

Shawnee (also called *Shawanese, Chaouanon*): a highly migratory Algonquian-speaking tribe. Between 1680 and 1754,

254

many Shawnees lived in Pennsylvania and the Ohio Country.

Shickellamy: an Oneida who was sent to Shamokin by the Iroquois League Council in 1728 to watch over Indian affairs in Pennsylvania. Shickellamy was an important intermediary in negotiations involving Pennsylvania officials, the Iroquois, and Pennsylvania Indians. He died at Shamokin in 1748.

Six Nations: see Five Nations

Southern Indians: the tribes living south of Pennsylvania and the Ohio River. *See also Flatheads* and *Catawbas*.

Susquehannocks (also called *Conestogas*): a powerful Iroquoian-speaking tribe on the lower Susquehanna River in Pennsylvania and Maryland. After 1675, many tribal members moved northward into New York and Pennsylvania, where they became known as Conestogas.

Swegatchy: see Oswegatchie

Tionontadee (also called the *Tobacco Nation* or the *Petun*): an Iroquoian-speaking tribe closely related to the Hurons. The tribe originally lived in Ontario, between Lake Huron and Lake Simcoe. After its defeat by the Iroquois in 1649, it merged with the Hurons, eventually migrating to the Ohio County, where the tribe became known as the Wyandot.

Tobacco: see Tionontadee

Tuscaroras: an Iroquoian-speaking tribe that originally lived in North Carolina. After 1712, the tribe moved northward to New York, where it became part of the Iroquois Confederacy. *See also Five Nations*.

Twightwee: see Miami

Upper Nations: see Far Indians

Waganha: see Ottawa

Weiser, Conrad: Pennsylvania's official Indian interpreter and a consultant for Indian affairs.

Western Country: territory that extended from Iroquoia in the east to the lands north and south of Lake Michigan in the west; bounded by the Ohio River in the south and the Ottawa River in the north.

Western Indians (also called western tribes): Indians living in the Western Country.

Wyandots: see Hurons

Notes

ABBREVIATIONS

Cal. of State Papers	J. W. Fortescue, ed., *Calendar of State Papers, Colonial Series*
CC Papers	*The Cadwallader Colden Papers*
DHSNY	E. B. O'Callaghan, ed., *The Documentary History of the State of New York*
Eccl. Recs.	*Ecclesiastical Records of the State of New York*
Ill. Hist. Collec.	*Collections of the Illinois State Historical Library*
JP	James Sullivan, ed., *The Papers of Sir William Johnson*
JR	Reuben Gold Thwaites, ed., *Jesuit Relations and Allied Documents*
MPHC	*Michigan Pioneer and Historical Collections*
NYCD	E. B. O'Callaghan and John Brodhead, eds., *Documents Relative to the Colonial History of the State of New York*
Pa. Archives, 1st series	Samuel Hazard, ed., *Pennsylvania Archives, 1st series*
Pa. Archives, 2nd series	John Linn and William Egle, eds., *Pennsylvania Archives, 2nd Series*
Pa. Minutes	*Minutes of the Provincial Council of Pennsylvania*
Wisc. Hist. Collec.	*Report and Collections of the State Historical Society of Wisconsin*

Chapter 1

Information about Iroquois culture was drawn from numerous sources. Eyewitness accounts of Iroquois culture can be found in Reuben Gold Thwaites, ed., *Jesuit Relations and Allied Documents*. The classic account of Iroquois culture is Lewis Henry Morgan's *The League of the Iroquois*. The most recent and comprehensive study of Iroquois culture can be found in Bruce Trigger, ed., Volume XV, *Handbook of North American Indians*. Anthony F. C. Wallace studies one Iroquois tribe in *The Death and Rebirth of the Seneca*. Also useful are Bruce Trigger's studies of the Huron, a related Iroquoian tribal group. His monograph *The Hurons: Farmers of the North* provides a good summary of

Huron culture, while his two-volume work *The Children of Aataentsic: A History of the Huron People to 1660* includes much valuable information about the Iroquois.

1. George T. Hunt, *The Wars of the Iroquois: A Study in Intertribal Relations*, 34–37; Peter Wraxall, *An Abridgement of the New York Indian Records*, xliii; *NYCD*, IX, 80; *JR*, XXVII, 289–91, XXVIII, 287, XLVII, 111; *Pa. Archives, 2nd series*, VI, 9; *DHSNY*, I, 97. Additional information concerning the Iroquois' economic motivations for war can be found in Bruce Trigger, ed., *Handbook of North American Indians*, XV, 352–56, and Bruce Trigger, *Children of Aataentsic*, II, 726–30.

2. Lewis Henry Morgan, *League of the Iroquois*, 72; George Snyderman, "Behind the Tree of Peace: A Sociological Analysis of Iroquoian Warfare," 78–79; Anthony F. C. Wallace, *The Death and Rebirth of the Seneca*, 31; *DHSNY*, I, 217; Robert Livingston, *The Livingston Indian Records, 1663–1723*, 112; *Cal. of State Papers, 1689–1692*, Entry 288, 102, Entry 2257, 647; A. Wallace, *Death and Rebirth*, 103–4; Francis Parkman, *The Jesuits in North America*, 549; A. Wallace, *Death and Rebirth*, 103.

3. A. Wallace, *Death and Rebirth*, 46–47; William N. Fenton, "The Lore of the Longhouse: Myth, Ritual, and Red Power," 143.

4. Hunt, *Wars*, 68; Morgan, *League*, 40, 41; *DHSNY*, I, 232.

5. Morgan, *League*, 8, 442; Parkman, *Jesuits*, 56, 59; *DHSNY*, I, 97, 99, 127; Livingston, *Records*, 114; *NYCD*, IV, 181; Elizabeth Tooker, "The Iroquois Defeat of the Huron: A Review of Causes," 120–22; *DHSNY*, I, 219.

6. *Pa. Archives, 2nd series*, VI, 27; *DHSNY*, I, 222, 157; Tooker, "Iroquois Defeat," 117; Allen W. Trelease, "The Iroquois and the Western Fur Trade: A Problem in Interpretation," 50; Hunt, *Wars*, 9, 165–75, 171.

7. Parkman, *Jesuits*, 149, 150; Nicholas Perrot, "Memoir on the Manners, Customs, and Religion of the Savages of North America," I, 210; *Pa. Archives, 2nd Series*, VI, 11; *DHSNY*, I, 141.

8. Parkman, *Jesuits*, 548; Clarence Alvord, *The Illinois Country, 1673–1818*, 36, 37, 57; Trigger, *Handbook*, XV, 354–56.

9. *JR*, XLIII, 265; *Wisc. Hist. Collec.*, XVI, 10; A. Wallace, *Death and Rebirth*, 103; *JR*, XLIII, 265, XLV, 207; Parkman, *Jesuits*, 60; *DHSNY*, I, 11, 60; *Pa. Archives, 2nd series*, VI, 27.

10. *JR*, XLVIII, 75–77, 83, 107; Hunt, *Wars*, 134, 135; William M. Beauchamp, *A History of the New York Iroquois*, 217, 218.

11. Livingston, *Records*, 29; Hunt, *Wars*, 135; Beauchamp, *History*, 218; *Ill. Hist. Collec.*, XXIII, French Series, I, 68; Livingston, *Records*, 36; Hunt, *Wars*, 135–36; Beauchamp, *History*, 221.

12. Hunt, *Wars*, 138–39; Parkman, *Jesuits*, 546–48; Hunt, *Wars*, 137–38.

13. Hunt, *Wars*, 140–43; *NYCD*, XIII, 516; Livingston, *Records*, 48; Frederick W. Hodge, ed., *Handbook of American Indians*, I, 335–36; Trigger, ed., *Handbook*, XV, 356.

14. Propositions of Col. Henry Coursey to Iroquois, June 20, 1677, in Livingston, *Records*, 42; Beauchamp, *History*, 221.

15. Alvord, *Illinois*, 57; *JR*, LI, 169; *Pa. Archives, 2nd series*, VI, 9; *DHSNY*, I, 398; *NYCD*, IX, 80; *Ill. Hist. Collec.*, XXIII, French Series, I, 15; *Pa. Archives, 2nd series*, VI, 9.

16. *Pa. Archives, 2nd series*, VI, 9, 10.

17. *MPHC*, XXXIV, 279; Livingston, *Records*, 100; *DHSNY*, I, 213, 228; Livingston, *Records*, 116; *Eccl. Recs.*, II, 938; *DHSNY*, I, 228, 154.

Chapter 2

1. Complete coverage of Iroquois involvement in King William's War can be found in Allen W. Trelease's *Indian Affairs in Colonial New York: The Seventeenth Century*, David Hardcastle's "The Defense of Canada Under Louis XIV, 1643–1701," and W. J. Eccles' *The Canadian Frontier, 1543–1760* and *Frontenac, the Courtier Governor*. For specific events see Cadwallader Colden, *The History of the Five Indian Nations*, 54–57; Hardcastle, "The Defense of Canada," 263–68; Trelease, *Indian Affairs*, 279–97; Hardcastle, "The Defense of Canada," 314–15; *Cal. of State Papers*, col. series, 1685–1688, Entry 1431, 441, Entry 1479, 457; Trelease, *Indian Affairs*, 279–97; Francis Parkman, *Count Frontenac and New France Under Louis XIV*, 178; Pierre Charlevoix, *History and General Description of New France*, IV, 29–30. Additional information about Iroquois warfare in the late seventeenth century can be found in Bruce Trigger, ed., *Handbook of North American Indians*, XV, 431–32.
2. Colden, *History*, 101–4, 113–17; Hardcastle, "The Defense of Canada," 380, 381; *NYCD*, IV, 16–18; Parkman, *Frontenac*, 223; Trelease, *Indian Affairs*, 311–23; Hardcastle, "The Defense of Canada," 380, 381; *NYCD*, IV, 240, 294, 338, 373; Parkman, *Frontenac*, 445–49. For a view of Frontenac that contradicts Parkman's, see W. J. Eccles, *Frontenac, the Courtier Governor*. Two other works by Eccles, *France in America* and *The Canadian Frontier, 1534–1760*, provide valuable overviews of the French military strategies and actions during King William's War.
3. *NYCD*, IV, 579; Charlevoix, V, 100; Robert Livingston, *The Livingston Indian Records, 1663–1723*, 176; *NYCD*, IV, 693; Charlevoix, *Description*, V, 100, 101; *NYCD*, IV, 690; Charlevoix, *Description*, V, 100, 102.
4. *NYCD*, IV, 638, 647, 648, 649, 654–59, IX, 704. Livingston was appointed one of New York's Commissioners of Indian Affairs by Governor Bellomont. The commissioners were formally commissioned by the governor to conduct all official negotiations with the Five Nations. Much has been written about the role of the Albany commissioners, as well as the role of Albany merchants in New York-Iroquois relations. Valuable background information about the Albany Commissioners of Indian Affairs can be found in H. L. Osgood, *The American Colonies in the Eighteenth Century*, I, III, and IV, and in Thomas Elliot Norton, *The Fur Trade in Colonial New York, 1686–1776*, ch. 5. Early studies tended to condemn the Albany merchants for placing their own interests in the fur trade above those of the British. For examples, see Cadwallader Colden's writings or Charles H. McIlwain's introduction to Wraxall's *An Abridgement of the New York Indian Records*. More recent historians have treated the Albany merchants more sympathetically. See Arthur H. Buffinton, "The Policy of Albany and English Westward Expansion"; David A. Armour, "The Merchants of Albany, New York, 1686–1760"; and Patricia W. Bonomi, *A Factious People: Politics and Society in Colonial New York*.
5. Livingston, *Records*, 176; *NYCD*, IV, 693.
6. Charlevoix, *Description*, V, 99–102; *NYCD*, IV, 690.
7. Charlevoix, *Description*, V, 101, 102.
8. *NYCD*, IX, 708, 709; Charlevoix, *Description*, V, 102, 103, 99–103; *NYCD*, IX, 710, 711.
9. Frank Severance, "The Story of Joncaire," 87, 88; Colden, *History*, 179.
10. *NYCD*, IX, 708–11; Charlevoix, *Description*, V, 99–103.
11. Charlevoix, *Description*, V, 103, 104; Livingston, *Records*, 180.

12. Livingston, *Records*, 179; Charlevoix, *Description*, V, 103–5; *Pa. Archives, 2nd series*, VI, 50.
13. Charlevoix, *Description*, V, 105–8; Parkman, *Frontenac*, 441, 442.
14. Wraxall, *An Abridgement*, 34, 35; *NYCD*, IV, 729, 735, 736; for a fuller understanding of the Covenant Chain, see Francis Jennings, "The Constitutional Evolution of the Covenant Chain."
15. Charlevoix, *Description*, V, 108; *NYCD*, IX, 715–20; Charlevoix, *Description*, V, 109; Leopold LaMontagne, ed., *The Publications of the Champlain Society: Royal Fort Frontenac*, 199; *NYCD*, IX, 718–20; LaMontagne, *Royal Ft. Fron.*, 200; Charlevoix, *Description*, V, 109, 110, 111; *NYCD*, IX, 720, IV, 798; *Wisc. Hist. Collec.*, XVI, 200; *NYCD*, IX, 711.
16. *NYCD*, IX, 711; *MPHC*, XXXIII, 97.
17. *NYCD*, IV, 783.
18. Charlevoix, *Description*, V, 136.
19. *Pa. Minutes*, II, 14–17.
20. *Pa. Minutes*, II, 18; Charlevoix, *Description*, V, 138–40.
21. All decisions made by the Iroquois League Council had to be unanimous. Therefore, it is likely that many decisions had to be of a compromise nature. For a fuller explanation of unanimity on the League Council and the decision-making process, see Lewis Henry Morgan, *League of the Iroquois*, 111–13.
22. Charlevoix, *Description*, V, 141; Parkman, *Frontenac*, 443–45; Charlevoix, *Description*, V, 141–45; Parkman, *Frontenac*, 444, 445.
23. Charlevoix, *Description*, V, 144, 145; Parkman, *Frontenac*, 445–47; Charlevoix, *Description*, V, 148–49; Parkman, *Frontenac*, 448.
24. Charlevoix, *Description*, V, 150, 151.
25. Charlevoix, *Description*, V, 152; Parkman, *Frontenac*, 450, 451.
26. Parkman, *Frontenac*, 451; Charlevoix, *Description*, V, 152–54; see also Anthony F. C. Wallace, "The Origins of Iroquois Neutrality: The Grand Settlement of 1701"; Paul Wallace, *Indians In Pennsylvania*, 102; Bacqueville de La Potherie, *Histoire de l'Amerique Septentrionale* (Paris, 1722). The Montreal treaty is described by La Potherie in volume IV.
27. Wraxall, *An Abridgement*, 39–41; *NYCD*, IV, 908, 888–906.
28. Charlevoix, *Description*, V, 138–41; *Cal. of State Papers, Colonial Series, 1689–1692*, Entry 1968, 580.

Chapter 3

1. *NYCD*, IV, 337, 345; *DHSNY*, I, 690; *NYCD*, IV, 237, 305, 487; Robert Livingston, *The Livingston Indian Records, 1663–1723*, 220; Peter Wraxall, *An Abridgement of the New York Indian Records*, lxii.
2. *NYCD*, IV, 1067, 37, 55, 648, 195; Wraxall, *An Abridgement*, 120; *NYCD*, IV, 173–74, 38, 39, 20.
3. *NYCD*, IV, 62, 37, 65, 74, 487, 1067, 173, 6, 19, 435.
4. Wraxall, *An Abridgement*, 70; *NYCD*, V, 217; Wraxall, *An Abridgement*, 113. For additional information concerning Indians and alcohol, see Wilcomb E. Washburn, *The Indian in America*, 107–10; Nancy O. Lurie, "The World's Oldest On-Going Protest Demonstration: North American Indian Drinking Patterns," 311–32.
5. *NYCD*, IV, 608, 579, 654, 701; Francis Parkman, *A Half-Century of Conflict*, 10, 11; *NYCD*, IV, 658; Wraxall, *An Abridgement*, 63; *NYCD*, V, 382, 383.

6. *NYCD*, IV, 294, 492, 564, 729; Wraxall, *An Abridgement*, 34, 44; *NYCD*, V, 226; Wraxall, *An Abridgement*, 78; *NYCD*, IV, 488, 768, 505, 22, 654; Wraxall, *An Abridgement*, 117.
7. *NYCD*, IV, 373, 487; Wraxall, *An Abridgement*, 57, 58, 48.
8. See Parkman, *Jesuits*, chapter 20; Leopold LaMontagne, ed., *Publications of the Champlain Society: Royal Fort Frontenac*, 208.
9. *JR*, LXV, 33–35.
10. *Pa. Archives, 2nd series*, VI, 12; *Eccl. Recs.*, II, 879; *DHSNY*, I, 230, 154; *JR*, LXVII, 205; *Eccl. Recs.*, II, 879; *Pa. Archives, 2nd series*, VI, 22; *NYCD*, IV, 40; Robert Livingston, *Records*, 171; Pierre Charlevoix, *History and General Description of New France*, V, 91, 155; Cadwallader Colden, "History of the Five Indian Nations, for the Years 1707–1720" (hereafter cited as "History . . . 1707–1720"), 360.
11. Livingston, *Records*, 134, 157; Charelvoix, *Description*, IV, 250, V, 78, 99–111; *NYCD*, IV, 690, 47, 1067; Charlevoix, *Description*, V, 76; *NYCD*, IV, 85; Charlevoix, *Description*, V, 50; *NYCD*, IV, 342; Colden, "History . . . 1707–1720," 361, 362; Wraxall, *An Abridgement*, 69, 91; Charlevoix, *Description*, V, 165; Livingston, *Records*, 208; *MPHC*, XXXIII, 106; Livingston, *Records*, 197; Wraxall, *An Abridgement*, 52; Charlevoix, *Description*, V, 203.
12. For information concerning factionalism among Native Americans, see Robert J. Berkhofer, Jr., "The Political Context of a New Indian History," 357–82; and P. Richard Metcalf, "Who Should Rule at Home? Native American Politics and Indian-White Relations," 651–65.
13. *NYCD*, IV, 13, 38, 168, 169, 183, 294, 500; *DHSNY*, I, 338; Lawrence H. Gipson, *The British Empire Before the American Revolution*, V, 49; Herbert Osgood, *The American Colonies in the Eighteenth Century*, I, 473; Parkman, *Half-Century*, 22, 327; *NYCD*, IV, 906.
14. Parkman, *Half-Century*, 17, 22, 29; *DHSNY*, IV, 240; Wraxall, *An Abridgement*, 39–41; *NYCD*, IV, 906, 911.
15. Parkman, *Half-Century*, 15; Wraxall, *An Abridgement*, lxv; *NYCD*, V, 559, 586; Douglas Leach, *The Northern Colonial Frontier, 1607–1763*, 152.
16. *NYCD*, IV, 500, 597, 693; Wraxall, *An Abridgement*, 83, 243; *NYCD*, V, 544, IV, 789, V, 275; Wraxall, *An Abridgement*, 47, 95, 468; Colden, "History . . . 1707–1720," 368, 408.

Chapter 4

1. *NYCD*, IV, 982–90, V, 42, IX, 736, 737, 746, 767, 766, 814; Pierre Charlevoix, *History and General Description of New France*, V, 155, 159, 164, 165, 167, 168, 179, 203; Robert Livingston, *The Livingston Indian Records, 1663–1723*, 187, 193, 194, 201; Peter Wraxall, *An Abridgement of the New York Indian Records*, 46, 47, 48, 58, 60, 63; Cadwallader Colden, "History . . . 1707–1720," 361, 362, 363, 364, 368, 370; *MPHC*, XXXIII, 367, 370, 396.
2. *NYCD*, IX, 817, V, 73; Colden, "History . . . 1707–1720," 372; *Pa. Minutes*, II, 461; Livingston, *Records*, 206–9; Wraxall, *An Abridgement*, 69; Colden, "History . . . 1707–1720," 378.
3. Livingston, *Records*, 210–11; Colden, "History . . . 1707–1720," 376–78, 380; Charlevoix, *Description*, V, 215, 216; *NYCD*, IX, 38, 828.
4. Francis Parkman, *A Half-Century of Conflict*, 104–10; Colden, "History . . . 1707–1720," 380.
5. Charlevoix, *Description*, V, 222–24, 221.

6. Charlevoix, *Description*, V, 223, 224, 236; *NYCD*, IX, 843.
7. Parkman, *Half-Century*, 104–10, 121–22. For complete coverage of the Iroquois' visit to London, see R. P. Bond, *Queen Anne's American Kings.*
8. Colden, "History . . . 1707–1720," 403; Wraxall, *An Abridgement*, 91; *NYCD*, V, 270.
9. Charlevoix, *Description*, V, 236–37; Colden, "History . . . 1707–1720," 398, 392; *NYCD*, IX, 852, V, 267–70.
10. Charlevoix, *Description*, V, 236; Colden, "History . . . 1707–1720," 402–8; *NYCD*, IX, 856; Wraxall, *An Abridgement*, 91.
11. *NYCD*, V, 267–70; Wraxall, *An Abridgement*, 91; Colden, "History . . . 1707–20," 404–6; Parkman, *Half-Century*, 127–33; Wraxall, *An Abridgement*, 92; Colden, "History . . . 1707–20," 408.
12. Colden, "History . . . 1707–20," 408; *NYCD*, V, 278.
13. *MPHC*, XXXIII, 528–32; Charlevoix, *Description*, V, 256.
14. *NYCD*, VI, 289–303, 282, 646, X, 2, 18; *CC Papers*, III, 106, 133, 137; *Pa. Minutes*, V, 5–10, 20–25.
15. *JP*, I, 42; *NYCD*, VI, 647, 305, 649; Wraxall, *An Abridgement*, 244; *NYCD*, VI, 650; Wraxall, *An Abridgement*, 247.
16. Milton Hamilton, *Sir William Johnson: Colonial American, 1715–1763*, 8, 45; Wraxall, *An Abridgement*, 245; *JP*, IX, 4.
17. *NYCD*, VI, 654; Wraxall, *An Abridgement*, 247; *CC Papers*, III, 230, 233; *JP*, I, 54, 55; *NYCD*, IX, 36, 67; Wraxall, *An Abridgement*, 248; *NYCD*, VI, 317–25; *CC Papers*, III, 263; *JP*, I, 62.
18. *JP*, I, 59, 68; *NYCD*, VI, 314, 659, 343, 358, 390; *Pa. Archives, 1st series*, I, 746; *JP*, I, 63, 68, 72, 73, 77, 80, 81, 82, 83, 93, 95, 107–10, 120, XIII, 7, IX, 8.
19. *NYCD*, VI, 366–72, 663; *Pa. Archives*, 1st series, I, 749, 750, 751, 761; *Pa. Minutes*, V, 137; *NYCD*, X, 91, 94.
20. *CC Papers*, III, 404, 406; *Pa. Minutes*, V, 86, 87; *JP*, I, 167; *NYCD*, VI, 383, 671, X, 86, 91, 94, 97, 99, 103, 111, 112, 124, 127, 129, 132, 172, 184–88.
21. *NYCD*, VI, 485, 486, 489–98, 505, 506, 515; *JP*, I, 231, 908, IX, 41, 47; *Pa. Archives, 1st series*, II, 28; *Pa. Minutes*, V, 467; *JP*, I, 227, 288, 914, IX, 129, X, 108; *NYCD*, VI, 538, 546, 547, 589, 590, 706, 743, X, 205–8, 228, 265–69.
22. *Ill. Hist. Collec.*, XXIX, 48, 49, 54, 185, 188, 198, 627, 631; *JP*, XIII, 11; *Wisc. Hist. Collec.*, XVIII, 11, 12; *Pa. Minutes*, V, 299, 307–15, 323, 433–36; *NYCD*, VI, 456, 509, 487, X, 178, 179, 200–202, 229, 240–44.
23. *NYCD*, VI, 476, 484, 485, 692; *JP*, I, 909; *Ill. Hist. Collec.*, XXIX, 97; *Wisc. Hist. Collec.*, XVII, 36–56; *NYCD*, VI, 547, 589, X, 219, 220; *JP*, I, 276–79, 290, IX, 61; *Pa. Minutes*, V, 433, 434, 437, 450.
24. *JP*, I, 296, 338, IX, 80–82; *NYCD*, VI, 713; *Pa. Minutes*, V, 530, 531, 533, 534; *JP*, I, 916; *Pa. Archives, 1st series*, II, 233; Howard H. Peckham, *The Colonial Wars, 1689–1762*, 127, 128; *NYCD*, VI, 778, 779, X, 205–8, 233, 235, 240–45, 255, 256; *JP*, IX, 106, 107; *Pa. Minutes*, V, 608, 614, 615, 701, 702, 693, 735; VI, 36, 134, 154–59, 183; *NYCD*, VI, 796, 797.
25. *JP*, IX, 69, 108, XIII, 25; *NYCD*, VI, 781–88, 808, 809.
26. *JP*, IX, 110–15.
27. *NYCD*, VI, 799, 853–84. For excellent background material on colonial delegates, see Hamilton, *Sir William Johnson*, 100–112.
28. *NYCD*, VI, 897–99.
29. *NYCD*, VI, 887, 867, 887.
30. *JP*, IX, 129, I, 430; *NYCD*, X, 263, 265–69, VI, 923; *Pa. Minutes*, VI, 181, 182, 219.

31. Thomas Elliot Norton, *The Fur Trade in Colonial New York, 1686–1776*, 27–34; *NYCD*, IX, 751, 1081, IV, 1067, V, 441, 727–30, 861; Wraxall, *An Abridgement*, 47, 58, 100, 101, 140, 174, 188, 195, 203; Livingston, *Records*, 229, 232–35; Leopold LaMontagne, ed., *The Publications of the Champlain Society: Royal Fort Frontenac*, 217; *MPHC*, XXXIII, 460.

32. Wraxall, *An Abridgement*, 47, 60, 174; *NYCD*, V, 220, 384, 866.

33. *NYCD*, IV, 982–91, V, 217–23, 859–69, 960–69; Livingston, *Records*, 226; *Pa. Minutes*, III, 120–33, 192–202, 435–51, IV, 86, 653; *NYCD*, IX, 817, V, 272; Colden, "History . . . 1707–20," 422; *MPHC*, XXXIII, 118; Colden, "History . . . 1707–20," 370; *Wisc. Hist. Collec.*, XVI, 382; Colden, "History . . . 1707–20," 369; *NYCD*, IX, 1075; Wraxall, *An Abridgement*, 221–24; *Pa. Minutes*, IV, 501; Wraxall, *An Abridgement*, 96, 203, 228; *Pa. Minutes*, IV, 563–654, 560.

34. Wraxall, *An Abridgement*, 39, 40, 131, 168; *NYCD*, V, 783–85, VI, 897.

35. *NYCD*, IV, 987–88; Livingston, *Records*, 184; Wraxall, *An Abridgement*, 70; *NYCD*, V, 217–26; Wraxall, *An Abridgement*, 77; Colden, "History . . . 1707–20," 399–402; *NYCD*, V, 246–49, 278; Colden, "History . . . 1707–20," 411; Wraxall, *An Abridgement*, 96; Colden, "History . . . 1707–20," 412; Wraxall, *An Abridgement*, 115; Livingston, *Records*, 224, 225; *NYCD*, V, 542–44, 550; Wraxall, *An Abridgement*, 131, 168, 169, 170; *NYCD*, V, 799, 859–69, 963; Wraxall, *An Abridgement*, 52; Colden, "History . . . 1707–20," 363; Wraxall, *An Abridgement*, 54; Colden, "History . . . 1707–20," 367; *NYCD*, VI, 876.

36. Livingston, *Records*, 190; *NYCD*, V, 246–49; Colden, "History . . . 1707–20," 416; *NYCD*, V, 382; Livingston, *Records*, 226.

37. *NYCD*, IV, 986; Livingston, *Records*, 193; Wraxall, *An Abridgement*, 47, 60, 63, 86, 87, 95; Colden, "History . . . 1707–20," 426; *Pa. Minutes*, III, 125, 129; Wraxall, *An Abridgement*, 174; *NYCD*, V, 863–64; Wraxall, *An Abridgement*, 188; *NYCD*, V, 967–68; Wraxall, *An Abridgement*, 195; *Pa. Minutes*, IV, 92; *NYCD*, VI, 265.

38. *Pa. Minutes*, III, 149; Wraxall, *An Abridgement*, 160, 163; *Pa. Minutes*, III, 274–75.

39. *NYCD*, V, 905; Wraxall, *An Abridgement*, 187, 195; *CC Papers*, II, 257–60.

40. Wraxall, *An Abridgement*, 70; Colden, "History . . . 1707–20," 414; Wraxall, *An Abridgement*, 113; *Pa. Minutes*, III, 120–33, 193, 271–75, 411, 577–80, IV, 90–94; Wraxall, *An Abridgement*, 160–62, 173, 174, 176, 183, 207; *JR*, LXVII, 39–41.

41. Wraxall, *An Abridgement*, 179; *NYCD*, VI, 15–100; Cadawallader Colden to Governor Clarke, November 3, 1736, in *CC Papers*, II, 158–60; *Pa. Minutes*, IV, 92–94, 699–740; *NYCD*, V, 960, 850–51.

42. Wraxall, *An Abridgement*, 218, 230, 70, 176; William Beauchamp, *A History of the New York Iroquois*, 290; *NYCD*, IV, 888, 908–11; Wraxall, *An Abridgement*, 34, 29, 70, 77, 144, 171; *NYCD*, IV, 691, 748, V, 42, 222, 659.

43. Frank Severance, "The Story of Joncaire," 93; *NYCD*, IV, 968, 1067; Livingston, *Records*, 197; *MPHC*, XXXIII, 207; Colden, "History . . . 1707–20," 414, 542; Severance, "Joncaire," 108; *Wisc. Hist. Collec.*, XVI, 314; Colden, "History . . . 1707–20," 425; Wraxall, *An Abridgement*, 120, 48; Severance, "Joncaire," 96; *Wisc. Hist. Collec.*, IX, 246; *NYCD*, IX, 819–26; LaMontagne, *Royal Ft. Frontenac*, 205–8; Joncaire to d'Aigremont in Severance, "Joncaire," 101, 115–28; *NYCD*, V, 588.

44. Begon to Dupuy, October 31, 1725, in LaMontagne, *Royal Ft. Frontenac*, 217; *NYCD*, IX, 1081; Severance, "Joncaire," 169.

45. Wraxall, *An Abridgement*, 163.

46. Severance, "Joncaire," 165–67.
47. LaMontagne, *Royal Ft. Frontenac,* 218; *DHSNY,* IV, 240, 241; LaMontagne, *Royal Ft. Frontenac,* 225; *NYCD,* IX, 1081, 1099; Charles Hanna, *The Wilderness Trail,* I, 315, 316, 329; *Pa. Archives, 1st series,* I, 662, *NYCD,* VI, 742, 743.
48. *Pa. Archives, 2nd series,* VI, 51; *NYCD,* IX, 736.
49. *MPHC,* XXXIII, 207, 391; Charlevoix, *Description,* V, 223, 236; *NYCD,* IX, 843; Wraxall, *An Abridgement,* 48, 172, 207, 219; *NYCD,* V, 591–623, IX, 1052; Charlevoix, *Description,* V, 159; *MPHC,* XXXIII, 190, 191; Charlevoix, *Description,* V, 165; *NYCD,* IX, 759, 761, 765, 767, 768, 766; Charlevoix, *Description,* V, 179; *NYCD,* IX, 775; *Wisc. Hist. Collec.,* XVI, 228–30, 240–42; *MPHC,* XXXIII, 285–87, 303–13, 328–30, 403; *Wisc. Hist. Collec.,* XVI, 263–64; *NYCD,* V, 243; LaMontagne, *Royal Ft. Frontenac,* 209; *MPHC,* XXXIII, 589–93; Wraxall, *An Abridgement,* 148; *NYCD,* IX, 1082, 1086–88.
50. *NYCD,* IX, 746; Colden, "History . . . 1707–20," 370; Wraxall, *An Abridgement,* 63, 93; *NYCD,* IX, 936, 1088, 876.
51. Charlevoix, *Description,* V, 155; *NYCD,* IX, 736, IV, 1067; Wraxall, *An Abridgement,* 48; Colden, "History . . . 1707–20," 370; *JR,* LXVII, 203, 205, LXVIII, 261–79, LXIX, 35–39; *JP,* I, 199, 288; *NYCD,* X, 203, 204, 263, VI, 589.
52. Parkman, *Half-Century,* 26.
53. *JR,* LXVII, 205, LXVIII, 275, LXIX, 37.
54. *NYCD,* IV, 987; Callieres and Beauharnois to the Minister, Nov. 3, 1702, in LaMontagne, *Royal Ft. Frontenac,* 204; *NYCD,* IX, 736; Wraxall, *An Abridgement,* 46, 47, 75; *NYCD,* V, 960.
55. *NYCD,* IV, 987, 988, V, 845, 846, IX, 1011, VI, 870, 871, 873, 897.
56. Wraxall, *An Abridgement,* 221, 222; *NYCD,* IX, 1105. 1112.
57. Charlevoix, *Description,* V, 167–68; *CC Papers,* I, 129–30; Wraxall, *An Abridgement,* 219.
58. J. C. B., *Travels in New France,* 25; *JP,* IX, 125, 129; *NYCD,* IV, 701, 484; *Wisc. Hist. Collec.,* XVII, 172; *MPHC,* XXXIV, 109; Wraxall, *An Abridgement,* 221; *NYCD,* IX, 1075; *Pa. Minutes,* IV, 563, 564.
59. Parkman, *Half-Century,* 27; *NYCD,* IV, 1067; Charlevoix, *Description,* V, 165, 236, 237; Livingston, *Records,* 212; Colden, "History . . . 1707–20," 386; *NYCD,* X, 129, 263; *JP,* I, 914, IX, 108, 129; *NYCD,* IX, 864, 1041, 1099, V, 570, 727, 728; Colden, "History . . . 1707–20," 402, 424, 430, 432; Charlevoix, *Description,* V, 256; Severance, "Joncaire," 107, 108; *CC Papers,* I, 129, 130; Wraxall, *An Abrigement,* 189, 207; *Wisc. Hist. Collec.,* XVII, 420.
60. *NYCD,* IX, 745; Wraxall, *An Abridgement,* 46, 58.
61. *NYCD,* V, 42, 228; Wraxall, *An Abridgement,* 69, 91; *NYCD,* V, 85; Colden, "History . . . 1707–20," 362; *NYCD,* IV, 1067, V, 907, 908; Charlevoix, *Description,* V, 157; Colden, "History . . . 1707–20," 361; Wraxall, *An Abridgement,* 164, 166, 168, 169; Severance, "Joncaire," 146; *NYCD,* VI, 135, 853–99; Peckham, *Col. Wars,* 122.
62. *NYCD,* IX, 765; *Wisc. Hist. Collec.,* XVI, 240; *MPHC,* XXXIII, 453, 529, 403; Wraxall, *An Abridgement,* 103, 204, 52, 171; *NYCD,* IX, 884; Colden, "History . . . 1707–20," 363, 432; *JR,* LXVII, 191–93, 205; Wraxall, *An Abridgement,* 50; Colden, "History . . . 1707–20," 394; Parkman, *Half-Century,* 54; Norton, *Fur Trade,* 126.
63. *NYCD,* V, 907, 908.
64. LaMontagne, *Royal Ft. Frontenac,* 204; *NYCD,* IX, 736, 1081, 1082; Wraxall, *An Abridgement,* 48; *Wisc. Hist. Collec.,* IX, 246; *NYCD,* IX, 811; Norton, *Fur Trade,* 122, 126; Parkman, *Half-Century,* 28; Wraxall, *An Abridgement,* 48, 68,

102, 127; Colden, "History . . . 1707–20," 419; Wraxall, *An Abridgement*, 124, 125; *NYCD*, VI, 112, IX, 1081.

65. *NYCD*, IX, 818; LaMontagne, *Royal Ft. Frontenac*, 207; Charlevoix, *Description*, V, 236, 237; *NYCD*, IX, 885, 952, 954, 1085, VI, 897.

66. The English and French understood that their western policies were tied to Iroquois actions. Much has been written about the nature and wisdom of English and French western policies. Good starting points for understanding these strategies are Ray Allen Billington, *Westward Expansion: A History of the American Frontier*, chapters V, VI, VII, and David Hawke, *The Colonial Experience*, 315–33. Overviews of British western policies and relations with Indians can be found in Douglas Leach, *The Northern Colonial Frontier, 1607–1763*; Lawrence H. Gipson, *The British Empire Before the American Revolution*, vols. III, IV, V, VI; Herbert L. Osgood, *The American Colonies in the Eighteenth Century*, 4 vols; and Charles Andrews, *The Colonial Period of American History*, 4 vols. Accounts of how specific aspects of British western policy affected the Iroquois are included in Allen W. Trelease, *Indian Affairs in Colonial New York: The Seventeenth Century*; Robert Livingston, *The Livingston Indian Records*; C. H. McIlwain, ed., Peter Wraxall's *An Abridgement of the New York Indian Records*; Thomas E. Norton's *The Fur Trade in Colonial New York*; Lawrence Leder, *Robert Livingston, 1654–1728, and the Politics of Colonial New York*; R. P. Bond, *Queen Anne's American Kings*; and Milton Hamilton, *Sir William Johnson: Colonial American*. Studies of French western policy and relations with Indians include W. J. Eccles, *The Canadian Frontier, 1534–1760*; Yves F. Zoltvany, "New France and the West, 1701–1713"; and Francis Parkman, *Count Frontenac and New France Under Louis XIV*. For a view that contradicts Parkman's, see W. J. Eccles' *Frontenac, the Courtier Governor*. For a better understanding of the Anglo-French rivalry, see Francis Parkman, *A Half-Century of Conflict*; Walter Dorn, *Competition for Empire, 1740–1763*; Max Savelle, "The American Balance of Power and European Diplomacy, 1713–1778"; Joseph Rutledge, *Century of Conflict: The Struggle Between the French and British in Colonial America*; G. H. Guttridge, *The Colonial Policy of William III in America and the West Indies*; and Justin Winsor, ed., *The English and French in North America, 1689–1763*. Comparisons of French and English relations with Indians can be found in Wilbur Jacobs, *Wilderness Politics and Indian Gifts*, and in Randolph Downes, *Council Fires on the Upper Ohio*.

Chapter 5

1. *NYCD*, IV, 488; *Pa. Archives, 2nd series*, VI, 51–60; *NYCD*, IX, 885–92, V, 622, IX, 1052–58; Robert Livingston, *The Livingston Indian Records*, 220; *NYCD*, IX, 1056; *DHSNY*, IV, 240; Pierre Charlevoix, *History and General Description of New France*, V, 236; *MPHC*, XXXIII, 497; *NYCD*, IX, 854, IV, 488, 768, 654, 729; Livingston, *Records*, 197, 198; *MPHC*, XXXIII, 391; Leopold LaMontagne, ed., *The Publications of the Champlain Society: Royal Fort Frontenac*, 205, 206; *NYCD*, V, 271; Peter Wraxall, *An Abridgement of the New York Indian Records*, 94; LaMontagne, *Royal Ft. Frontenac*, 209; *NYCD*, V, 545, 543.

2. *NYCD*, IX, 722; Charlevoix, *Description*, V, 141–54; Anthony F. C. Wallace, "The Origins of Iroquois Neutrality: The Grand Settlement of 1701," 233–35; William A. Beauchamp, *A History of the New York Iroquois*, 255; *NYCD*, IX, 722.

3. Charlevoix, *Description*, V, 165; *NYCD*, IX, 765, 767, 768; Charlevoix, *Descrip-*

tion, V, 179; *MPHC*, XXXIII, 285; *Wisc. Hist. Collec.*, XVI, 230; Charlevoix, *Description*, V, 225; Wraxall, *An Abridgement*, 78; *NYCD*, IX, 848, V, 243; *MPHC*, XXXIII, 592; *NYCD*, IX, 1089.
4. Wraxall, *An Abridgement*, 34.
5. *NYCD*, V, 728, 729, 730.
6. *NYCD*, V, 691, 748; *MPHC*, XXXIII, 118; *NYCD*, IV, 979–81, IX, 751, 743; Livingston, *Records*, 196; *NYCD*, IX, 763, 774, 811; Cadwallader Colden, "History . . . 1707–20," 367, 370, 372; Wraxall, *An Abridgement*, 55, 58, 59, 66, 67, 68; *NYCD*, V, 65; *MPHC*, XXXIII, 395, 431. The Iroquois' middleman position has been interpreted in various ways. Some historians have argued that seventeenth-century Iroquois traders obtained English goods at Albany and carried them westward, where they were then exchanged for western Indians' peltry. For example, see Charles McIlwain's introduction to Peter Wraxall's *An Abridgement*, xlii; George T. Hunt, *The Wars of the Iroquois;* and Barbara Graymont, *The Iroquois in the American Revolution*, 24, 27. In 1962, Allen W. Trelease exposed the flaws in the McIlwain-Hunt thesis that the Iroquois were economic middlemen. In his article, "The Iroquois and the Western Fur Trade: A Problem in Interpretation," 48–51, Trelease shows that the Iroquois might have had ambitions to become economic middlemen and might even have served as middlemen on occasion, but overall they never played a major role as middlemen between the English and western tribes during the seventeenth century. Recent historians have generally accepted Trelease's position. For example, see Bruce Trigger, ed., *Handbook of North American Indians*, XV, 353; Bruce Trigger, *The Children of Aataentsic*, II, 729; and Thomas Norton, *The Fur Trade in Colonial New York, 1686–1776*, 13, 14, 17, 34–38. While accepting Trelease's position, one must be careful not to reject all types of middleman activity by the Iroquois. Trelease was correct in concluding that the Iroquois were not "economic" middlemen during the 1600s, but he overlooked their important role as "geographic" middlemen in the 1700s. As my evidence shows, the Iroquois, throughout the first half of the eighteenth century, sought to develop a geographic middleman position by drawing western tribes through Iroquoia to the Albany or Oswego trade. This policy was an excellent blend of geopolitics and economic diplomacy, for it enabled the Iroquois to obtain peace with the western tribes, hunting and traveling privileges in the Western Country, and trade with Indian travelers who came into Iroquoia.
7. Colden, "History . . . 1707–20," 381–83, 384–86.
8. Colden, "History . . . 1707–20," 403, 417, 420, 424, 430–32; Wraxall, *An Abridgement*, 112, 122; *Wisc. Hist. Collec.*, XVI, 383; Frank Severance, "The Story of Joncaire," 111; *MPHC*, XXXIII, 594; Wraxall, *An Abridgement*, 123; *Wisc. Hist. Collec.*, XVI, 395.
9. *NYCD*, V, 586; Livingston, *Records*, 232–35; *Wisc. Hist. Collec.*, XVI, 399; *NYCD*, V, 693; Wraxall, *An Abridgement*, 144, 159; *NYCD*, IX, 952, 953; Wraxall, *An Abridgement*, 171, 173, 197; *NYCD*, IX, 1049, IV, 112, 113, VI, 135; *Wisc. Hist. Collec.*, XVII, 409, 446; *NYCD*, VI, 366, 388, 537, 538, 714; *JP*, I, 105, 183, XIII, 11, IX, 61, 78, 79, 125–28; *Ill. Hist. Collec.*, XXIX, 347, 348.
10. Wraxall, *An Abridgement*, 148, 70, 102; Colden, "History . . . 1707–20," 419.
11. *MPHC*, XXXIII, 445; *Wisc. Hist. Collec.*, XVI, 334, 335; *NYCD*, V, 741, IX, 998; Colden, "History . . . 1707–20," 383; Burnet to Board of Trade, June 25, 1723, in Severance, "Joncaire," 143; *NYCD*, V, 911; *MPHC*, XXXIII, 415, 416.
12. *NYCD*, IV, 990, V, 218, 221, 374, VI, 135; Wraxall, *An Abridgement*, 62, 64; *CC Papers*, I, 131; *NYCD*, V, 374, 715, 716, 861, 963, VI, 102.

13. Colden, "History . . . 1707–20," 426; Wraxall, *An Abridgement*, 204, 205; *NYCD*, V, 225; Colden, "History . . . 1707–20," 392, 393; *NYCD*, V, 659; Trelease, "The Iroquois," 45.
14. Wraxall, *An Abridgement*, 111, 188, 195.
15. Colden, "History . . . 1707–20," 412, 425, 430.
16. *NYCD*, V, 586, 757, 740, 760–63; Wraxall, *An Abridgement*, 161.
17. *NYCD*, IX, 646–47; Trelease, "The Iroquois," 43; *NYCD*, IX, 822; Severance, "Joncaire," 102; Memorial written by John Maddox, Anthony Sadusdus, and John Fiskes, August 8, 1730, in *Pa. Archives, 1st series*, I, 265; *NYCD*, IX, 1081, 1088, 1089–91; Thomas Elliot Norton, *The Fur Trade in Colonial New York, 1686–1776*, 34–38.
18. *JR*, LXV, 253; Charlevoix, *Description*, V, 257; Beauchamp, *History*, 290; Wraxall, *An Abridgement*, 87; Colden, "History . . . 1707–20," 409–10; Wraxall, *An Abridgement*, 218, 230; Colden, "History . . . 1707–20," 420, 421.
19. Colden, "History . . . 1707–20," 364; Wraxall, *An Abridgement*, 64, 70, 176; *NYCD*, IX, 751; Colden, "History . . . 1707–20," 368; *NYCD*, IX, 894, 1086; Colden, "History . . . 1707–20," 368; Wraxall, *An Abridgement*, 214; *NYCD*, VI, 266.
20. *Wisc. Hist. Collec.*, XVI, 345; *NYCD*, IX, 953; Wraxall, *An Abridgement*, 163; *MPHC*, XXXIV, 73, 75, 76; Lawrence Henry Gipson, *The British Empire Before the American Revolution*, IV, 166; *NYCD*, IX, 1027; Douglas Leach, *The Northern Colonial Frontier, 1607–1763*, 158; Beauchamp, *History*, 293.
21. Livingston, *Records*, 192, 193; *NYCD*, V, 249; Wraxall, *An Abridgement*, 96; Colden, "History . . . 1707–20," 411; Wraxall, *An Abridgement*, 115; *NYCD*, V, 542, 544, 861, IV, 888, 908–11; Wraxall, *An Abridgement*, 39, 40; *NYCD*, V, 799–801.
22. *MPHC*, XXXIII, 171, 172; Livingston, *Records*, 210; *MPHC*, XXXIII, 592, 593; *NYCD*, IX, 1081; *Pa. Minutes*, IV, 565; *NYCD*, IX, 1099; Sieur Navarre's Report to Sieur de Celeron, 1743, in Charles Hanna, *The Wilderness Trail*, I, 316; *Pa. Minutes*, V, 351; Hanna, *Wilderness Trail*, I, 311; *NYCD*, VI, 303.
23. Colden, "History . . . 1707–20," 367; *JR*, LXVII, 145; *MPHC*, XXXIV, 150; Rev. John Heckewelder, "An Account of the History, Manners, and Customs of the Indian Natives who once inhabited Pennsylvania and the Neighboring States," 116.
24. *NYCD*, IX, 828; *Wisc. Hist. Collec.*, XVI, 262; Colden, "History . . . 1707–20," 409, 410; *MPHC*, XXXIII, 537; *Wisc. Hist. Collec.*, XVI, 333, XVII, 280.
25. For examples of Iroquois-western Indian war parties, see chapter 7, The Southern Wars; Francis Parkman, *A Half-Century of Conflict*, 196; *MPHC*, XXXIII, 537, 538, XXXIV, 69; *Wisc. Hist. Collec.*, XVI, 289, XVII, 102, 109, 110; *NYCD*, IX, 863; *MPHC*, XXXIII, 431; Wraxall, *An Abridgement*, 70, 71, 74; *NYCD*, IX, 863; *Wisc. Hist. Collec.*, XVI, 310, 394, 417; *NYCD*, V, 693–97; Wraxall, *An Abridgement*, 144, 145; *NYCD*, IX, 1082, VI, 300; *Pa. Minutes*, III, 440, IV, 84; *NYCD*, VI, 178; *Pa. Minutes*, IV, 586.
26. *Wisc. Hist. Collec.*, XVII, 446, 447, XVIII, 67; *NYCD*, VI, 372, 388, 456, 509, 484, 486, 487, 538, 714, X, 21, 138, 141, 143, 200; *Ill. Hist. Collec.*, XXIX, 38, 48, 49, 97; *NYCD*, X, 23, 24, 83, 114, 138, VI, 366; Hanna, *Wilderness Trail*, I, 324; *JP*, I, 97; *Pa. Minutes*, V, 72; *Pa. Archives, 1st series*, I, 751; *CC Papers*, III, 407.
27. *NYCD*, VI, 562, 926; *Ill. Hist. Collec.*, XXIX, 166, 167, 168, 169, 176, 188, 198, 199; *Pa. Archives, 2nd series*, VI, 141; *JP*, IX, 130, I, 430, 431.
28. *JR*, LXVII, 191–93, 203–5; *Wisc. Hist. Collec.*, XVIII, 17, 18.
29. Livingston, *Records*, 184, 190; *NYCD*, IX, 767; *MPHC*, XXXIII, 328; Colden,

"History . . . 1707–20," 362, 364, 365, 369; Wraxall, *An Abridgement*, 48; Colden, "History . . . 1707–20," 361; Wraxall, *An Abridgement*, 50.

30. Charlevoix, *Description*, V, 215, 216; Livingston, *Records*, 212; *NYCD*, IX, 834.

31. Colden, "History . . . 1707–20," 409; Iroquois message to the Caugnawagas in Severance, "Joncaire," 108; Wraxall, *An Abridgement*, 103; Colden, "History . . . 1707–20," 428, 429; *NYCD*, IX, 878.

32. *NYCD*, IX, 881; Livingston, *Records*, 231.

33. Wraxall, *An Abridgement*, 146, 148; *NYCD*, IX, 933–35, V, 720; Wraxall, *An Abridgement*, 155; *NYCD*, V, 711, 712.

34. *NYCD*, IX, 936.

35. *NYCD*, IX, 1030, VI, 148; J. F. H. Claiborne, ed., *Mississippi as a Province, Territory, and State*, I, 72; *NYCD*, VI, 178; Wraxall, *An Abridgement*, 220.

36. *NYCD*, IX, 1086–88; *Pa. Minutes*, IV, 731.

37. *NYCD*, VI, 282, 289–303, 654, X, 32–34, 38; *CC Papers*, III, 133, 233; *JP*, I, 42; Wraxall, *An Abridgement*, 247.

38. *CC Papers*, III, 233; *JP*, I, 55; *NYCD*, X, 91, 94.

39. *NYCD*, X, 79, 81, 91, 94, VI, 358, 366, 659, 663, 674, 742; *Pa. Minutes*, V, 85–87, 217; *JP*, I, 80, 107, 146; *CC Papers*, IV, 5; *NYCD*, X, 179, 180, 87, 113.

40. *Moravian Journals*, 31, 45; *JP*, IX, 84, 129, I, 329; *Pa. Minutes*, V, 549, 480, VI, 182; *Pa. Archives, 1st series*, II, 11; *CC Papers*, IV, 125, 126, 414; *NYCD*, X, 266, 200, 201, 202, VI, 742.

41. *NYCD*, IX, 1052–58; Wraxall, *An Abridgement*, 207, 208; *NYCD*, VI, 126; *JR*, LXVII, 191–93; *NYCD*, IX, 878; *JR*, LXVII, 121.

42. Colden, "History . . . 1707–20," 361, 428, 429; *NYCD*, VI, 148, 173, IX, 1085, 1093, 1097, 1098; Colden, "History . . . 1707–20," 409; Severance, "Joncaire," 108.

43. Livingston, *Records*, 187, 212; *NYCD*, V, 712; *DHSNY*, IV, 240.

44. Charlevoix, *Description*, V, 164; Wraxall, *An Abridgement*, 48; Livingston, *Records*, 231, 232, 236; Wraxall, *An Abridgement*, 146, 148, 155, 171; *NYCD*, IX, 933–35.

45. Wraxall, *An Abridgement*, 110; *JR*, LXVII, 75, 76; *NYCD*, IX, 1071; Wraxall, *An Abridgement*, 232–33; *NYCD*, V, 712.

46. *Pa. Archives, 2nd series*, VI, 12; *Eccl. Recs.*, II, 879; *DHSNY*, I, 155; Charlevoix, *Description*, V, 166; Wraxall, *An Abridgement*, 92; *JR*, LXVII, 25, LXVIII, 279; *NYCD*, IX, 1053; *JR*, LXIX, 39.

Chapter 6

1. *DHSNY*, I, 154; Robert Livingston, *The Livingston Indian Records*, 221.

2. Paul A. W. Wallace, *Indians in Pennsylvania*, 109. For examples of the Pennsylvania Indians' autonomy, see *Pa. Minutes*, II, 548; Anthony F. C. Wallace, "Women, Land, and Society: Three Aspects of Aboriginal Delaware Life," 6–16, 24, 3; *Pa. Archives, 1st series*, I, 62, 65, 67, 91, 92, 117, 134; *NYCD*, IV, 98; *Pa. Minutes*, I, 447; Livingston, *Records*, 168.

3. George T. Hunt, *The Wars of the Iroquois: Study in Intertribal Relations*, 68, 69; Charles Hanna, *The Wilderness Trail*, I, 156, II, 251, 252; *Pa. Minutes*, II, 138, 513; Peter Wraxall, *An Abridgement of the New York Indian Records*, 83; *Pa. Minutes*, II, 531, 565; Livingston, *Records*, 221; Wraxall, *An Abridgement*, 96, 97, 115; *Pa. Minutes*, II, 145, 204, 246, 247, 537; Wraxall, *An Abridgement*, 91; *Pa. Minutes*, II, 247, 387, 469, 546.

4. *Pa. Minutes,* II, 140, 145, 204, 388, 531, 533, 548, 557–59.
5. *Pa. Minutes,* II, 14–17, 35, 244–47, 537, 599–601, 606, 607, III, 45–48, II, 469–73, 509, 510, 516, 533.
6. *Pa. Minutes,* III, 66, 78, 79, 95, 99, 100, 114, 115–18, 120–33.
7. Cadwallader Colden, "History . . . 1707–20," 432; *Pa. Minutes,* III, 97.
8. *Pa. Minutes,* III, 100, 101.
9. *Pa. Minutes,* III, 181, 182.
10. *Pa. Minutes,* III, 148–53, 163–69, 181, 193, 168, 169, 182.
11. *Pa. Minutes,* III, 196–98, 199–201.
12. *Pa. Minutes,* III, 202.
13. *Pa. Minutes,* III, 210, 206, 204, 209–11.
14. *Pa. Minutes,* III, 182, 271–75, 204, 99, 100, 102, 182, 204.
15. *Pa. Minutes,* III, 80, 97, 182, 216–21, 78, 92–98, 102–4, 148–53, 216–21, 187, 104, 128, 163, 206, 207, 209, 210, 211.
16. *Pa. Minutes,* III, 302; *Pa. Archives, 1st series,* I, 213; *Pa. Minutes,* III, 303, 309, 402; *Pa. Archives, 1st series,* I, 298, 299, 300, 305.
17. *Pa. Minutes,* III, 312, 313, 319, 320.
18. *Pa. Minutes,* III, 295–97, 302; *Pa. Archives, 1st series* I, 230; *Pa. Minutes,* III, 312, 330, 333.
19. *Pa. Minutes,* III, 303–8.
20. *Pa. Archives, 1st series,* I, 223, *Pa. Minutes,* III, 306.
21. *Pa. Minutes,* III, 316–26, 330, 331; *Pa. Archives, 1st series,* I, 228.
22. *Pa. Minutes,* III, 333–37.
23. *Pa. Minutes,* III, 361–63.
24. *Pa. Minutes,* III, 402.
25. *Pa. Minutes,* III, 409; *Pa. Archives, 1st series,* I, 228.
26. *Pa. Minutes,* III, 425.
27. *Pa. Archive, 1st series,* I, 321–23.
28. *Pa. Minutes,* III, 310–13; 315–20, 333–36, 361–64; *Pa. Archives, 1st series,* I, 240.
29. *Pa. Minutes,* III, 435, 436, 437.
30. *Pa. Minutes,* III, 437–40.
31. *Pa. Minutes,* III, 440–42.
32. *Pa. Minutes,* III, 442.
33. *Pa. Minutes,* III, 442, 443.
34. *Pa. Minutes,* III, 445, 447–51.
35. *Pa. Minutes,* III, 500–504, 511–13, 577–80, 607, 608, 609.
36. *Pa. Minutes,* IV, 82–84, 90–94; *Pa. Archives, 1st series,* I, 498.
37. *Pa. Minutes,* IV, 245, 433, 434, 446, 447, 481.
38. *Pa. Minutes,* IV, 245, 433, 434, 446, 447, 481.
39. *Wisc. Hist. Collec.,* XVII, 242, 243; *Pa. Minutes,* III, 607–9, 597–605, IV, 307, 481.
40. *Pa. Minutes,* IV, 563–86, 578. Details about the fraudulent 1686 deed and the notorious Walking Purchase of 1737 can be found in Paul A. W. Wallace, *Indians in Pennsylvania,* 131, 132, 135; Francis Jennings, "The Scandalous Indian Policy of William Penn's Sons: Deeds and Documents of the Walking Purchase," 19–39; Anthony F. C. Wallace, *King of the Delawares: Teedyuscung,* 18–30; and Francis Jennings, "Miquon's Passing: Indian-European Relations in Colonial Pennsylvania, 1674–1755," 477–85.
41. *Pa. Minutes,* IV, 579.
42. The Iroquois-Delaware political relationship has long been a matter of contro-

versy. The Iroquois' designation of the Delawares as "women" has often been misunderstood. As Anthony F. C. Wallace explains in his excellent "Women, Land, and Society," the term "women" did not necessarily imply Delaware inferiority or dependence upon the Iroquois. Wallace points out that there are three distinct periods in the use of the term "woman": the prehistoric and protohistoric period, when the term was probably not offensive; the historic period, when it became offensive; and the twentieth century, when it is again a complimentary or neutral term. When the Iroquois referred to the Delawares as "women" in the 1600s and early 1700s, the term was not meant as an insult, and the Delawares still retained their political independence. Only after the 1730s does the term become an insult, implying an inferior position and lack of Delaware sovereignty. More information about how the Iroquois made "women" of the Delawares can be found in Anthony F. C. Wallace, "Women, Land, and Society: Three Aspects of Aboriginal Delaware Life," 20–32; Paul A. W. Wallace, *Indians in Pennsylvania*, 56, 57; and Bruce Trigger, ed., *Handbook of North American Indians*, XV, 223. Eventually the Delawares would strike back at the Pennsylvania colonists and the Iroquois in 1755. See Paul A. W. Wallace, *Indians in Pennsylvania*, 143, 146, and Francis Jennings, "The Delaware Interregnum."

43. *Pa. Minutes*, IV, 601, 624, 677.
44. *Pa. Minutes*, IV, 630, 635, 636.
45. *Pa. Minutes*, IV, 640, 646–50, 653, 654.
46. *Pa. Minutes*, IV, 700.
47. *Pa. Minutes*, IV, 699–714, 715, 718.
48. *Pa. Minutes*, IV, 719–21, 726.
49. *Pa. Minutes*, IV, 727, 728, 729.
50. *Pa. Minutes*, IV, 730, 731, 739, 732–37, 735.
51. *Pa. Minutes*, IV, 739, 772, 778, 781, 782; *Moravian Journals*, 13; *Pa. Minutes*, V, 5, 7, 20, 22, 45.
52. *Pa. Minutes*, V, 145–149, 156, 184, 194, 195.
53. *Pa. Minutes*, V, 212, 222, 223, 287, 288, 289; *Pa. Archives, 1st series*, II, 8.
54. *Pa. Minutes*, V, 299, 307–15, 323.
55. Reuben Gold Thwaites, *Early Western Travels, 1748–1846*, I, 19, 21, 24, 26, 29, 30, 31, 34, 35, 39, 40, 42; *Pa. Minutes*, V, 348, 351, 353, 354, 355, 357, 358.
56. *Pa. Minutes*, V, 433–36, 438–40, 449, 462, 463, 464, 485, 497.
57. *Pa. Minutes*, V, 517–21, 530–38.
58. *Pa. Archives, 1st series*, II, 33, 23, 24; *Pa. Minutes*, V, 388–93, 467, 478, 479, 480, 635, 636, 637, 768, 769, 776, VI, 116–19, 124; *Moravian Journals*, 48, 55; *JP*, I, 317.
59. *Pa. Minutes*, V, 608, 609, 614–16, 665–79, 685, 686, 693, 694, 700, 701, 706, 712, VI, 134, 140, 147–59, 188, 194–99, 204; *Pa. Archives, 1st series*, II, 114, 119, 144, 234, 237, 238, 239.

Chapter 7

1. *JR*, XLVII, 143, 145, 147; Douglas Summers Brown, *The Catawba Indians: The People of the River*, 160; Robert Livingston, *The Livingston Indian Records*, 42, 43. The Iroquois referred to both the Catawbas and Choctaws as Flatheads. See Charles M. Hudson, *The Catawba Nation*, 27; Henry Schoolcraft, *Notes on the Iroquois*, 156; and James Adair, *History of the American Indians*, 10, 305; Francis

Parkman, *A Half-Century of Conflict,* 25; *NYCD,* IX, 722, V, 382–84, 484–91, 637; *Pa. Minutes,* II, 191, III, 84–86, 102, 129–33; Peter Wraxall, *An Abridgement of the New York Indian Records,* 46, 52, 103, 124, 125, 191, 210, 211, 229; Cadwallader Colden, "History . . . 1707–20," 363, 381, 382, 417, 425, 428, 429, 431, 432; James Adair, *History of the Southern Indians,* 235.

2. *JR,* XLVII, 143, 147; Adair, *Southern Indians,* 158, 159; see Brown, *The Catawbas,* 160, 161; Herbert L. Osgood, *American Colonies in the Eighteenth Century,* I, 490; Schoolcraft, *Notes,* 156; Anthony F. C. Wallace, *Death and Rebirth of the Seneca,* 101, 102.

3. *NYCD,* IX, 704–7.

4. *Pa. Minutes,* II, 138, 191; Wraxall, *An Abridgement,* 46; Colden, "History . . . 1707–20," 361, 362; Wraxall, *An Abridgement,* 52; Colden, "History . . . 1707–20," 363; Wraxall, *An Abridgement,* 48.

5. Wraxall, *An Abridgement,* 60, 62; *MPHC,* XXXIII, 404; Colden, "History . . . 1707–20," 380, 381, 382.

6. *NYCD,* V, 217–26; Colden, "History . . . 1707–20," 389–94; Wraxall, *An Abridgement,* 77, 80, 81.

7. Colden, "History . . . 1707–20," 398, 399; Wraxall, *An Abridgement,* 77–78, 80; Frank Severance, "The Story of Joncaire," 478; Colden, "History . . . 1707–20," 398; *NYCD,* V, 267–75; Wraxall, *An Abridgement,* 78; Colden, "History . . . 1707–20," 398; Parkman, *Half-Century,* 111–12; Colden, "History . . . 1707–20," 403–8; *NYCD,* V, 267–75; Wraxall, *An Abridgement,* 80, 81; Pierre Charlevoix, *History and General Description of New France,* V, 256.

8. Colden, "History . . . 1707–20," 409; *NYCD,* V, 346; Livingston, *Records,* 223; Colden, "History . . . 1707–20," 410; *Pa. Minutes,* III, 82–84; Colden, "History . . . 1707–20," 413, 414.

9. *NYCD,* V, 382–86; Colden, "History . . . 1707–20," 417, 418; Wraxall, *An Abridgement,* 103.

10. *NYCD,* V, 441–44; Conference between Governor Hunter and Five Nations in Colden, "History . . . 1707–20," 420–22; Wraxall, *An Abridgement,* 109, 110; *NYCD,* V, 450; *Wisc. Hist. Collec.,* XVI, 315–17; *NYCD,* IX, 931.

11. *NYCD,* V, 463, 447, 464; Colden, "History . . . 1707–20," 423; *NYCD,* V, 476.

12. Livingston, *Records,* 222; Colden, "History . . . 1707–20," 425; Livingston, *Records,* 222–23; *NYCD,* V, 490–91; Colden, "History . . . 1707–20," 426–28.

13. Livingston, *Records,* 222–23; *NYCD,* V, 484–91; Colden, "History . . . 1707–20," 426–28, 428–29; *Pa. Minutes,* III, 85.

14. *Pa. Minutes,* III, 19–22.

15. Livingston, *Records,* 226–27; *NYCD,* IX, 884; *Pa. Minutes,* III, 85, 86.

16. Colden, "History . . . 1707–20," 431; Wraxall, 124, 125; Colden, "History . . . 1707–20," 432; *Pa. Minutes,* III, 102.

17. *Pa. Minutes,* III, 114, 115–18.

18. *Pa. Minutes,* III, 120–28, 129–33.

19. Conference between Governor Burnet and Five Nations, in *CC Papers,* I, 131–33; *NYCD,* V, 637–39.

20. *NYCD,* V, 657–60; *Pa. Minutes,* III, 206, 207, 209–11.

21. *NYCD,* V, 733, 793–96; Wraxall, *An Abridgement,* 171, 177; *Pa. Archives,* 1st series, I, 241, 240; Wraxall, *An Abridgement,* 177, 178; *MPHC,* XXXIV, 76; *Pa. Archives, 1st series,* I, 295; *NYCD,* V, 967.

22. Wraxall, *An Abridgement,* 191, 195; *MPHC,* XXXIV, 109; *NYCD,* V, 963.

23. Wraxall, *An Abridgement,* 198; *Pa. Archives, 1st series,* I, 544.

24. *Pa. Minutes,* IV, 245; Wraxall, *An Abridgement,* 209.

25. Wraxall, *An Abridgement*, 210, 211.
26. *NYCD*, VI, 137, 138, 148; Wraxall, *An Abridgement*, 214; "Journal of a French Officer, 1739," in J. F. H. Claiborne, ed., *Mississippi As a Province, Territory, and State*, I, 72.
27. *NYCD*, VI, 159; Wraxall, *An Abridgement*, 217; *NYCD*, IX, 1062, VI, 172–78; Wraxall, *An Abridgement*, 217–19.
28. *MPHC*, XXXIV, 184; *Wisc. Hist. Collec.*, XVII, 334, 337; *NYCD*, VI, 210, 211; Wraxall, *An Abridgement*, 224.
29. *NYCD*, VI, 216–18.
30. *NYCD*, IX, 1090–94; Wraxall, *An Abridgement*, 229; *Pa. Minutes*, IV, 630.
31. Wraxall, *An Abridgement*, 229; *Pa. Minutes*, IV, 630, 635, 636.
32. *NYCD*, VI, 238–39, 241.
33. *Pa. Minutes*, IV, 668; *NYCD*, IX, 1097; *DHSNY*, I, 465.
34. *Pa. Minutes*, IV, 699–740.
35. *Pa. Minutes*, IV, 718, 720, 721, 726, 727, 729, 733.
36. *Pa. Archives, 1st series*, I, 664.
37. *Pa. Archives, 1st series*, I, 665; *Moravian Journals*, 9; *Pa. Minutes*, IV, 776, V, 5; *NYCD*, VI, 390, 441, 443.
38. *Pa. Minutes*, V, 137, 303, 495; *JP*, I, 135, 260, 287, 326, 912, IX, 61, 69; *NYCD*, VI, 546, 588, 701, 709; *Pa. Minutes*, V, 303, 470–78; *JP*, I, 278, 287, IX, 75; *NYCD*, VI, 588.
39. *NYCD*, VI, 703, 704, 713, 714, 717, 718, 725, 726; Wraxall, *An Abridgement*, 250.
40. *JP*, I, 369, 377, 386; *Moravian Journals*, 115; *Pa. Minutes*, V, 607, 608, 634, 641, 699, 706, VI, 36.
41. *NYCD*, IX, 706, 707; *Wisc. Hist. Collec.*, XVII, 161; *JR*, LXIX, 49; *NYCD*, VI, 242, IX, 1097, 1098; Wraxall, *An Abridgement*, 48; *Pa. Minutes*, III, 96, 99; Wraxall, *An Abridgement*, 48; Colden, "History . . . 1707–20," 380, 413, 414, 428, 432; *NYCD*, V, 638, 732; Wraxall, *An Abridgement*, 171; *NYCD*, VI, 148, IX, 1085; Wraxall, *An Abridgement*, 224, 229.
42. Wraxall, *An Abridgement*, 48; *Wisc. Hist. Collec.*, XVII, 163, 164; Wraxall, *An Abridgement*, 49, 52; Colden, "History . . . 1707–20," 363; Wraxall, *An Abridgement*, 224, 229.
43. *NYCD*, IX, 706; Colden, "History . . . 1707–20," 361; *NYCD*, IX, 885, 886; *Wisc. Hist. Collec.*, XVI, 161; *MPHC*, XXXIV, 108, 109; *NYCD*, IX, 1093; Wraxall, *An Abridgement*, 34; *NYCD*, IV, 500; Colden, "History . . . 1707–20," 420–22; *NYCD*, V, 221, 224, 225.
44. *NYCD*, IX, 1085, 1093, 1094.
45. *NYCD*, V, 443, 463; Colden, "History . . . 1707–20," 422; *NYCD*, IX, 931; Wraxall, *An Abridgement*, 109, 110; *Pa. Minutes*, III, 83.
46. *Pa. Minutes*, III, 21, 22, 79, 92–98, 204–6.
47. *Pa. Minutes*, III, 82–87, 92–98; Colden, "History . . . 1707–20," 431; *Pa. Minutes*, IV, 699–740.
48. *NYCD*, V, 464, 375; Livingston, *Records*, 221–23; Wraxall, *An Abridgement*, 178, 115; *Pa. Minutes*, III, 99–102; Wraxall, *An Abridgement*, 115; Colden, "History . . . 1707–20," 414; *Wisc. Hist. Collec.*, XVI, 315.
49. *Pa. Minutes*, III, 82–87, 120–133; *Pa. Archives, 1st series*, I, 295; *Pa. Minutes*, IV, 635; *NYCD*, VI, 241, V, 548; *Pa. Minutes*, III, 45–48, 66, 78–80; *NYCD*, IX, 1059, VI, 241; *Pa. Minutes*, III, 221, V, 689.
50. For a full explanation of the social causes of Iroquois warfare, see George Snyderman, "Behind the Tree of Peace: A Sociological Analysis of Iroquoian

Warfare," 78–79; Allen Trelease, "The Iroquois," 50, 51; A. F. C. Wallace, *Death and Rebirth*, 31; *CC Papers*, VIII, 279–80. For interesting insights on the psychological functions of Iroquois warfare, see Anthony F. C. Wallace, *The Death and Rebirth of the Seneca*, 44–48; Colden, "History . . . 1707–20," 381; *NYCD*, IX, 1084.

51. *Pa. Minutes*, III, 99, 95, 99; Archer B. Hulbert, *Indian Thoroughfares*, 48–50; Hunt, 68, 69.

Conclusion

1. For additional information about the French and Indian War, see Howard Peckham, *The Colonial Wars, 1689–1762*.

2. Overviews of Iroquois participation in the French and Indian War can be found in Barbara Graymont, *The Iroquois in the American Revolution*, 29–32; Randolph Downes, *Council Fires on the Upper Ohio*, chapters 4, 5; Bruce Trigger, ed., *Handbook of North American Indians*, XV, 433–34; and Anthony F. C. Wallace, *The Death and Rebirth of the Seneca*, 114.

3. For Iroquois relations with western Indians during this period see Downes, *Council Fires on the Upper Ohio*, chapters 6, 7, and 8.

4. The best study of the Iroquois between 1776 and 1783 is Barbara Graymont's *The Iroquois in the American Revolution*. Anthony F. C. Wallace's *Death and Rebirth*, 125–54, is also useful.

Bibliography

1. Primary Sources

Since the Five Nations left few written records, any study of the Iroquois must rely heavily on English and French primary materials. Therefore, the student of Iroquois history must constantly be on the lookout for white bias in the records. Since the colonies of New York, Pennsylvania, and New France were in constant contact with the Five Nations, the government records and documents of those colonies, along with the papers of individuals, are of particular importance. In many cases the colonial papers are indexed, but I recommend that the serious student go through the materials page by page to make sure no significant information is missed.

Adair, James. *History of the Southern Indians.* Edited by Samuel Cole Williams. 1775. Reprint. New York: Promontory Press, 1930. Adair arrived in South Carolina from Great Britain in 1735. Shortly thereafter he became involved in the Indian trade. This book is Adair's firsthand account of southern Indians such as the Catawba, Cherokee, Choctaw, and Chickesaw.

The Cadwallader Colden Papers. Vols. I–IX. Collections of the New York Historical Society. New York: New York Historical Society, 1917–37. References to Iroquois lifestyles and politics.

Charlevoix, Pierre. *History and General Description of New France.* 6 vols. Translated by John G. Shea. New York, 1866–72. Charlevoix's history contains much useful information about Iroquois relations with New France. The writings of this early French Jesuit must be used with caution, however, since his views of the Iroquois are greatly colored by his pro-French leanings.

Claiborne, J. F. H., ed. *Mississippi As a Province, Territory, and State.* Vol. I. Jackson, Mississippi: Power and Barksdale Printers, 1880. Information about Iroquois raids on southern tribes.

Colden, Cadwallader. *The History of the Five Indian Nations.* 1727. Reprint. Ithaca: Cornell University Press, 1958.

———. *History of the Five Indian Nations, for the Years 1707–1720.* Collections of the New York Historical Society, vol. LXVIII. New York: Little and Ives, 1937. Colden's history of the Five Nations is extremely useful, but must be used with great caution. As a colonial official, Colden was writing his history to prove the Five Nations' value to his colony. Although biased toward the English, the book includes information about Iroquois dealings with whites and Indians.

Collections of the Illinois State Historical Library. Vol. XXIII. French Series, vol. I. Edited by T. C. Pease and R. C. Werner. Springfield, Illinois: Illinois State Historical Library, 1934. Iroquois contacts with the French and Indians in the Western Country.

274

Ecclesiastical Records of the State of New York. 7 vols. Edited by Hugh Hastings. Albany: James B. Lyon Printer, 1901. Documents concerning Iroquois relations with New York.

Fortescue, J. W., ed. *Calendar of State Papers, Colonial Series.* Vols. 1685–88, 1689–92, 1697–98. London: Norfolk Chronicle Company, 1899. Iroquois activities during the Twenty Years' War.

Hazard, Samuel, ed. *Pennsylvania Archives, 1st Series.* Philadelphia: Joseph Severns Company, 1852. Iroquois relations with Indians and whites on the Pennsylvania frontier.

Heckewelder, John "An Account of the History, Manners, and Customs of the Indian Natives who Once Inhabited Pennsylvania and the Neighboring States." Transactions of the Historical and Literary Committee of the American Philosophical Society, vol. I. Philadelphia; Abraham Small Printer, 1819.

J. C. B. *Travels in New France.* Edited by S. K. Stevens, D. H. Kent, and E. E. Woods. Harrisburg: Pennsylvania Historical Commission, 1941. A French soldier's firsthand account of New France and relations with Indians; also Iroquois relations with New France.

Kalm, Peter. *Travels in North America.* Edited by Adolph Benson. New York: Wilson Erickson, Inc, 1937. Indian culture on the northern colonial frontier.

LaMontagne, Leopold, ed. *The Publications of the Champlain Society: Royal Fort Frontenac.* Translated by Richard Preston. Toronto: The Champlain Society, 1958. French and Indian relations.

Linn, John, and Egle, William, eds. *Pennsylvania Archives, 2nd series.* Harrisburg: E. K. Meyers Printers, 1891. Iroquois in Pennsylvania.

Livingston, Robert, *The Livingston Indian Records, 1666–1723.* Edited by Lawrence L. Leder. Gettysburg: Pennsylvania Historical Association, 1956. Iroquois relations with the English, the French, and the Indians, documented by New York's Robert Livingston (1654–1728), Secretary for Indian Affairs.

Michigan Pioneer and Historical Collections. Vols. XXXIII and XXXIV. Lansing: Robert Smith Printing Company, 1904. Iroquois, French, and Indian activities in the Western Country.

Minutes of the Provincial Council of Pennsylvania. Philadelphia: Joseph Severns Company, 1852. This collection includes extremely important primary sources dealing with Iroquois relations with the Pennsylvania government, Pennsylvania Indians, and Ohio Indians.

Moravian Journals Relating to Central New York. Edited by William Beauchamp. Syracuse: Dehler Press, 1916. Descriptions of Iroquois lifestyles.

O'Callaghan, E. B., ed. *The Documentary History of the State of New York.* 4 vols. Albany: Weed, Parsons, and Company, 1849.

O'Callaghan, E. B., and Brodhead, John, eds. *Documents Relative to the Colonial History of the State of New York.* 15 vols. Albany: Weed, Parsons, and Company, 1856–83. These documents are essential for understanding Iroquois activities, lifestyles, and relations with Indians and whites on the colonial frontiers in the seventeenth and eighteenth centuries.

Perrot, Nicholas. "Memoir on the Manners, Customs, and Religion of the Savages of North America." In *The Indian Tribes of the Upper Mississippi Valley and Region of the Great Lakes,* edited by Emma H. Blair. 2 vols. Cleveland: Arthur Clark Company, 1911. A French fur trader describes Indian activities in the Western Country, including Iroquois relations with western tribes.

Report and Collections of the State Historical Society of Wisconsin. Madison: Atwood and Rublee Printers, 1902–8. Indian activities in the Western Country.

275

Sullivan, James, ed. *The Papers of Sir William Johnson*. Albany: University of State of New York, 1921. New York's liaison with the Iroquois and a successful fur trader, soldier, and politician; Iroquois activities and relations with Indians and whites.

Thwaites, Reuben Gold, ed. *Early Western Travels, 1748–1846*. Vol. I. Cleveland: Arthur Clark Company, 1904. Journals of Pennsylvania's George Croghan and Conrad Weiser; Indian affairs in Pennsylvania and Ohio.

———. *Jesuit Relations and Allied Documents*. 73 vols. Cleveland: Burrows, 1896–1901. Iroquois culture and relations with Indians and whites on the colonial frontier.

Wraxall, Peter. *An Abridgement of the New York Indian Records*. Edited by C. H. McIlwain. Cambridge, Massachussetts: Harvard University Press, 1915. Iroquois relations with their English, French, and Indian neighbors, 1678–1751.

2. Secondary Sources

No one work provides an up-to-date, comprehensive study of the Iroquois from 1650 until 1754. However, information relating to Iroquois power, politics, and relations with Indians and whites on the colonial frontier can be found in the following works.

Alvord, Clarence. *The Illinois Country, 1673–1818*. Springfield, Illinois: The Illinois Centennial Commission, 1920.

Andrews, Charles M. *The Colonial Period of American History*. 4 vols. New Haven, 1934–38.

Armour, David. "The Merchants of Albany, New York, 1686–1760." Ph.D. dissertation, Northwestern University, 1965.

Baldwin, C. C. "Early Indian Migrations in Ohio." *Western Reserve Historical Society Tract, No. 47*. Cleveland, 1888.

Beauchamp, William A. *A History of the New York Iroquois*. New York State Museum Bulletin 78. Albany: New York State Museum, 1905.

Berkhofer, Robert F., Jr., "The Political Context of a New Indian History." *Pacific Historical Review* XL (August, 1971): 357–82.

Billington, Ray Allen. *Westward Expansion: A History of the American Frontier*. New York, 1974.

Bond, R. P. *Queen Anne's American Kings*. Oxford, 1952.

Bonomi, Patricia W. *A Factious People: Politics and Society in Colonial New York*. New York, 1971.

Brown, Douglas Summers. *The Catawba Indians: The People of the River*. Columbia, South Carolina, 1966.

Buffinton, A. H. "The Policy of Albany and English Westward Expansion." *Mississippi Valley Historical Review* VIII (1922): 337–66.

Dorn, Walter. *Competition for Empire, 1740–1763*. New York, 1940.

Downes, Randolph. *Council Fires on the Upper Ohio*. Pittsburgh, 1940.

Eccles, W. J. *The Canadian Frontier, 1534–1760*. New York, 1969.

———. *France in America*. New York, 1972.

———. *Frontenac, the Courtier Governor*. Toronto, 1959.

Fenton, William N. "The Lore of the Longhouse: Myth, Ritual, and Red Power." *Anthropological Quarterly* XXXXVIII, no. 3 (July, 1975): 131–47.

———. "Problems Arising from the Historical Northeast Position of the Iroquois." *Smithsonian Miscellaneous Collections* C (1940): 159–251.

276

Gipson, Lawrence Henry. *The British Empire Before the American Revolution.* Vols. III, IV, V, VI. New York, 1954–67.

Graymont, Barbara. *The Iroquois in the American Revolution.* Syracuse, 1972.

Guttridge, G. H. *The Colonial Policy of William III in America and the West Indies.* Cambridge, England, 1922.

Halsey, Francis Whiting. *The Old New York Frontier: Its Wars with Indians and Tories, Its Missionary Schools, Pioneers and Land Titles, 1614–1800.* New York, 1912.

Hamilton, Milton. *Sir William Johnson: Colonial American, 1715–1763.* Port Washington, New York, 1976.

Hanna, Charles. *The Wilderness Trail.* 2 vols. New York, 1911.

Hardcastle, David. "The Defense of Canada Under Louis XIV, 1643–1701." Ph.D. dissertation, Ohio State University, 1970.

Hawke, David. *The Colonial Experience.* New York, 1966.

Hodge, Frederick W., ed., *Handbook of American Indians North of Mexico.* 2 vols. 1907. Reprint. New York, 1959.

Hudson, Charles M. *The Catawba Nation.* Athens, Georgia, 1970.

Hunt, George T. *The Wars of the Iroquois: Study in Intertribal Relations.* Madison, Wisconsin, 1940.

Hulbert, Archer B. *Indian Thoroughfares.* Historic Highways of America, vol 2. Cleveland, 1902.

Jacobs, Wilbur R. *Wilderness Politics and Indian Gifts.* Lincoln, Nebraska, 1950.

Jennings, Francis. "The Constitutional Evolution of the Covenant Chain." *Proceedings of the American Philosophical Society* CXV, no. 2 (April, 1971): 88–96.

———. "The Delaware Interregnum." *Pennsylvania Magazine of History and Biography* LXXXIX, no. 2 (1965): 174–98.

———. "Miquon's Passing: Indian-European Relations in Colonial Pennsylvania, 1674–1755." Ph.D. dissertation, University of Pennsylvania, 1965.

———. "The Scandalous Indian Policy of William Penn's Sons: Deeds and Documents of the Walking Purchase." *Pennsylvania History* XXXVII, no. 1 (1970): 19–39.

Leach, Douglas. *The Northern Colonial Frontier, 1607–1763.* New York, 1966.

Leder, Lawrence. *Robert Livingston, 1654–1728, and the Politics of Colonial New York.* Chapel Hill, North Carolina, 1961.

Lurie, Nancy O. "The World's Oldest On-Going Protest Demonstration: North American Indian Drinking Patterns." *Pacific Historical Review* XL (1971): 311–32.

Metcalf, P. Richard. "Who Shall Rule at Home? Native American Politics and Indian-White Relations." *Journal of American History* LXI (December, 1974): 651–65.

Morgan, Lewis Henry. *The League of the Iroquois.* 1851. Reprint. New Jersey, 1972.

Morton, W. L. *The Kingdom of Canada.* New York, 1963.

Nammack, Georgiana C. *Fraud, Politics, and the Dispossession of the Indians: The Iroquois Land Frontier in the Colonial Period.* Norman, Oklahoma, 1969.

Norton, Thomas Elliot. *The Fur Trade in Colonial New York, 1686–1776.* Madison, Wisconsin, 1974.

Osgood, Herbert L. *The American Colonies in the Eighteenth Century.* 4 vols. Massachusetts, 1958.

Parkman, Francis. *Count Frontenac and New France Under Louis XIV.* 1880. Reprint. Boston, 1966.

———. *A Half-Century of Conflict.* 1892. Reprint. New York, 1966.

———. *The Jesuits in North America.* 1867. Reprint. Boston, 1963.

Peckham, Howard. *The Colonial Wars, 1689–1762.* Chicago, 1964.

Rutledge, Joseph L. *Century of Conflict: The Struggle Between the French and British in Colonial America.* Garden City, New York, 1956.

Savelle, Max. "The American Balance of Power and European Diplomacy, 1713–1778." In *The Era of the American Revolution,* edited by Richard B. Morris. New York, 1939.

Severance, Frank. "The Story of Joncaire." Publications of the Buffalo Historical Society, vol. IX. Buffalo, 1906.

Schoolcraft, Henry R. *Notes on the Iroquois.* Albany, New York, 1847.

Shetrone, H. C. *The Indian in Ohio.* Columbus, Ohio, 1918.

Snyderman, George. "Behind the Tree of Peace: A Sociological Analysis of Iroquoian Warfare." Ph.D. dissertation, University of Pennsylvania, 1948.

Swanton, John R. *The Indian Tribes of North America.* U.S. Bureau of American Ethnology, Bulletin 145. Washington, D.C.: U.S. Bureau of American Ethnology, 1953.

Tooker, Elisabeth. "The Iroquois Defeat of the Huron: A Review of the Causes." *Pennsylvania Archaeologist* XXXIII, no. 103 (July, 1963): 11–123.

Trelease, Allen W. *Indian Affairs in Colonial New York: The Seventeenth Century.* Ithaca, New York, 1960.

———. "The Iroquois and the Western Fur Trade: A Problem in Interpretation." *Mississippi Valley Historical Review* XLIX (June, 1962): 32–51.

Trigger, Bruce. *The Children of Aataentsic: A History of the Huron People to 1660.* 2 vols. Montreal, 1976.

———, ed. *Handbook of North American Indians.* Vol. XV. Washington, D.C., 1978.

———. *The Huron: Farmers of the North.* New York, 1969.

Wallace, Anthony F. C. *The Death and Rebirth of the Seneca.* New York, 1969.

———. *King of the Delawares: Teedyuscung.* Philadelphia, 1949.

———. "The Origins of Iroquois Neutrality: The Grand Settlement of 1701." *Pennsylvania History* XXIV (1957): 223–35.

———. "Woman, Land, and Society: Three Aspects of Aboriginal Delaware Life." *Pennsylvania Archaeologist* XVII (1947): 1–35.

Wallace, Paul A. W. *Conrad Weiser, 1696–1760.* Philadelphia, 1945.

———. *Indians in Pennsylvania.* Harrisburg, Pennsylvania, 1961.

Washburn, Wilcomb E. *The Indian in America.* New York, 1975.

Weslager, C. A. *The Nanticoke Indians.* Harrisburg, Pennsylvania, 1948.

Winsor, Justin, ed. *The English and French in North America, 1689–1763.* Narrative and Critical History of America, vol. V. Boston, 1887.

Zoltvany, Yves F. "New France and the West, 1701–1713." *Canadian Historical Review* XLVI (1965): 301–22.

INDEX

Page numbers of illustrations are in italics

ern Indians, 206–7, 222, 227, 231; in Western Country, 41. *See also* Far Indians; Northern Indians; Western Indians
Frontenac, Count Louis de, 45, 46, 259 n. 2.
Fur trade. *See under names of specific participants*

G
Ganawese, 156–57, 161, 163, 165, 171, 173, 183, 188, 191
Glen, Governor James (South Carolina), 225
Gooch, Lt. Governor Sir William (Virginia), 218–19
Gookin, Lt. Governor Charles (Pennsylvania), 158
Gordon, Governor Patrick (Pennsylvania), 167–74, 176
Grand Council Treaty of 1701, 46–69, 131, 132
Grand Peace Treaty, 46–69, 131, 132
Great Lakes tribes. *See* Western Indians
Great Southern Trail, 31

H
Hamilton, Governor Lord George (Pennsylvania), 199–201
Hendrick (Mohawk chief), 22, 89, 104, 108, 208
Hetaquantagechty, 175–78, 180
Hiawatha, 33
Ho-de-no-sau-nee, 30, 245. *See also* Iroquois
Hunter, Governor Robert (New York), 91, 138, 207–8, 210–14
Hurons, 35, 37–38, 42, 56, 65, 101, 145, 206. *See also* Wyandots

I
Illinois, 35, 42
Ingoldsby, Governor Richard (New York), 85, 86
Irondequoit, 117
Iroquoia, 30, 31, 36, *246*
Iroquois: Confederacy (League), 30, 32–34, 36, 37, 183, 260 n. 21; cul-

ture, 31–36, 71, 72, 257; decline of strength, 70, 71, 73, 124, 130, 239, 241; disease among, 39, 71, 92, 124, 194, 217, 239; factionalism, 46–49, 53, 60, 66–69, 75–77, 86, 92, 100, 111–12, 124–25, 153, 155, 236, 241–42; fur trade, 35, 39, 65, 67, 77–79; images of, 30, 34; names, 30; peace settlements, 46–69, 131, 132; population, 30, 38–39, 70–71, 73, 86, 230; seventeenth century wars, 35–45, 258 n. 1; significance of, 188, 237, 238, 242–45. *See also under names of individual tribes;* Restoration Policy, Iroquois

J
Jesuits, 38, 44, 55, 57, 65, 66, 71, 74, 77, 95, 112, 121–22; Bruyas, 50, 59; effect of, on Iroquois, 47, 50, 75–76, 121–22; Germain, 75, 122; Jogues, 29–30; Lamberville, 74; Lafitau, 115–16; Loyard, 152; Mareuil, 87–88; Millet, 75; missions, 52, 121, 122; Nau, 122, 155; Piquet, 121. *See also* Missionaries
Johnson, William: captures Ft. Niagara, 240; colonel of Five Nations, 98; contacts Iroquois, 95; and Iroquois, 109; on Iroquois' importance, 110–11; home of, *20;* persuades Iroquois to fight French, 97, 100; portrait of, *25;* renews Covenant Chain, 105; and southern wars, 225
Joncaire, Daniel ("Chabert"), 96, 99, 103
Joncaire, Louis Thomas de: admired by Iroquois, 50–51, 76; deputy to Iroquois, 50–51, 53–54, 59, 65, 76, 212; and Fort Niagara, 117–19; maintains peace with Iroquois, 76, 148; and Shawnees, 167, 183

K
Keith, Governor (Pennsylvania), 160–66, 213–17
King George's War, 92, 100–101, 144, 149, 151, 193, 225, 238
King William's War, 42, 45, 259 n. 1
Kirkland, Samuel, 241

281

CPSIA information can be obtained
at www.ICGtesting.com
Printed in the USA
LVOW13s2253050617

536990LV00021B/227/P